# UNHOLY COMMUNION:
## *Alice, Sweet Alice*

# UNHOLY COMMUNION:

## *Alice, Sweet Alice* from script to screen

## by Troy Howarth

BearManor Media

2021

*Unholy Communion:* Alice, Sweet Alice, *from script to screen*

© 2021 Troy Howarth

All rights reserved.

No portion of this publication may be reproduced, stored, and/or copied electronically (except for academic use as a source), nor transmitted in any form or by any means without the prior written permission of the publisher and/or author.

Published in the United States of America by:

BearManor Media
1317 Edgewater Dr #110
Orlando FL 32804

bearmanormedia.com

Printed in the United States.

Typesetting and layout by John Teehan

Front cover design by Tony Strauss

ISBN—978-1-62933-766-1

# Table of Contents

Acknowledgements ................................................................... vii

Foreword by Dante Tomaselli ................................................... ix

Preface ..................................................................................... xv

Chapter 1: Horror in the Time of Free Love: An Overview ........ 1

Chapter 2: Alfred Sole: From XXX to Anti-Catholic Horror ..... 17

Chapter 3: Cast Talent Bios ....................................................... 43

Chapter 4: The Locations of *Alice, Sweet Alice* ...................... 61
          by Michael Gingold

Chapter 5: The Script ................................................................ 73

Chapter 6: Analyzing *Alice* ................................................... 211

Chapter 7: What the Critics Said ............................................ 233

Chapter 8: Interview with Alfred Sole .................................... 253

Bibliography ........................................................................... 277

Index ....................................................................................... 279

About the Author ................................................................... 285

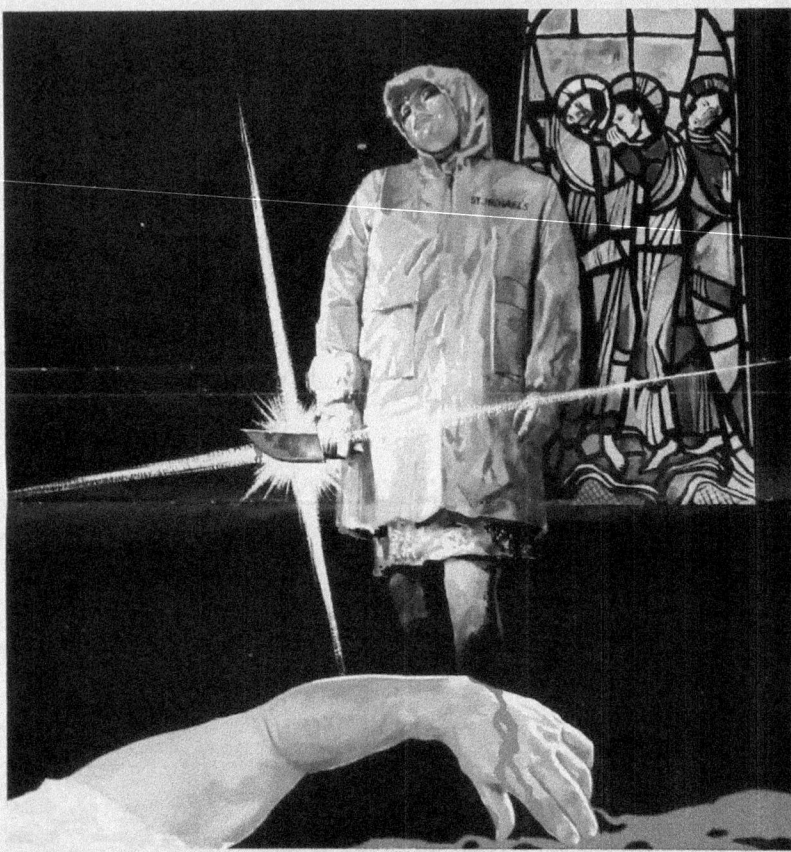

Beautiful Italian *locandina* for *Alice, Sweet Alice*. Artist unknown.

# Acknowledgements

**This project started** in a somewhat circuitous fashion. My friend and fellow writer Lee Gambin suggested that I reach out to Ben Ohmart of Bear Manor to see about getting a book project off the ground. Since Bear Manor has done so many volumes dedicated to specific films, it made sense for me to do one in the same vein. But which one? I decided upon *Alice, Sweet Alice* for reasons which will hopefully be apparent as you read this book. Fortunately Ben was keen on the idea, and we were up and running with a minimum of fuss. Lee and Ben both have my thanks to helping to bring this project into the world.

I was very fortunate indeed to have a number of devoted *Alice* fans in my corner to assist where need. Nathaniel Thompson has my thanks for providing various frame grabs from the film.

Unless otherwise noted, all other images were provided courtesy of Dante Tomaselli and Alfred Sole. The author does not assert the rights to any images; they are reproduced in the spirit of publicity for which they were originally created.

Casey Scott was kind enough to provide me with a possible mailing address for the film's elusive star, Paula Sheppard. I reached out to Ms. Sheppard in the hopes of getting her to make a few comments about her most iconic film role, but never heard back. It just wasn't meant to be.

Michael Gingold, whose passion for the film extended to helping prepare the extensive supplements on the Arrow Video restoration of *Alice, Sweet Alice*, was also very helpful in tracking down various critical write-ups from the film's original theatrical run. Michael also provided some invaluable factoids about the film's decidedly torturous theatrical release, and he also agreed to write an essay about the locations which feature so memorably in the film. The town of

Paterson, New Jersey, is virtually a character in the film, so Mike's insights into these impeccably chosen locations was a tremendous addition to the book.

Dante Tomaselli, the gifted filmmaker and musician whose relationship with this film is deeply personal, was probably the project's number one cheerleader; as soon as I suggested the idea to him, he moved heaven and earth to ensure that I had access to all the materials I could ever wish for. Dante is the cousin of the film's co-writer and director, Alfred Sole, and thanks to him, I was given access to a great archive of images and press clippings about the making of the film. Dante also facilitated an interview with his cousin Alfred and helped in more ways than I can ever adequately thank him for. This volume is dedicated to him as a small token of my appreciation.

And, of course, a very big "thank you" is reserved for Mr. Alfred Sole. In addition to graciously answering all of my questions about his life in film and about the making of *Alice* in particular, Mr. Sole was also kind enough to allow us to reproduce the entire shooting screenplay. Seeing the words on paper and comparing them with the images on screen give a great insight into how seemingly minor details can assume tremendous importance in a finished work, and I think you will agree that having the ability to study this document helps to appreciate the film even more.

# Foreword

### by Dante Tomaselli

**My cousin, Alfred Sole,** unleashed his landmark horror shocker in 1976 when I was only six-years-old. *Communion* (aka *Alice, Sweet Alice* or *Holy Terror*) is forever embedded in my psyche and was a staple of my childhood, inspiring me to pursue directing and scoring my own fantasies. Back in the day, my father owned a jewelry store and bridal shop and he supplied the white veils, gloves and Communion dresses for the production. A lot of my relatives were featured extras. At first, I didn't understand the commotion, I only knew that my cousin was directing a "horror movie" and it was a "big deal." I heard through hushed whispers that Alfred once directed an X-rated film called *Deep Sleep* and that it played at the local Willowbrook Mall in Totowa, New Jersey but that didn't really register with my six-year-old brain. A porno? Mainly, I knew I loved scary films and wished to attend the much-hyped *Communion* World Premiere in Paterson. Unfortunately I was informed by my parents that I was too young. My earliest impression of the film was a stylish *Communion* pamphlet replete with colorful, eye-popping stills from the actual production. The cover had a veiled, white gloved Catholic girl evilly holding a spectral dagger. I remember I thought it was beautiful and had the feel of *The Omen* (1976) and *Don't Look Now* (1973): high quality...painterly. This was a low budget film? I discovered this booklet in my father's den and would stare in amazement. I couldn't get enough and poured over everything, including the title's typography...*Communion* in that special haunted font. Soon I began illustrating and replicating *Communion* on all my school notebooks. I was in the 1st Grade.

The cover to the film's original pressbook.

Naturally, I asked my parents about the World Premiere and my mother, who's a fan of horror, said it was a powerful, well-made horror film. Mom also relayed that a lot of my relatives, some of them elderly and from Italy were extremely uncomfortable and did not appreciate the film's hardcore violence. I was told that during an especially grisly stabbing a few older relatives had enough and left the theater screaming, "No more Alfie! No more!" Still, the screening was a success and judging by my mother's enticing description, it seemed to be a horror fan's dream.

It was around this time *Communion*, the book, entered my world. I was snooping through my parents' bedroom drawer and the paperback novel poked out at me like a Dark Ride spook. Inside there was a thank you note and autograph by Alfred. I could not keep my eyes off the blasphemous artwork! It was a diminutive Catholic girl grinning and wearing a clownish, translucent mask. My blood ran cold. Over darkness, this warped figure appeared knock-kneed in a pure white Communion dress...brandishing a bloody knife! The tagline read: "I love you. I don't want to kill. But I can't help myself." This macabre imagery was deeply twisted, borderline Satanic and I dared myself to gaze at the book again.

Dante Tomaselli poses with his mother and grandmother on the occasion of his first Holy Communion; aptly, it was around this time that *Alice, Sweet Alice* was released.

Over the next few years, I was treated to new artwork popping up with the film's title morphing from *Communion* to *Alice, Sweet Alice* to *Holy Terror*. I liked each title. That sinister, grotesque mask…the two-faced crying baby doll with a kitchen knife lodged in it. As a young fan of horror movies, I was whipped into a frenzy and beaming with pride for my filmmaker cousin. At that point, Alfred had moved to Hollywood, California and I would ask Aunt Gloria (my father's sister) how he was managing. I remember she said Alfred was very busy but distraught and compared the Hollywood film industry to a "rat race." Apparently he was unhappy with its dumb, cookie-cutter politics.

In 1980 when VCRs were available, I finally experienced *Alice, Sweet Alice* and from the very first frame, with its hypnotic opening titles, I was transported to a disorienting, dreamlike realm. Encased in chilling sound design, I heard shrill *Psycho*-like violins… Breathy, ethereal moans… A sparkling ice-cold lullaby… It was at times an almost *Godfather*-like soundtrack: sweeping… Epic. The film unfolded like a visual poem. I firmly believed *Alice, Sweet Alice* was as high quality and stylish as a Brian DePalma picture like *Carrie* (1976) or some kind of warped, Hitchcock fever dream. The fact that it was so low budget and utilized only one camera intrigued me and I considered my cousin a "master of horror." The film's ominous atmosphere was mysterious and gloomy and I focused on the kooky Italian-American characters. Alfred brought me right in with his camera and production design and the acting was so realistic. Sometimes these lost souls rang frighteningly familiar, like they were my real relatives. Even though I was born in Paterson General Hospital, which is technically the location where the interiors of the film's church were shot, I lived and was raised in Montville, New Jersey, which is about 20 minutes away and more suburban. One of my grandmothers would reside at our house every weekend and I'd visit with my other Paterson relatives a lot. Many were kind-hearted and loving like my two grandmothers but some seemed rigid, close-minded and ferociously conservative. In other words, they scared me.

The Blessed Madonna Statue world of Paterson was always poking at me and just a car ride away. Alfred captured this unique and vibrant Italian-American enclave on film so perfectly. Not to mention the ever-present weird, decaying industrial abandoned buildings. It's all very much in league with artists like Martin Scorsese and his depiction of Italian New York. However, this swirling landscape is pure Paterson, New Jersey and a world unto itself.

Alfred Sole's movie tapped into my anxieties. Kneeling in church… Feelings of guilt…jealousy… Scary Confessionals…The fear of family and judgment… and damnation. *Family sickness…* The hysterics of certain characters, like Aunt Annie dramatically wailing might sometimes register as over-the-top

Dante Tomaselli on the set of his directorial debut, *Desecration* (1999).

but I knew people like her. And Mrs. Tredoni, a willing slave to the church, often dressed in puritanical black and white, clutching rosaries and muttering prayers... Alfred revealed to me that he was inspired by our very own Aunt Matilda (who actually appears in the film's funeral scene as Mrs. Bruno). Matilda was devoted to the church and lived in the Rectory part-time. She was

Dante Tomaselli poses with his cousin, Alfred Sole.

a very gentle woman, meek, a servant of God and he wondered what it would be like if she suddenly snapped. Alfred and I are so connected. I'm *also* inspired by my enigmatic Aunt Matilda Tomaselli (R.I.P), eternally religious and the name of the lead character of my first film, *Desecration* (1999). *Communion* is in my blood.

# Preface

**As a child of the 80s,** I remember only too well the ritual of the late night weekend horror movie as well as the thrill of discovering (potential) hidden gems in the VHS bargain bins at various department stores. It was just a short while ago in the big scheme of things, and yet the world has changed so very much since those days. That I miss them is no doubt down largely to nostalgia, and yet there is something to be said for the way so many of us came to these films in those dark days prior to the Internet and having instant access to just about every film with the click of a button.

One of the films that used to show up with eerie regularity was *Alice, Sweet Alice*. Sometimes it would show up as *Communion*. Sometimes as *Holy Terror*. But most of us knew it as *Alice, Sweet Alice*—this despite the fact that the film's co-writer and director, Alfred Sole, has always preferred the short and punchy title of *Communion*.

Seen in the small hours of Friday night/Saturday morning, *Alice* wove a spell that was unlike just about any other film. It felt vaguely "European," with its emphasis on devout Catholicism and shattered relationships, yet it wasn't one of the many Euro imports that used to show up on Channel 9 at 2 in the morning—think of Emilio Miraglia's *The Night Evelyn Came Out of the Grave* (*La notte che Evelyn uscì dalla tomba*, 1971), for example. It was roughly contemporary with John Carpenter's *Halloween* (1978), yet it seemed to exist in a completely different world. Both films were independently produced in the U.S. on very small budgets. Both films featured creepy knife-wielding killers wearing masks. Both films had supremely creepy soundtracks. And both films seemed openly influenced by the stylized Italian thrillers (known as *giallo* films, or *gialli* in its plural form), though only Carpenter was consciously aware of those films. As shall be discussed later in this text—and in the accompanying interview with Alfred Sole—the makers of *Alice* were aware of the likes of Nicolas Roeg's Venice-set arthouse horror thriller *Don't Look Now* (1973), but when it came to the likes of Mario Bava, Lucio Fulci, and Dario Argento, they weren't on the radar at all. So much for that apparent avenue of influence; sometimes great ideas simply manifest themselves coincidentally without any real cross-pollination to speak of.

*Alice* was also a mainstay of the public domain VHS scene, much to the annoyance of its makers. Like George A. Romero and company with *Night of the Living Dead* (1968) and Tobe Hooper and company with *The Texas Chain Saw Massacre* (1974), Alfred Sole and his collaborators were the victims of bad deal-making and spotty distribution. In the case of *Night*, the filmmakers made a blunder where copyrighting was concerned. On the other hand, Hooper and his associates fell afoul of some…sketchy characters when they agreed to allow a company named Bryanston to distribute their movie. The end result of all of this was simple: the films raked in a lot of cash, but the filmmakers saw very little of it. That's not quite the case where *Alice* was concerned. Like so many low budget gems of the prolific 70s, it simply got lost in the shuffle. Mainstream critics who resented being assigned to review low budget genre fare seldom did their due diligence and would give these films the bare minimum where their attention and efforts were concerned. The ones who actually bothered to stay awake for the entire running time would sniffily dismiss the films in a few "witty" sentences, reserving their acclaim for the latest *auteur* offerings from Robert Altman or Ingmar Bergman. It isn't that Altman and Bergman weren't deserving of the respect—but many of these lower budgeted items deserved more love than they received, too. John Carpenter again comes to mind: his early films

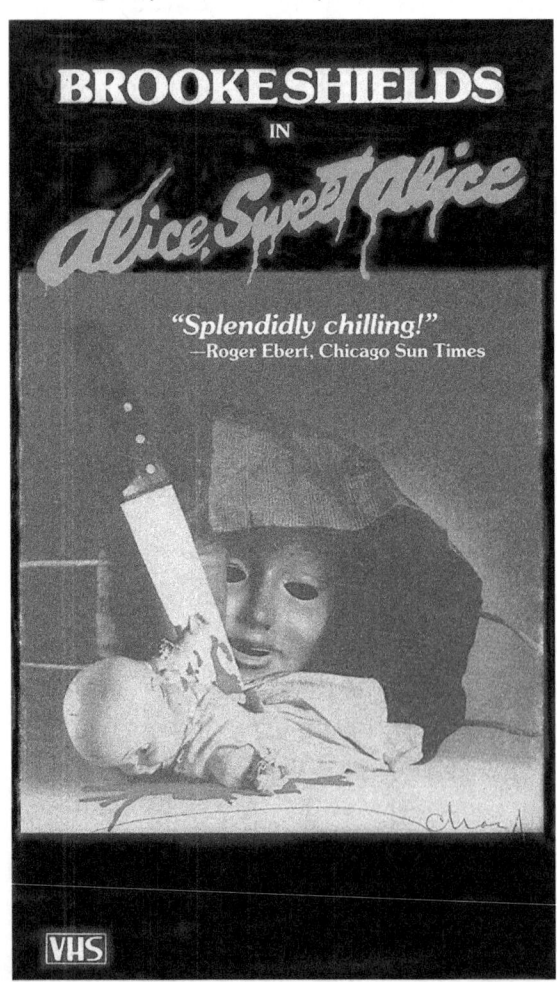

Cover for the Goodtimes Video VHS edition of *Alice, Sweet Alice*.

*Assault on Precinct 13* (1976) and *Halloween* were both curtly dismissed by the few critics who grudgingly agreed to write about them…and then something mysterious happened. The former ended up receiving bona fide critical acclaim overseas, while the latter got a remarkably positive notice from critic Tom Allen in *The Village Voice*. The critics were forced to eat crow and go back to reassess… Oh yeah, these films are actually pretty good. Who knew?

In the case of *Alice*, critical rehabilitation was a little longer in offing. As time wore on and the film was duped, sold, resold, and sold again in various inferior-quality VHS editions, it seemed to fall into a black pit from which there was no escape. The film fell out of copyright for a period of time, and it became easy to just slap the movie on another shoddy VHS label without paying a penny to the people who were responsible for making it. Then, in the 1990s, William Lustig came to the rescue. Lustig, the director responsible for *Maniac* (1980) and *Vigilante* (1982), had been an uncredited crew member on *Alice*—as an assistant in the make-up and effects department for a couple of weeks—and he set out to preserve a remastered version of the film on laser disc, in then state-of-the-art quality. Alfred Sole managed to get the film back under copyright, which he retains to this day, and the film was rescued from the purgatory of public domain. The Roan Group laser disc release showed up in March of 1997, complete with commentary by Lustig and Sole, and for years it remained the gold standard by which all other editions were to be based. This release also saw Sole tinkering with the film, removing some footage in an effort to speed up the pace. All told, he reduced the running time by about 90 seconds, notably deleting the bit where Dominick receives a phone call from his second wife. The changes were not warmly embraced by the fans who were accustomed to the original version, however, and subsequent editions have reinstated the footage Sole removed from that particular version. Since that time, there have been other releases which have blown it out of the water—culminating in the Arrow Video edition in August of 2019. Now that the film has been properly preserved in more-or-less pristine quality, it's possible to appreciate one of the true genre gems of the 1970s.

Given the film's somewhat tortured and torturous history, it seems as good a time as any to examine it in detail—paying homage to the men and women who made it happen, and examining the film in-depth, analyzing what makes it so unique and why it continues to retain its ability to get under the skin of viewers. *Alice* is not a gorefest, but it contains moments which are shocking—and they remain shocking, even in light of all the *Friday the 13$^{th}$* and *Hostel* movies which have followed in its wake. It was never subjected to a string of ever-worsening sequels, either, thus ensuring that it remains

Cover art for the glorious restoration of *Alice, Sweet Alice* from Arrow Video.

unique. If any one film best manages to recapture the off-kilter ambience and fetishistic creepiness of the best of the Italian *giallo* films, this is it; and it did so without even *trying* to emulate those movies. Perhaps that's the key to its success.

# Chapter 1

## Horror in the Time of Free Love: An Overview

**In many respects,** the '70s began in 1968. The shift to greater freedom and fresh new thematic concerns did not occur overnight, however. In order to understand this, it is necessary to put things into context.

It has been said, with much justification, that the horror genre takes its strength from the horrors of society. The first explosion of what would become known as horror cinema came after the First World War—and much of it was centered squarely in the German film scene. In the 1940s, the horrors of World War II gave way to a new cycle of monster movies from Universal and psychological terrors courtesy of RKO's Val Lewton. Then in the 1950s, fear of "the other" (i.e., Communism) and of the potential of nuclear holocaust gave way to a fresh wave of sci-fi horrors dealing with loss of identity (as in Don Siegel's masterful version of *Invasion of the Body Snatchers*, 1956), "foreign" menace from other worlds (*It Came from Outer Space*, 1953), and giant bug movies such as *Them!* (1954) which warned of what could happen when science was left unchecked.

In the 1960s, major changes were afoot, both within the film industry and in society at large. The classical studio system of Hollywood resulted in a smooth, efficient behemoth of a machine which cranked out a mixture of pulp product and *auteur*-level cinema—not that a real understanding of that was really in the air outside the pages of *Cahiers du Cinema*. The major studios like MGM and Paramount had created a signature style based around a cluster of influences, including the personal tastes and whims of the men in charge, and the cumulative talents and sensibilities of those who were under contract to them. Even the average person on the street could pretty much tell the

The classical style of Hollywood horror, represented by the likes of James Whale's *Frankenstein* (1931), mutated into something different as society itself underwent major changes. Courtesy Universal Pictures.

difference between a glossy MGM soap opera and a gritty gangster movie from Warner Bros., for example. The smaller companies like Universal and RKO had their own unique aesthetic, too, and of course there was no mistaking the impoverished look of "poverty row" outfits such as Republic or Monogram—though when Orson Welles ended up making *Macbeth* (1948) on a shoestring for Republic, he admittedly brought a very different sensibility to bear on their typical programmer.

As the conservativism of the '50s gave way to the experimentation of the '60s, the way in which movies were made in Hollywood began to change. The studios lost their stranglehold and the typical way of working, wherein talent was placed under long-term contracts and a steady stream of product was generated throughout the year, was more-or-less abandoned. Independent companies like American International Pictures (AIP) started to enjoy mainstream success and the old-school stuffed shirts who ran the roost were gradually replaced by *wunderkinds* like Robert Evans at Paramount. Long gone were the days of classical middle-aged journeymen in suits and ties calling the shots while the contracted players dutifully obeyed, lest they be hit with penalties for breaking their contracts. Younger men (and women) with long hair, wild clothes, and wilder ideas started to find their way into the talent pool—and this was reflected in the tone and tenor of their work. While a few of the new generation worshipped at the altar of old school Hollywood (think of cineastes like Peter Bogdanovich and François Truffaut, for example), anarchy was very much the order of the day: *forget about the rules, man, and let's get real for a moment.*

Inevitably, the overall goal was pretty much still the same: selling tickets. No matter how deeply personal and experimental a filmmaker might be, they were usually aware of one practical reality: if you want to keep making movies, your movies have got to turn a profit. One sure-fire way of doing this was to appeal to a key demographic: the young. The older generation, being more buttoned-down, might have been resistant towards the new trends which arose out of slackening censorship; they didn't necessarily hold with all this sex and violence and, well, *subversion*. For the young and the restless, however, it was a dream come true. Having been weaned on the likes of *The Adventures of Ozzie and Harriet* or old *Andy Hardy* movies, wherein things weren't much more complicated than getting good grades in school or getting the pretty girl (or hunky guy) to take notice, the young generation thrilled as films ranging from exploitation-level programmers from AIP to "art house" experiments by established *auteurs* like Antonioni started to grapple with issues which really engaged and interested them.

The so-called counterculture was established on screen in the '50s thanks to "rebels" like James Dean, Montgomery Clift, and Marlon Brando. Dean's iconic *Rebel Without a Cause* (1955) might seem the ideal template, yet wasn't Brando's Johnny Strabler in *The Wild One* (1953) the one who summed it up best? When asked what he was rebelling about, he quipped: "Whadda you got?" A new genre was born: the juvenile delinquent picture. True, there had been antecedents in some of the well-meaning but hopelessly conservative "social" melodramas of the 30s and 40s—just think of the anti-marijuana camp classic *Reefer Madness* (1936), for example. But those films didn't really seek to grapple with why young people were unhappy; they sought to offer a pat diagnosis and offer insight into how to prevent them from getting to be out of control. This new breed of "misfit" cinema was much freer and more unfettered, and as the '50s yielded to the hedonism of the '60s, things continued to morph into something much less black-and-white.

The notion of drug addiction was nothing new in the horror genre, of course, though it was typically codified or subverted in ways that made it more palatable to the audience—and the censor. The classic template is to be found in Robert Louis Stevenson's *The Strange Case of Dr. Jekyll and Mr. Hyde*, published in January of 1886. The story dealt with the idea of unleashing the Id, with the typical well-intended scientist learning the hard way that "there are some things man is not meant to meddle with." Of all the screen versions, the 1931 Rouben Mamoulian adaptation starring Fredric March (winning an Oscar for Best Actor—a first for the genre…and a last, until Anthony Hopkins won the gold for playing Hannibal Lecter in *The Silence of the Lambs*, 1991) is probably the best remembered, while Victor Fleming's glossy take for MGM with Spencer Tracy in 1941 is notable for its kinky sexual symbolism. All the versions deal with the notion of addiction in some way, as Jekyll struggles to keep sight of his basic humanity while the transformative serum continues to wreak havoc on him.

In early 1945, producer Ernst Lubitsch and director Joseph L. Mankiewicz cast Vincent Price in a role which had an eerie foreshadowing of things to come for the actor. In *Dragonwyck* (released in 1946), the then-thirty-three-year-old character star and sometime-leading man plays a callous aristocrat with a shameful skeleton in his closet: he's a drug addict. It's pretty remarkably upfront stuff for a major feature from 20th Century Fox, but to his credit, Mankiewicz doesn't skirt the issue. Price's portrayal of an outwardly charming but inwardly morally decrepit aristocrat paved the way for his later stardom in low budget horror movies. The actor was well aware of this and would later joke that it was the first of his many "dead wife pictures."

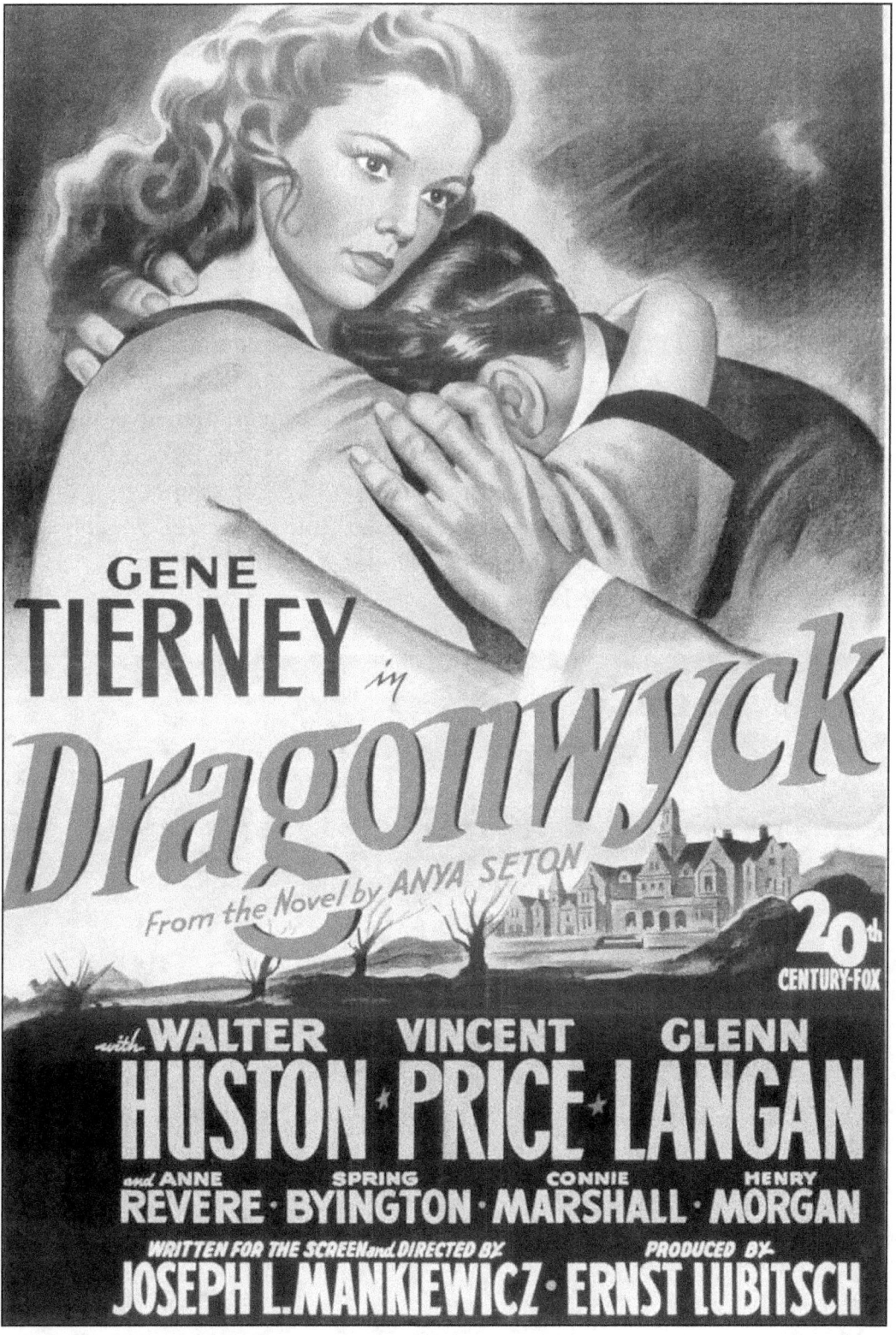

The Gothic melodrama *Dragonwyck* (1946) helped to set the stage for Vincent Price's later career in horror movies. Courtesy 20th Century Fox.

Which brings us to a major player in the counterculture horror movie movement, namely Roger Corman. A ferociously creative—both artistically and fiscally—force to be reckoned with, Corman burst into films as a producer before moving into directing an array of very low budget westerns, horror movies, and science fiction pictures—many of them shot in 10 days or less. He was also very prominent in the "youth run wild" movement, as evidenced by his production of *The Fast and the Furious* (1954) or his rock and roll pictures like *Rock All Night* (1957). In 1960, he enlisted Vincent Price to play the lead in his most ambitious movie to date: a color, widescreen adaptation of Edgar Allan Poe's *The Fall of the House of Usher*. Corman's partners at AIP, Samuel Z. Arkoff and James H. Nicholson, had their misgivings, but decided to trust Corman's commercial instincts by allowing him a longer-than-usual schedule (15 days!) and added money to film in color and Cinemascope. It was money well spent, and the success of *Usher* led to a series of 8 Poe adaptations directed by Corman—9 if we count the bizarre Poe-like Gothic *The Terror* (1963), and yes also admitting that one of them (*The Haunted Palace*, 1963) was *really* the big screen's first taste of H.P. Lovecraft.

*The Fall of the House of Usher* (1960) kicked off Roger Corman's cycle of Edgar Allan Poe films. Courtesy MGM.

Corman's Poe films were undoubtedly part of the classical Gothic tradition, with the additional validation of being literary adaptations (meaning that it was OK for the snootier critics to embrace them), but they all had touches of psychedelic cinema. This is most evident in the film's many dream and/or fantasy sequences, which are as revered these days as they are parodied. The use of distorting lenses, colored gels, and unnatural soundtracks has all the hallmarks of what would become known as "trippy cinema." The psychedelia is even more prominently featured in the last two entries, both of which were shot in England, where the cost-conscious Corman was able to take advantage of some tax breaks: the hyper-stylized *The Masque of the Red Death* (1964, photographed in very vivid colors by Nicolas Roeg, whose later forays into directing, beginning with *Performance* (1970), would help to push psychedelic cinema into bold new directions) and the more somber and pastel-tinted *The Tomb of Ligeia* (1965).

The Poe films are significant in this context because they allowed Corman to experiment with the sort of drug-fueled imagery which would come to the foreground in later efforts like *The Trip* (1967), which was essentially his attempt to translate his one LSD experience into a cinematic "happening." Apart from the Poe movies, one must also consider his horror/sci-fi classic *X: The Man with the X-Ray Eyes* (1963), in which scientist Ray Milland invents a drug which allows him to see through things—with horrific results. Interestingly, Corman originally wanted the anti-hero to be a jazz musician—but the counterculture movement hadn't quite exploded just yet, so going with the "mad scientist" angle was safer commercially. The fractured, impressionist imagery of *The Trip* has its roots in these earlier genre movies, underlining the fact that such hallucinogenic stylization has its roots in genre cinema, where such excesses were more sympathetically received.

It also makes sense that there should be this link between "science gone wrong" strain of genre cinema and the sensation-pushing counterculture movement. Ultimately, the motivating impulse is much the same: to see, to experience, to go beyond that which is normal and mainstream. In their own way, the counterculture types—the hippies, the anarchists, etc.—were pioneers just as the men of science in those earlier films had been. In questioning authority and pushing the envelope to see just how much sensory stimulation we could take, the youth movement was looking to shake things up and force society into facing its own limitations head-on. Though frequently misunderstood by the conservatives as purely being concerned with self-gratification while avoiding things like "good, honest, hard work," they launched a revolution which helped to break down some of the barriers of old while coming to a deeper understanding of the human condition.

Far out, man! Movies like *The Trip* (1967) signaled a change in the filmic landscape. Courtesy MGM.

By the 1970s, the world—both cinematic and at large—was a radically different landscape compared to even twenty years prior. The horror genre felt the change pretty radically. In many respects, the new order was established in 1968, thanks to a trio of very different, yet hugely influential pictures. George A. Romero's *Night of the Living Dead* demonstrated that horror movies didn't need big budgets or name actors to sell their ideas. Paradoxically, the Polish-born *auteur* Roman Polanski ended up making his big transformative splash in the genre thanks to the machinery of one of the major studios: *Rosemary's Baby* found Paramount tackling the sort of subject matter which had previously been consigned to the likes of AIP or Hammer Films in England. And then there was AIP's co-production with British company Tigon, *Witchfinder General*, in which Vincent Price played a historical monster named Matthew Hopkins, who capitalized on fear and religious hypocrisy by condemning many innocent people to death for practicing witchcraft. The three films were realized with radically different resources, but crucially they were all the work of supremely

Horror films crossed into bold new terrain thanks to films like *Night of the Living Dead* (1968). Courtesy Latent Image.

talented *auteurs* with a strong and inflexible vision. *Night* and *Witchfinder* pushed gore and brutality to terrifying extremes, while *Rosemary* cleverly subverted the sort of fluffy Rock Hudson/Doris Day romantic comedies into a horrifying satire of just how far an ambitious wannabe movie star (John Cassavetes) is willing to go in order to realize his dream.

Crucially, all three films connected with audiences. The landscape started to change. Imitations ran wild, and the genre as a whole would never be the same. As more "thirsty young Turks" worked their way into the film industry and tried to make their mark, the comparatively staid old school craftsmen of the '50s and '60s found themselves trying to play catch-up: for example, look at the sudden burst of extreme gore in Mario Bava's delightful *giallo*/proto-slasher/black comedy *Reazione a catena* (*Twitch of the Death Nerve*, 1971), which was a direct response to the success of the much younger Dario Argento, who burst on to the scene with *L'uccello dalle piume di cristallo* (*The Bird with the Crystal Plumage*, 1970) and generated box office far beyond anything the older filmmaker had ever achieved. Whether one prefers Bava or Argento, or rates them both equally, is a moot point in this context: the significant thing is the way the younger man connected to audiences and thus helped to change the landscape. Through the '70s, more young filmmakers would come along and contribute to this revolution: Tobe Hooper, John Carpenter, Joe Dante… and among the lesser-known, but no less valid, was Paterson, New Jersey native Alfred Sole (born 1943).

On the face of it, Sole's thematic concerns could be seen as conservative or even old hat. In situating the action of his horror-thriller in 1961, he was looking to evoke the very real controversy over the topic of divorce among Catholics. True, it's a point that was missed on some commentators—more than one critic of the time scratched their head in wonder at why Sole went to the trouble of setting the film in the '60s to begin with. Arguably it was a film made by Catholics and *for* Catholics, first and foremost, but it would be a gross mistake to interpret the film as a love letter to the Catholic Church. And yet, how typical such an interpretation would be: many insisted on viewing seminal slasher fare like John Carpenter's *Halloween* (1978) as inherently conservative and anti-sex, even if that particular agenda couldn't have been further removed from reality. In writing *Halloween*, Carpenter and his then-girlfriend Debra Hill—who, horror of horrors, were "living in sin"—weren't looking to condemn pre-marital sex or suggest that the pleasure of sex must be met with the pain of brutal death; far from it. The critics who were looking for a way of savaging such films took this as an easy approach to criticism, failing to realize that the success of Carpenter's film inspired filmmakers who were looking to copy its most "sellable" assets. Sex and violence have always sold, and they always will. That the linkage between the two might have been misunderstood or misinterpreted was beside the point: it allowed for a great deal of hysterical condemnation among the critics who were frankly sick and tired of being assigned to write about these films.

The film that started life as *Communion* and ended up being known as *Alice, Sweet Alice* before it was retitled once more as *Holy Terror* didn't concern itself with the whole "teen in peril" milieu of so many other genre pieces of the period. However, it pays to remember that while it made its way across the globe very slowly between 1976 and 1981, it was actually made before the whole

Early newspaper ad from Allied Artists, prior to changing the title to *Alice, Sweet Alice*.

slasher boom got up and running. Yes, there had been antecedents, including the aforementioned *Reazione a catena* and Bob Clark's *Black Christmas* (1974), but Sole's primary sources of inspiration were decidedly more "respectable": specifically Alfred Hitchcock, by way of *Psycho* (1960), and Nicolas Roeg's *Don't Look Now* (1973). Hitchcock, of course, had long been lionized as a serious filmmaker worthy of serious study. By the time Sole came on to the scene, Brian De Palma had already made at least one overt Hitchcock pastiche (*Sisters*, 1973) and he would soon be responsible for more—including the *Vertigo* (1958) riff *Obsession*, which made its debut the same year as Sole's picture. John Carpenter would also consciously channel Hitchcock in *Halloween*, but later imitators seemed less concerned with suspense than with gory shocks. Similarly, Roeg's film had the added protection of art house validity. *Don't Look Now* is genuinely frightening, with at least one shock sequence that still packs one hell of a punch, but its elliptical storytelling and artful visuals mark it out as something unique within the horror genre. Its influence would be profound, too, and nowhere more evidently than in *Alice, Sweet Alice*.

Nicolas Roeg's elegantly terrifying *Don't Look Now* (1973) was a major inspiration for Sole. Courtesy Paramount Pictures.

In namechecking such "established" examples, Sole was seemingly hedging his bets by looking to make a "classy" genre picture. His precise visual style, informed by his background in the fine arts, gives the film the look and feel of an *avant garde* European import. As mentioned earlier, it feels more like an Italian *giallo* than some really Italian *gialli*—especially the ones that try much too hard to look and feel "American." The critics who were sympathetic to the film picked up on this and found something to admire, even if they had issues with other aspects of the picture; those who couldn't get past what they deemed to be its gory excesses, however, used it as a battering ram to really pummel Sole for having the audacity to aspire for something more than the usual grindhouse genre fare. There's simply no pleasing everybody.

Sole's relationship with Catholicism is, to use contemporary parlance, problematic. He seems fascinated by the ritual and the pageantry, yet he also recognizes that its attempt to stifle healthy sexuality can result in a form of repression which can become poisonous and destructive. In setting the action in 1961, Sole at once complicates things for himself while also situating the drama in a very specific context. He's complicating it because, quite frankly, as a low budget filmmaker, his access to "period" trappings is limited. He doesn't have the ability to build sets from scratch, to shut down local traffic for extended periods and draft in a fleet of vintage cars, and to meticulously load the frame with details which scream "period." Instead, he is judicious about what he shows—and if the occasional anachronism slips through, it pays to remember just how tight the resources were. And yet, the context is absolutely critical to the overall impact of the picture. Had Sole elected to simply set the film in the '70s, then the central theme of divorce wouldn't have carried the same weight. By 1975, when production was gearing up on the film, the old standards had loosened somewhat. The Catholic Church would never truly embrace the concept of divorce, of course, but it was no longer quite the same as a source of shame and scandal. "*Your marriage isn't working? Get divorced! You've only got one life to live!*" Sole was canny enough to understand that, in setting the action in 1961, the audience members in the know about the history of divorce in relation to the Church would get it—while everybody else could conceivably go with the flow and simply appreciate it as a straight-ahead horror film.

All that being said, *Alice* is not strictly anti-religion, either. As such, it's not entirely in line with the anti-establishment mentality which dominated the new wave of filmmaking in the 1970s. Sole stops short of suggesting that everybody in the Church is corrupt. The primary representative of the Church, Father Tom (Rudolph Willrich), is depicted as a kindly and benevolent sort; there is nothing dark or foreboding about him at all. It is the dogma itself which is at the heart of Sole's commentary. The sense of grief, shame, even revulsion which is instilled in the parishioners over perfectly natural feelings (be they lust or the grim reality that relationships sometimes simply don't work out) has the capacity to trigger devastating acts of violence. Similarly, Sole relishes the presentation of religious hypocrites who get their jollies "tut tutting" the moral foibles of others while failing to live up to the letter of the Good Book themselves.

Like George A. Romero before him, Sole is also at heart a regional filmmaker. Romero had turned down overtures from Hollywood to relocate and make films there, preferring the familiarity of Pittsburgh and the group of local talent to whom he felt a special kinship, whereas Sole would eventually be lured by the siren call of Los Angeles. It's hard to fault him for this, and yet it's clear that something was lost when he made this transition. Just as Romero had a flair for finding the right locations in and around the 'burgh, Sole's status as a Patersonian gives *Alice* a tremendous sense of mood and atmosphere—as well as a verisimilitude which somehow makes the horror all the more unsettling. Going back to Hitchcock for a moment, it was his innovation in *Psycho* to take horror out of the Gothic and to put it into common, everyday places—the bathroom, the bedroom…the shower. Hitch managed to have his cake and eat it, too, by also allowing for the Bates house to stand out as iconic a presence as, say, Castle Dracula had been; yet, within that framework, much of *Psycho* unfolds in locations which are remarkable for their *ordinariness*.

Roman Polanski managed a similar feat on *Rosemary's Baby*—opening the film with a sensual exterior view of the high-Gothic architecture of the Dakota apartment building (where, appropriately, genre icon Boris Karloff once resided—and where, tragically, John Lennon would later be gunned down), before allowing the action to unfold in blandly benign settings.

Films like this helped to pave the way for the independent filmmakers of the '70s, none of whom had access to the production machinery afforded to even low budget film factories like England's Hammer Films. In lieu of imposing castles and chateaus, the likes of Romero, Carpenter, Hooper, and, yes, Sole would allow their films to take place in the sort of settings most of us encounter on a daily basis.

This is part of the lasting impact and appeal of *Alice, Sweet Alice*. It doesn't unfold in the sort of idyllic "every town U.S.A." environs as *Halloween*, nor does it inhabit the rustic space of *Night of the Living Dead*'s secluded farmhouse. It's definitely an *urban* film. The sense of urban decay and blight hangs heavily over the picture—and sadly that blight has only gotten worse in the forty-plus years since the picture was made. It's a world of moldy bricks and chipped paint, a world that was once prosperous but which has since fallen into disrepair. Amid the gradually worsening economic conditions, we're left with people with pride in what once was—and who are too stubborn to admit what it has now become. Sole's eye for locations is second to none, and working within the often tight confines of real locations, he always manages to find a way to make things look off-kilter. Nowhere is this more evident than in the scenes set in the nightmarish dwelling of the grotesque landlord Mr. Alphonso (Alphonso DeNoble), which *almost* tip the film into self-parody at times. Sole walks a tightrope in these sequences, but his eye for interesting details remains undiminished. That sense of a space that was once ornate and well-appointed, which has deteriorated into a grisly shadow of its former self, provides the perfect backdrop for the story; it's something that could never have *quite* been replicated on a Hollywood soundstage.

As shall become apparent, *Alice, Sweet Alice* did not take the box office by storm. Critical response was mixed—some reviewers appreciated its ambition and its attention to detail, while others decried its bloodshed and felt that the filmmakers were too self-conscious to tell a coherent or engaging story. It would become a true cult movie, attracting a loyal following among those who typically first encountered it in dodgy quality on VHS or on late night screenings on television.

As such, it is one of many so-called "unsung gems" which dot the genre landscape in the '70s. Not every film enjoyed the sort of success and exposure as *The Texas Chain Saw Massacre* (1974), *Halloween*, or *Dawn of the Dead* (1979). Among the many gems initially consigned to relative obscurity—to which we can certainly add the likes of *Deathdream* (1972), *Messiah of Evil* (1973), and *The Wicker Man* (1973)—*Alice* stands tall as one of the most distinctive and accomplished.

The scenes of Mr. Alphonso (Alphonso DeNoble) threatening Alice (Paula Sheppard) are queasily effective.

# Chapter 2

## Alfred Sole: From XXX to Anti-Catholic Horror

**Alfred Sole didn't set out** to become a film director. He studied to become an architect and went into practice. It was a good, solid, dependable way of life—but he had been bitten by the film bug as a young boy, and he knew in his heart of hearts that he wanted to make his own movies someday. He even managed to get hold of a 16mm camera when he was just a kid, and he cajoled his friends and neighbors into helping him make his own little films—a foreshadowing of things to come, as it happens. He continued to explore making films in the short form into adulthood, but he knew that if he really wanted to "make it," he needed to penetrate the marketplace with a feature.

Part of his on-going film obsession was reading the august publication *American Cinematographer*. He had hoped that it might provide some guidance in terms of breaking into the business, and sure enough, it did. Reading a profile on Academy Award-winning filmmaker Francis Ford Coppola, he discovered that the young Italian-American had cut his teeth making some "nudie cutie movies." Suddenly, it clicked. Sex sells and if Coppola could use it to break into the business, then Sole would follow his example.[1]

The problem was, the days of the so-called "nudie cuties" were long gone. Those were films—including Coppola's *The Bellboy and the Playgirls* (1962)—in which there was no actual sex. They played to the public's fascination with sex and eroticism by offering plenty of leering nudity, but they were fairly innocent,

---

1. This is consistent with the narrative presented to the author by Alfred Sole; however, on other occasions, he has said that originally he tried to interest his friends in funding a more mainstream movie, and that his poker buddies told him that if he were to make a porno movie, they'd chip in to make it happen.

18 • *Unholy Communion:* Alice, Sweet Alice

even naïve in their approach. By the early 1970s, when Sole was looking to break into the business, things had progressed—or regressed, depending on one's point of view. *Deep Throat* (1972) had thrown open the door to the "porno chic" movement. For a relatively brief moment in time, porn went mainstream, playing in theaters across America; the films were reviewed by mainstream publications, and it wasn't unusual for couples to go see these films on date

Italian poster for *Deep Throat* (1972), the porno movie that took the world by storm. Courtesy Arrow Productions.

night. Martin Scorsese and Paul Schrader made explicit reference to this trend in *Taxi Driver* (1976), in the painfully awkward sequence where Travis (Robert De Niro) takes conservative Betsy (Cybil Shepherd) to see a porno in a grimy XXX theater. The era of "porno chic" was by far the closest porn ever came to achieving real "respectability," though inevitably there was ample backlash and moral indignation.

Shot in January of 1972 and released to theaters in June of that year, *Deep Throat* made a superstar out of Linda Lovelace and entered into the pop cultural lexicon. Produced on a paltry budget of approximately $22,500, it ended up generating millions at the box office. Sadly, its success was overshadowed by a laundry list of controversies, ranging from the Mafia money connected to the making of the picture to star Linda Lovelace's (real name Lina Boreman) subsequent revelations that she was forced into making the film by her abusive husband and that much of what she did on camera amounted to rape.

All of that was still a ways off in 1972 when Alfred Sole decided to pitch in and make his own contribution to the burgeoning porno movement. He got some practical on-set experience by reaching out to New York-based contacts in the porno scene; he was allowed to come and participate in the making of some of these films, the titles of which Sole has long since forgotten, and he found the experience to be more than a little awkward. Nevertheless, he knew he had a concrete goal in mind, and if making sex movies was the way to facilitate his dreams, then he was willing to go down that path.

Sole managed to raise $25,000 from various contacts, friends, and members of the Paterson business community, all of whom were ready and eager to profit from the sudden mainstreaming of sex on celluloid. They all requested anonymity, of course, but the money invested was more-or-less guaranteed to return a handsome profit. Sole looked to stand out from the rest of the crowd by making a slightly "artier" movie, one which would hopefully signal to the critical establishment that he was a director of talent and intelligence. He titled the film *Deep Sleep*, in an obvious bid to ride on the coattails of *Deep Throat*'s notoriety, and he found a distributor in the form of Chelly Wilson, a New York-based distributor with a significant stake in the state's porn theater scene. Sole was given a list of changes that needed to be made if the deal was to be finalized, so he dutifully obliged by going back and inserting more explicit close-ups.

It may not have been the film Sole really wanted to make, but no matter: he had an actual movie playing in theaters. It was on film. It had actors. It had a soundtrack. Like it, love it, or hate it, there was no denying that he had finally managed to get his foot in the door.

Then all hell broke loose.

Promo for *Deep Sleep*; Alfred Sole had no idea what he was getting into when he decided to use the porno market to break into movies.

The sudden mainstreaming of sex movies didn't come without considerable pushback from various moral watchdog groups, and *Deep Sleep* soon found itself as an easy target. Sole had elected to sign the film with his own name and he made no effort to disguise his involvement. After all, he was using it as a sort of calling card to producers, so why would he hide his identity? Most porn was shot either in Los Angeles or in the mean streets of New York City, but here was a sex flick shot in Paterson, New Jersey. With so many locals in on the production end of things, it should come as no surprise that it started making a lot of money in New Jersey. Location filming revealed a number of familiar sights, and the locals were equal parts thrilled and horrified—and Sole had a target on his back.

The controversy over the film—which had less to do with the film itself than the general discomfort with the sudden depictions of graphic sex on cinema screens—could have been good for the film. All the chest-thumping certainly didn't hurt *Deep Throat*'s box office receipts, after all. Instead it deteriorated into a media circus with a beleaguered Sole at the center. The local Catholic diocese complained to the Passaic County Public Prosecutor's office because Sole made the mistake of showing the outside of the Bishop's house in the picture. It was bad enough that the house should appear in a porno film, period, but a porno shot by a local Catholic boy? Sole, for his part, maintained that he didn't even realize that it *was* the Bishop's house.

Complaints continued to flood in from a variety of sources; many had never even seen the film, while others actually had taken part in the original shoot and later claimed that they had no clue it was going to be an "all-in" sex movie, so to speak. Protests were organized and the local news had a field day covering the furor. Eventually the FBI became involved and warrants were sworn out for the known participants in the production; the charges were based in archaic anti-fornication laws dating all the way back to the 1700s.

So far as Sole was concerned, it amounted to nothing more than a career-making witch hunt for hungry young Assistant Prosecutor John T. Niccollai, then working under Chief Prosecutor D.J. Gourley. Niccollai turned to the archaic, long-forgotten laws because, quite frankly, he didn't have any other legal recourse. There was really no law against making porno films in Paterson. Even the age-old question of "what constitutes pornography" could have been trotted out with some success, to say nothing of the inherent subjectivity of what constitutes obscenity or bad taste. The controversy over pornography was at an all-time high due to the sudden mainstream success of films like *Deep Throat*, but attempting to prosecute and suppress such fare on objective legal grounds was a very slippery slope, indeed. The fallout was immense: Sole found himself being besieged by the media and by the friends who had put their money into the production, all of whom were terrified that their lives were going to be ruined. Sooner than give in to pressure from Niccollai, however, Sole fought back.

Sole was put on trial, and cannily he did his best to play up the sensationalism by arranging for various friends to protest his innocence outside of the Paterson courthouse. The media coverage was intense and Sole's celebrity continued to soar—even if it wasn't for the reasons he would have liked. It wasn't just a media stunt, however. Sole really was in serious trouble, and things got worse when he was informed that because the film had somehow managed to play in Oklahoma City, he was about to be indicted on federal charges of interstate transportation of pornography. Sole dutifully went to Oklahoma City to stand trial and a deal was reached where Sole was hit with some fines—and worse, a two-year probation period in which he was not permitted to make any more films. All the publicity and money generated by Paterson's little porno movie that could vanished into thin air—the profits were all absorbed by Uncle Sam, and the film was pulled from distribution. While Sole was grateful that he wasn't going behind bars, he was despondent that any momentum he might have gained as a filmmaker was stopped dead in its tracks.

When Sole returned to Paterson, he got another surprise when he was informed that the Catholic Church, still smarting over the use of their Bishop's house as an unwitting location in a local-made smut film, had excommunicated

Sole. Given the bitterness he felt over their role in helping to make his life into a living hell, the director couldn't have cared less. And yet, the sudden distaste he felt for the Church would become very instrumental in the development of his next feature film.

With Sole legally forbidden from making any more films for a period of two years, he returned, as best as possible, to day-to-day normality. He had his architecture career to fall back on and he knew that, when the time was right, he would eventually get back into the movie game. One thing was for sure: porno was out. It may have been a sure thing where generating money was concerned, but quite apart from all the legal grief it generated, he hated the experience of making *Deep Sleep*. He felt uncomfortable dealing with the actors. By his own admission, he had no clue how to communicate with them. He wasn't a prude, necessarily, but breaking things down in such a clinical manner wasn't really his cup of tea. Even worse, he also had to deal with issues like "performance anxiety" when his male talent couldn't achieve or sustain erections. It was all too much stress and even if he hadn't been put through the ringer by the Church and by Niccollai, it's unlikely that he ever would have attempted such a film again.

Even so, he continued to think about potential projects—one was a psychological drama called *Neighbors*, while another was an adaptation of Dorothy Matzner's fact-based novel *Victims of Justice*. Considering Sole's own recent run-ins with the legal system, one could see where the story of a woman put on trial for a murder she didn't commit would have resonated with him. Both proved to be pipe dreams, but at least they gave him something to look forward to during part of that dark period.

By the time his probationary period was up and he could put the legal woes of *Deep Sleep* behind him, Sole was already chomping at the bit to make a very different type of movie. His first move towards the mainstream was a May/December romance melodrama called *American Soap*, about which very little is known. Sole said his aim was to make a slightly surreal melodrama in the style of Federico Fellini, but even he remains sketchy on the details after a lapse of so many years. The film starred Kay Williams (1916-1983), an actress who had appeared in about a dozen features released between 1943 and 1953; she was also the fifth and final wife of screen legend Clark Gable.

Sole found an investor in the form of a client named Irwin Greenberg; he was in the process of designing Greenberg's home, and he talked the businessman into ponying up somewhere in the range of thirty to forty grand to make the picture. Greenberg had no prior experience producing movies, but Sole's ambitious concept of an artsy melodrama with tasteful eroticism—

# Prosecutor launched career, says director of 'Deep Sleep'

**By NICHOLAS JOLLYMORE**
United Press International

United Press International
PATERSON — Former interior designer Alfred E. Sole, who made the hard-core pornographic film "Deep Sleep," says he thanks his county prosecutor every day for helping launch his career as a director.

Sole says he hasn't done any interior decorating for some time. He now is editing the film for his second movie and negotiating with the author of a book for film rights for his third.

The bearded, 30-year-old director was an unknown before Passaic County Prosecutor D. J. Gourley charged Sole, actor Joseph Rose, and actress Kim Pope with violations of the state's fornication law in the filming of "Deep Sleep," which Gourley called the worst kind of pornography.

The fornication law forbids sexual intercourse between unmarried persons.

### Called it a satire

Sole describes "Deep Sleep" as a satire in which a man dreams he is impotent and attends a sex therapy school, where he is made to watch various sex acts.

The flood of publicity surrounding seizures of the X-rated film and the following court battles put Sole in the public spotlight and high on the interview list of a number of metropolitan newspapers.

When he began planning his second film, "Neighbors," Sole said financial backers came to him.

"I have to thank the prose-

ALFRED E. SOLE
Readies second film

cutor for that. I thank him every day," Sole said in an interview. "I want to thank him for helping me to direct my second film."

### Playing it straight

In his second and third films, Sole is playing it straight. He doesn't expect an X rating on either one.

"Neighbors," which like "Deep Sleep" was partially filmed in Sole's home in an old residential section of Paterson, is described as a psychological drama about two families living across the street from each other. The budget is about $200,000, compared to some $25,000 for "Deep Sleep."

The third film, for which Sole has a distribution option with United Artists, will be based on Dorothe Matzner's book, "Victims of Justice." The book is based on the 1966 murder of Clifton housewife Judith Kavanaugh and the 12-week trial which followed.

Mrs. Matzner, her husband, and two others were acquitted in the trial. Look magazine alleged in a story immediately afterward that the charges were manufactured by the Passaic County prosecutor's office. John G. Thevos was the Passaic prosecutor at the time.

### Won't be shown

"Deep Sleep," as far as Sole is concerned, will not be shown again.

"The notoriety was great, but I'm involved in my second film," he said. "And I don't want to be indicted again for interstate transportation violations." Some charges against Sole still are pending.

He is defending himself in Superior Court here on the grounds there was selective prosecution of "Deep Sleep" by Gourley's office. Since the U.S. Supreme Court decision giving local governments jurisdiction in defining pornography, Sole said his film and others such as "Deep Throat" have become targets.

" 'The Devil in Miss Jones' is playing all over the place and they're not busting it," he said. "And 'The Devil in Miss Jones' is 90 minutes of pure sex."

No matter where "Deep Sleep" plays, Sole added, "I'm sure they're going to nail it."

Let a smile be your umbrella; Alfred Sole puts on a sunny disposition while trying to put the *Deep Sleep* fiasco to bed.

no porn this time—convinced him that it was worth the risk. According to Sole, the film was shot quickly on 16mm; apart from Williams and Alphonso DeNoble, who went on to make such a vivid impression in *Communion*, he can no longer recall the names of the other actors who participated.

In a press pamphlet put together to promote what was then known as *Communion*, it is claimed that United Artists was planning to release *American Soap* in the near future; obviously this failed to happen. According to Sole, he was going through a rough patch following the controversy of *Deep Sleep*; his marriage had fallen apart and he was bouncing around trying to establish roots. There were only one or two prints struck of *American Soap*, and the materials ended up going missing. Exactly when the prints went missing is not known. They seem to have lingered at least through the process of making *Communion* before then vanishing in a puff of smoke. Sole doesn't even know where the negative has ended up, and were it not for a brief reference to its existence in a 1977 *Variety* review of *Alice, Sweet Alice*, it likely would have escaped notice altogether.

With *American Soap* finished and attracting no immediate interest from distributors, Sole decided that, if he wanted to attract the right kind of notice, his next movie needed to be more overtly commercial. Like porn, horror was a sure-fire commercial genre. In the 1970s, horror movies were being churned out at an all-time high. Naturally, the majority of them weren't any good—and as such, the genre had long achieved a reputation for being a red-headed stepchild of sorts. Many critics turned their noses up at horror movies, especially those of a low budget profile, but every now and again a film would come along that stood out from the pack and asserted itself as something worth taking seriously. One such film was Nicolas Roeg's big budget *Don't Look Now* (1973), based on the story by Daphne Du Maurier. The tale of a couple grieving the sudden death of their young daughter who become mixed up in a plot involving ESP and a series of brutal murders in Venice had obvious arthouse aspirations, and Roeg's elliptical storytelling resulted in a film that was equal parts enigmatic and shocking. Sole saw the film when it opened in the U.S. in December of 1973, and he was instantly enamored with it. He was still on probation, so he knew he couldn't start production any time soon, but he started to think of a way of doing something similar when he was finally allowed to get back behind the camera.

To help develop the screenplay, Sole turned to his neighbor, a writer and teacher at Montclair State University by the name of Rosemary Ritvo. They had also worked together on the script for *American Soap* and, for a period, they seemed like they would remain collaboratively joined when it came to developing screenplays for the director. Like Sole, Ritvo had a strong background in Catholicism. Sole was looking to give voice to his frustration with the Church over the way it had conspired against him on *Deep Sleep*. Nothing is more vindictive when it comes to the Church than somebody who has been victimized by it in some way or another—and Sole was eagerly looking forward to splashing some vitriol in its direction with his new project. Ritvo proved to be an ideal collaborator and the writing of the script proceeded harmoniously and with a merciful lack of drama. They would meet daily for two to three hours, usually churning out about ten pages per session. All told, by Sole's reckoning, the script went through about three drafts throughout 1974 before it was ready to be put before the cameras.

*Deep Sleep* had been funded largely by a group of 10 friends, many of whom used to get together with Sole to play poker. In light of what had happened on *Deep Sleep*, he wasn't able to find such eager financing this time around. However, Richard K. Rosenberg, one of his attorneys during that fiasco, was willing to lend him a sympathetic ear. Rosenberg liked the script and agreed to produce the picture. It was an opportunity for the attorney to realize a long-standing dream. "I was one of those kids you saw every Saturday afternoon at the neighborhood playhouse. I love the movies. I know this sounds corny, but I always wanted to be a movie producer. Alfred gave me that chance."[2] A budget of approximately $350 thousand[3] was secured, with Sole refinancing his home and putting up all of his savings in order to get the necessary money in place, and filming was slated to begin that summer.

The budget may have been low, but compared to Sole's first features, it must have felt positively lavish. The film finally allowed Sole to graduate to 35mm, and the director later recalled that he used a 16mm lens for much of the shooting. This has caused some confusion among fans, who assumed that meant that the film had been shot in 16mm. By using this lens, Sole was able to get very particular wide-angle effects with a minimum of distortion; this enabled him to get the strange, off-kilter visual style he was looking to achieve.[4]

There was no money for stars, so Sole aimed his attention at the theatrical scene of New York City. He spent a lot of time going to various theatrical performances, then approaching actors who caught his eye when he thought they might be suitable for a particular role.

---

2. Chadwick, Bruce, "Out of 'Deep Sleep,' Into Wonderland of 'Alice,'" *Daily News*, November 7, 1977.
3. Contemporary reports indicated that the budget was $1 million. This was almost certainly inflated to make the film seem more "important."
4. As related by Sole in his audio commentary for the Roan Group laser disc.

One such actor was Paula Sheppard, an eighteen-year-old college student who was part of the Herbert Berghof Studio, where she was enrolled with a dance troupe. Prior to the preparations for *Alice, Sweet Alice*, Sole had enrolled at Berghof because he was eager to learn more about acting and how to deal with actors, so on the advice of his cousin, he enrolled there for some lessons. He caught sight of Sheppard and asked her if she'd be interested in appearing in his new movie. Surprisingly, given her age, the role was that of psychologically damaged pre-pubescent Alice Spages. Sheppard's unusual looks and diminutive height—four feet, eleven inches—were well-suited to the character, however, and none of the critics were any the wiser; even those who hated the film didn't pick up on the fact that the twelve-year-old was played by a young adult.

Sheppard admitted that she had some concerns at first. "This really strange guy came up to me at lunchtime and said he wanted to put me into movies. I didn't know what to do. Several other guys had approached me with the same line, and they were obviously creeps. Alfred seemed kind and honest, though, and I talked to him about it."[5] Given the scandal surrounding *Deep Sleep*, Sole was forthright about his background making porn but assured Sheppard's parents that they had nothing to fear and that there would be nothing sexually explicit in this film. They took him at his word and the rest of the casting soon proceeded on similar lines.

For the role of Alice's ill-fated younger sister, Sole sought the young Brooke Shields, who was then enjoying success as a model. Sole had seen her modeling work and he reached out to her mother, Teri Shields, who was only too eager to get Brooke involved in the movies. She was only ten years old at the time of filming, and within a few years she would become a major celebrity thanks to the controversy surrounding her appearance as a teenage courtesan in Louis Malle's *Pretty Baby* (1978). Her sudden ascent to screen stardom also enabled Sole's film, her big screen debut, to be put back in the spotlight several years after its original spotty release.

The role of the girls' mother, Catherine Spages, went to Broadway veteran Linda Miller, who proved to be a source of difficulty for Sole during the shooting. Miller was going through a lot of personal problems, having recently divorced the actor Jason Miller (who had recently been nominated for an Oscar for *The Exorcist*, 1973), and Sole would describe her as "a pain in the ass," though he remains complimentary of her acting abilities. Miller contributed to the most horrific incident that occurred during filming, when she slit her wrist just as Sole was gearing up for a take. According to Sole, the incident occurred during

---

5. Chadwick, Bruce, "Out of 'Deep Sleep,' Into Wonderland of 'Alice,'" *Daily News*, November 7, 1977.

Alfred Sole is flanked by Paula Sheppard and Brooke Shields during the making of *Alice, Sweet Alice*.

the final day of filming in the church. She recovered and was able to complete the filming, but it caused major scheduling headaches as Sole tried to shoot around her while she recuperated.

Unfortunately, the stop and go nature of filming was a consistent headache for Sole, as he was constantly dealing with cash flow difficulties. The director would later maintain that the actual number of shooting days was around 20, but with filming constantly being interrupted by gaps up to as much as two weeks while the money woes were being ironed out, it stretched over a much longer period.

Though anxious to distance himself from the world of porn, Sole didn't entirely sever ties with his *Deep Sleep* collaborators. Joe Rose, who appeared in Sole's first film, was brought in to play one of the minor priest characters in the film; could this have been another instance of the director thumbing his nose at the establishment?[6] He certainly didn't try to keep the casting secret, and entertainment writer Bruce Chadwick, who covered the film extensively

---

6. Rose is credited in *Deep Sleep* as Willard Butts.

when it was released, brought up the casting in at least one of his columns.[7] If anybody in the Church got wind of the casting of a sex film veteran—albeit one who did *not* have sex on camera—as a priest, however, they evidently didn't think it worth making waves. Rose (billed as Joe Rossi) appears as Father Joe, who helps Father Tom with serving Communion at the end of the picture.

By his own admission, Sole was forced to cut corners wherever he could, though he was determined to preserve the integrity of his overall vision. In addition to difficulties with Miller, he also had major problems with the cameramen on the picture. Sole has claimed that he burned through anywhere from three to six cinematographers, though only two are credited—and not as cinematographer, but as cameramen. Chuck Hall and John Friburg stuck around for the bulk of the shoot, earning screen credit in the process, but according to Sole they were less than supportive of their relatively inexperienced director. Of the two, Sole reserves his venom mostly for Friburg, a New Yorker who appears to have signed on purely for the money. Friburg fought Sole on every set-up and did his best to undermine the director in front of the crew. With tensions simmering throughout, Sole finally exploded on Friburg, asking him why he even signed on to do the film, if all he wanted to do was make his life miserable. Even so, Sole's quirky visual sensibility is evident throughout, suggesting that he ultimately had his way, even if he had to fight to justify every set up.

The filming progressed fitfully and the stress and strain continued to wear on Sole, who ended up becoming violently ill with hepatitis at one point. Sole's connections in the Paterson community ensured that he had support, however, and a doctor friend helped him to get through the days with B12 injections. Sole was also dependent on the kindness of strangers to provide background "period" materials, including cars, as the story had been set in 1961 to play up the Church's complicated relationship with the topic of divorce. A local by the name of Charles Hannah helped out by providing the vintage cars.[8] The Paterson Fire Department chipped in to provide rain effects with their hoses, while the local police department even donated a lie detector for one scene in addition to allowing Sole to film some scenes in their station. Sole may not have had much in the way of money, but the communal spirit of banding together to make a movie—better still, a *non-porno* movie—helped to smooth over some of the bumps on the road.

---

7. Chadwick, Bruce, "Nearly Jailed, Now Tank's for the Memory," *Daily News*, November 3, 1977.
8. Spero, Bette, "Paterson welcomes violent film by a penitent director," *Star-Ledger*, November 13, 1976.

By the time filming wrapped, Sole was eager to get into post-production. He remained with the picture through every step of the process, determined as he was to make the film everything he had hoped it would be. He enjoyed a very harmonious relationship with up-and-coming editor Edward Salier, with whom he had already worked on the ill-fated *American Soap*. Unlike his contentious camera crew, Salier was supportive and didn't turn his nose up at the picture. Where Sole had sometimes fallen down in terms of getting adequate coverage, Salier always managed to find a way to patch things over and make it work. He would utilize a variety of tricks, sometimes triple-printing images to get weird effects, and Sole savored the entire editing process as a result. All told, they spent about six months tinkering with and perfecting the final cut. It was time very well spent and Sole was fortunate indeed to have the benefit of time, without the added pressure of a pre-booked theatrical release date to meet. As for Salier, he would go on to direct such low-budget genre items as *Silent Scream* (1980) and *The Last Horror Film* (1982) before finding his niche in TV, working on such series as *Max Headroom, Quantum Leap, Lois & Clark: The New Adventures of Superman*, and *NCIS*.

To compose the score, Sole turned to New York-based Stephen Lawrence. Lawrence had struck gold in 1972 with the song *Free To Be… You and Me*, which was part of an audio-visual project of the same name devised by actress Marlo Thomas with the aim of teaching children not to feel constrained by traditional gender roles. The album and book were a smash hit and remain in print to this day; there was also a television adaptation which aired to acclaim and huge ratings in 1974. Prior to *Alice*, he had also composed the score for *Bang the Drum Slowly* (1973). Sole was very keen on the music of Bernard Herrmann and he encouraged Lawrence to use Herrmann's iconic work for Alfred Hitchcock as his inspiration. Lawrence responded with a score that is definitely Herrmann-esque, with an equal measure of Michael Small's score for *Klute* (1971), but which stops short of being a mere copy. The use of eerie vocals and aggressive strings helps to maximize the suspense as well as the horror.[9]

Sole's attention to detail extended to the final mixing, as he and sound editor Dan Sable worked in unison to create a very precise aural landscape. The use of ambient sound is particularly noteworthy in the scenes involving the grotesque landlord, Mr. Alphonso (Alphonso DeNoble). The use of the scratchy phonograph music and sound effects like a dripping tap and the scuttling of insects crawling around the filthy apartment help to make these

---

9. The long-overdue soundtrack release finally emerged from Waxwork Records in 2021; as per Dante Tomaselli, Stephen Lawrence found the original master tapes after an extensive search.

scenes particularly queasy. Sole also contrasts moments of extreme bombast with quiet, serene moments in much the same way as William Friedkin had used sound in *The Exorcist*.

Despite the controversy created by his first feature, Sole was able to get some positive support from the press in Paterson for his follow-up. Much was made of the fact that it was—reportedly—the first feature film shot entirely in New Jersey since 1933[10]; this obviously wasn't including grubby little porno movies. In the November 10, 1976 edition of the *Courier-Post*, Larry Delarose reported that Sole had shot 210,000 feet of film while playing up that it was entirely shot in Paterson—the original home of cinema, thanks to Thomas Edison.[11]

If *Deep Sleep* had been a built-in compromise of sorts, no such issues dogged Sole's follow-up. That's not to say that everything proceeded completely free of drama, even if it seemed pretty idyllic compared to the experience surrounding *Deep Sleep*. For one thing, as reported in the September 16, 1977 issue of *The Record*, Sole ended up bringing suit against attorney John Surgent to the tune of $23,000. Sole's suit alleged that Surgent and his company Horizon Films had agreed to pay Sole his $10 thousand directing fee among sundry other fees. The outcome of this suit is not known, and when asked about it in 2020, Sole told the author that he can't even remember such a suit being filed.

There was also the issue of the film's title. Sole had favored the title of *Communion*, and this was the title when the film premiered at the Chicago International Film Festival on November 12, 1976. The film lost out as Best Picture to Wim Wenders' *Kings of the Road* (*Im Lauf der Zeit*, 1976), but it collected a silver plaque as one of the runner-ups.

The Paterson premiere was held the very next day, and the local press had a field day boasting about it being filmed on location; a report in the *Star-Ledger* claimed it took 81 days to shoot, but this was an error—it could be that this was the total amount of days from start to finish, including the many periods of downtime, however.[12] The premiere was held at the Fabian Theater, and contemporary reports claimed that nearly 2,000 people showed up to see Paterson represented on the big screen.[13]

---

10. The film in question was *The Emperor Jones* (1933), starring Paul Robeson.
11. Delarose, Larry, "Edison started it—now it's back," *Courier-Post*, November 10, 1976, p. 24.
12. Spero, Bette, "Paterson welcomes violent film by a penitent director," *Star-Ledger*, November 13, 1976.
13. Chadwick, Bruce, "Spotlight Bash Heralds State's First Film Since 1933," *Daily News*, November 15, 1976.

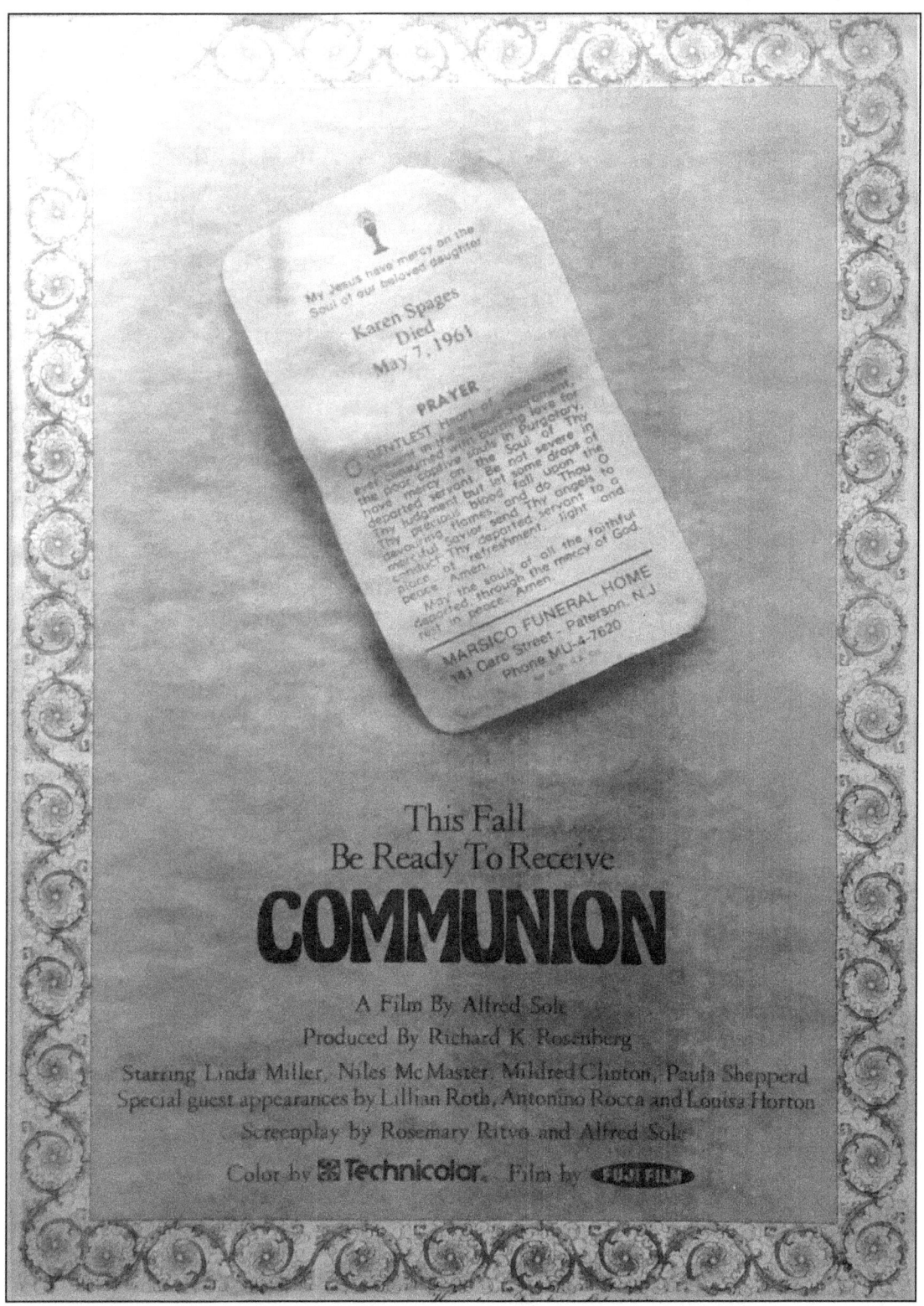

Full page ad in the May 19, 1976 issue of *Variety*.

After having been burned in effigy, Sole found himself warmly embraced by the people of Paterson.

The plaudits continued on November 22, 1976, when Sole and Rosenberg were awarded the gold medal for Best New Film at the Virgin Islands International Film Festival. Mildred Clinton also won a prize at the same festival as Best Supporting Actress. On top of that, there was talk of deals with major studios. Paramount and Universal were both reportedly interested, but ultimately Rosenberg managed to strike a deal with Columbia Pictures. A tie-in novelization was commissioned—written by Frank Lauria—and Sole was on top of the world. Finally he had made it. "I'm hoping it will make people remember me as the man who made *Communion*, and not the man who made *Deep Sleep*."[14]

As for the people of Paterson, all the fuss over *Deep Sleep* was forgiven and forgotten. Sole had managed to make a "legitimate" movie that showed off their city. It had the potential to become a major mainstream release from one of the major Hollywood studios. Lawrence Kramer, then-mayor of Paterson, saw dollar signs. "It's wonderful to have a major movie made in Paterson. We are so pleased by this film and we welcome other filmmakers to the city."[15]

---

14. Chadwick, Bruce, "Spotlight Bash Heralds State's First Film Since 1933," *Daily News*, November 15, 1976.
15. Chadwick, Bruce, "Spotlight Bash Heralds State's First Film Since 1933," *Daily*

The Gold Medal awarded to Alfred Sole and Richard K. Rosenberg.

Unfortunately Sole's joy was short-lived. Though Columbia had insisted on some trims to the film, Sole was agreeable because he knew that they would give the film the sort of wide release that would really make a difference. He felt like they understood the movie and would treat it fairly. Unbeknownst to him, however, troubles were brewing behind the scenes. Rosenberg dickered with Columbia over the money and the studio ultimately decided to pull out of the venture, leaving the film suddenly orphaned. Rosenberg tried to soothe Sole by claiming that Columbia hated the movie and thought it was much too gory, but the director soon found out the truth and had to seethe in silence over the deception.

*News*, November 15, 1976.

Back cover for the novelization by Frank Lauria.

Rare newspaper ad, courtesy of Michael Gingold.

Finally, Allied Artists expressed an interest. Sole didn't feel like they understood the movie at all. To them, from his point of view, it was just another cheap horror pick-up—a piece of disposable property that they could use as a tax write-off if it didn't generate interest. Sole tried to generate some positive communication with them, but claimed that after one terse phone call, they refused to continue talking with him. Suddenly he was informed by Rosenberg that Allied Artists didn't like the title *Communion*, and they were going to retitle it as *Alice, Sweet Alice*. Allied Artists executive Jerry Grunberg explained, "We tested the movie before several dozen preview audiences. Almost everyone loved the film and almost no one liked the *Communion* title. You need a title you can sell. We think *Alice, Sweet Alice* can sell."[16] Sole was displeased, but in his eagerness to get the movie out to the public, he had sold off his rights in the venture to Rosenberg and he was no longer in a position to fight any such changes.

Allied Artists put the movie out as *Alice, Sweet Alice* in November of 1977—and it generated very little interest. By 1981, it had changed monikers once more; now it was being shown as *Holy Terror*. It even ended up playing in Pensacola, Florida, and La Crosse, Wisconsin in August of 1977 as *The Mask Murders*, though that title never really caught on.[17] *Alice, Sweet Alice* became the best-known title, but Sole has never been happy with any of the alternate titles. His preferred title remains *Communion*, but apart from its very early screenings, it was never distributed as such in the United States.

It did, however, play as *Communion* in the U.K., where Hemdale put it in out in September of 1977 on a double bill with René Cardona, Jr.'s sleazy *Jaws* (1975) knock-off, *Tintorera* (1977). International distribution proved to be spotty, but it did play Italy in 1977 as *Comunione con delitti* ("Communion with Murder"), and it gradually showed up in other territories, as well. Considering the size of the budget, it's fair to say that it was generating a profit for *somebody*, even if it wasn't for Sole himself.

Even so, by his own admission, he was overjoyed to see the film playing in theaters, more or less in the form he had always intended it to be seen. What did not please him, however, was the discovery that the film had never been properly registered for a copyright. He had sold his interests in the film to Rosenberg, who in turn struck a distribution deal with Allied Artists, but evidently in the confusion over rebranding the movie and putting it out over and over again, nobody had thought to register legal copyright. When Sole discovered this, he set out to correct the wrong by securing the copyright himself. This didn't stop the film from being bootlegged and released through various video labels during the home video boom of the 1980s. The film was generating money, but Sole wasn't seeing any of it. With the director trying to forge ahead with his career and dealing with various life issues, he didn't have the time or the inclination to go after the various companies who were illegally distributing his

---

16. Chadwick, Bruce, "Nearly Jailed, Now Tank's for the Memory," *Daily News*, November 3, 1977.

17. Thanks to Michael Gingold for the release information on *The Mask Murders*. Italian genre buffs will be heartened to know that one of the films it played with under that name was *The School That Couldn't Scream*, a retitled version of Massimo Dallamano's *What Have You Done to Solange?* (*Cosa avete fatto a Solange?*, 1972).

movie, but he remains insistent that the copyright is his and his alone. In more recent years, Warner Bros. has also asserted ownership, due to their taking over the Allied Artists library.

There were some other bizarre incidents connected to the film, as indicated in a report by Bruce Chadwick in the November 3, 1977 edition of the *Daily News*. Andrew Roman, a New Jersey-based actor who also appeared in *Dog Day Afternoon* (1975), played a very small role as a policeman in *Alice*—and on August 11, 1976, he was arrested on the charge of murdering his girlfriend, model Mary Bruen. Roman, then hospitalized for a suspected suicide by drug overdose, was accused of shooting Bruen twice in the chest with a 22-caliber rifle. He was ultimately found guilty of first degree murder, though

Allied Artists' revamped campaign under the title of *Alice, Sweet Alice*.

through the process of appeals it was determined that the full severity of the charge was not properly explained to the jury and it was then reduced to a lesser verdict of second degree murder. He was ultimately sentenced to life in prison.

Chadwick's article also picked up on the suicide attempt by Linda Miller, as well as a subsequent suicide attempt by Alphonso DeNoble—though the latter was listed as Alphonso DeRose; tragically, DeNoble's subsequent attempt on November 17, 1978 proved to be successful.

As for Sole, he never really realized his dream of becoming a full-time motion picture director. He had brushes with infamy thanks to his experiences with *Deep Sleep* and he occasionally found himself rubbing shoulders with the rich and famous; according to Sole, he ran into Louis Malle during the editing of *Alice, Sweet Alice*, and he showed the French *auteur* some footage of Brooke

Shields, which lead to her casting in *Pretty Baby*. Shields, for her part, has never gone out of her way to acknowledge anything that Sole's cult favorite may have done for her career. Such is the fickle nature of the film industry.

While continuing to work primarily as an architect in Paterson, Sole continued to harbor hopes of making more pictures. There was talk of a film called *Gray Rhapsody*, again co-written with Rosemary Ritvo, which was to star Omar Sharif and Diana Rigg. Sole described it as "a cross between *Klute* and *Taxi Driver*," but that stalled.[18] He eventually accepted an offer from producer Pierre Brousseau to make a sort of updated version of *Beauty and the Beast* called *Tanya's Island*. Sole entered into the film with real artistic aspirations, but he soon discovered that Brousseau was making promises that he had no interest in keeping. He had written another script he was pleased with in collaboration with Rosemary Ritvo, and he even managed to secure the services of the young Rick Baker and Rob Bottin to design the beast costume, but the cash-strapped production fell way short of Sole's original ambitions. Though partly filmed in Canada to satisfy the Canadian financing, the bulk of the shoot unfolded in Puerto Rico, where Sole was hit with one technical mishap after another. Brousseau forced Sole to up the erotic content and the end result was completely different from the film Sole and Ritvo had written.

*Tanya's Island* made its debut in December of 1980, and the critical reaction was unsurprisingly hostile. Sole couldn't even object as he pretty much hated the end result, himself. It finally sank without a trace and has failed to generate much in the way of cult interest.

This was followed by a horror spoof originally titled *Thursday the 12th*, which was an obvious allusion to the success of the *Friday the 13th* franchise. By Sole's own admission, he was a bad fit for the material, as he displayed virtually no feel for, or affection towards, the comedy genre. Tellingly, it was the first film he directed that he hadn't also written, so he found himself in the role of "gun for hire" as he put a variety of comedy veterans—including Tom Smothers and Eve Arden—as well as up-and-comers like Paul Reubens and Phil Hartman through their paces.

Ultimately released in April of 1982 as *Pandemonium*, the film was another box office dud, signaling the end of Sole's career as a big screen filmmaker. By his own admission, he was also arrogant about offers to go into television, where he might have been able to establish a reputation. As far back as 1976, Sole let it be known that he had no interest in directing for television: "Television is

---

18. Delarose, Larry, "Edison started it—now it's back," *Courier-Post*, November 10, 1976.

Sole's follow-up to *Alice, Sweet Alice* wasn't what anybody expected—
least of all Sole. Courtesy CFDC.

too contrived. It's not something I would like to do."[19] He shot down offers to direct for the small screen—though he had been involved in another ill-fated comedy venture called *Cheeseball Presents* in 1984, where he was one of several credited directors—and decided it was time for a change of direction. Even so, he had dreams of making a dramatic thriller with a gay theme, but the financing

---

19. Delarose, Larry, "Edison started it—now it's back," *Courier-Post*, November 10, 1976.

*Pandemonium* (1982) put the final nail in the coffin of Sole's directorial career. Courtesy MGM.

never materialized. With no offers on the table and nobody looking to take a chance on giving him the money to make another feature, Sole retreated into screenwriting, working on spec and occasionally getting something produced. In an irony that couldn't have been lost on Sole, despite his protestations over working on the small screen, he ended up being confined to television. He wrote episodes of *Hotel*, *Friday the 13<sup>TH</sup>: The Series*, and *Alfred Hitchcock Presents*, as well as the tele-films *Under Siege* (1986) and *Secret Witness* (1988).

Ultimately, it was Sole's background in architecture that proved to be his primary source of income. After proceeding fitfully as a screenwriter for hire, he branched out into production design circa 1993. It's been a profitable transition for Sole, who has continued working on such hit series as *Castle* (2009-2016) and the remake of *MacGyver* (2017-2019).

Put bluntly, Sole never made another film worthy of *Alice, Sweet Alice*. He never enjoyed the sort of run of cult favorites enjoyed by the likes of George A. Romero, John Carpenter, Tobe Hooper, or David Cronenberg. It wasn't for lack of trying, however. Perhaps if he had been savvier about the business or had managed to hook up with somebody who could have looked out for his interests, things might have been different. Might, might, might. We will never know for sure. The history of Hollywood is rife with such stories of disappointment and professional frustration.

Yet, despite all the heartbreak, Sole managed something that relatively few can lay claim to: he made one legitimately great movie. *Alice, Sweet Alice* (or to use its creator's preferred title, *Communion*) continues to endure. It continues to fascinate. That you are holding this volume in your hands speaks to that very fact.

# Chapter 3

## Cast Talent Bios

**Given the lack of money,** Alfred Sole never set his sights on casting big name actors in *Communion*. He didn't even have the benefit of a casting director on the film, so he was forced to rely on his wits, reaching out to New York theater veterans and offering them roles in his upcoming production. Even so, he ended up with one major star in the making—as well as a former super star who was returning from a decades-long absence from the big screen.

Arguably the absence of stars worked to the film's advantage. As with indie horror hits like *Night of the Living Dead* (1968) or *The Texas Chain Saw Massacre* (1974), the cast were free of the baggage associated with star recognition. As such, it was easier for viewers to settle into the story without second-guessing things based on the established credentials of the actors inhabiting the roles. After all, wouldn't it have been distracting to see Sidney Poitier as Ben in *Night* or Faye Dunaway as the imperiled Sally in *Chain Saw*? For the sake of the film, it's truly for the best to have actors who could disappear into the skin of their characters, free of past associations and expectations. Sole has spoken fondly of most of his actors, but even where there were conflicts, he has stood by his ensemble and praised them for their efforts.

The following mini-bios are designed to provide a bit of background about the major players—some of whom enjoyed greater longevity on screen than others.

## Linda Miller (Catherine Spages)

Born: 16 September 1942, New York City, NY

Born as Linda Mae Gleason, she is the daughter of the legendary actor and comedian Jackie Gleason (1916-1987). In addition to sporadic film work, Miller has also enjoyed some success on the stage.

44 • *Unholy Communion:* Alice, Sweet Alice

Linda Miller and Brooke Shields in a tense moment.

In 1975, shortly before filming *Alice, Sweet Alice*, she was nominated for a Tony for her work in the Broadway production of *Black Picture Show*. Written and directed by Bill Gunn—revered for his cult horror picture *Ganja & Hess* (1973)—*Black Picture Show* tells of a black writer who succumbs to madness and reflects on his life at the point of death; his son, a successful filmmaker, decides to make a film about his father's life. Reality and fantasy collide, and Gunn explores themes of racism as the white figures of power in Hollywood corrupt the integrity of the African American artist. Miller (billed as Jane Linda Miller at the time) played the role of a drug-addled actress. All told it ran for 41 performances at the Vivian Beaumont Theatre, from January 6 through February 9, 1975.

Twice married, she wed the actor and playwright Jason Miller (1939-2001, best known for his Oscar-nominated turn as Father Karras in William Friedkin's film of William Peter Blatty's *The Exorcist*, 1973) in March of 1963; they divorced in 1973, and she would later marry Robert King in June of 1990. Her son with

Cast Talent Bios • 45

Mildred Clinton and Rudolph Willrich during the unforgettable climax.

Jason Miller, Jason Patric (born 1966), would also go on to become a well-known actor, appearing in such films as the horror hit *The Lost Boys* (1987).

*Alice, Sweet Alice* remains Miller's best-known film work, though she also appeared in such films as *An Unmarried Woman* (1978, directed by Paul Mazursky) and *Night of the Juggler* (1980), as well as episodes of such TV shows as *Highway to Heaven*, *Freddy's Nightmares*, and *Law & Order: Criminal Intent*.

She has been inactive on screen since 2014.

## Mildred Clinton (Mrs. Tredoni)

Born: 2 November, 1914, Brooklyn, New York
Died: 18 December, 2010, New York City, New York

At the time of production, Mildred Clinton was one of the more experienced screen performers in the cast. But in fact, Clinton's screen career had progressed very fitfully and was only just beginning to pick up steam when she was cast as the fanatical Mrs. Tredoni.

The daughter of Judge Charles Solomon, she made a name for herself appearing on stage, on screen, and on the radio. She got her start in the 1950s, appearing on TV shows like *The Jack Benny Program* and *Car 54, Where Are You?*, and also doing vocal work on *CBS Radio Mystery Theatre*.

She dropped out of view, where big screen work was concerned, for the better part of the 1960s, then in the '70s she started to establish herself as a familiar face—if not name. She did a lot of commercial work, including ads for Kentucky Fried Chicken and Minute Rice. Her big screen profile started to increase as well. Clinton appeared in Elaine May's *A New Leaf* (1971) in an uncredited role, before playing Al Pacino's mother in Sidney Lumet's hit drama *Serpico* (1973). Mrs. Tredoni was certainly her meatiest role, but she would continue to appear in films sporadically over the next twenty-plus years. She would become a favorite of director Spike Lee, who cast her in his films *Crooklyn* (1996), *Summer of Sam* (1999), and *Bamboozled* (2000). The latter was her final work for the screen.

Clinton won a well-deserved gold medal as Best Supporting Actress for *Alice, Sweet Alice* at the Virgin Islands International Film Festival; she was the only member of the cast to be so lauded for her work in the film.

In fact, Clinton was not Sole's first choice for the role: he would later reveal that he first approached the veteran stage and screen performer Geraldine Page (*Sweet Bird of Youth*, 1962), who was otherwise engaged.

## Paula Sheppard (Alice Spages)

Born: 7 July, 1957, East Orange, New Jersey

Thanks to her diminutive stature, Paula Sheppard was cast in the crucial role of Alice—despite being eighteen years of age. One would never guess her real age, however, making the deception completely convincing.

As Sole would later reveal, Sheppard came to his attention

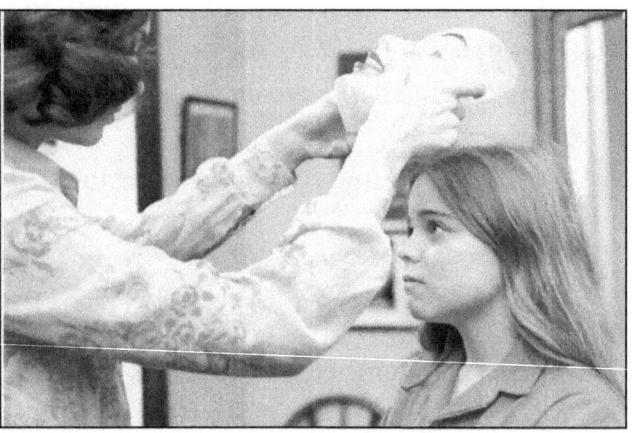

Alice (Paula Sheppard) is unmasked by her mother (Linda Miller).

when he met her during his stint in a New York acting course. She was enrolled in college at the time but was eager to participate in the picture. *Alice* would be her first film role—and it provided her with an ideal introduction to the public. Perhaps if it had been an immediate success, her career would have unfolded differently. As it stands, she didn't get another crack at screen acting until she was cast in the cult sci-fi/drug oddity *Liquid Sky* (1982).

At the time of *Alice*'s release, Sheppard admitted that the film was a fluke and she didn't see herself pursuing acting as a full-time proposition. "I never acted before in my life, and to this day I still don't know why Alfred wanted me in this picture. It was tough to act. I never went to acting school or even paid much attention to actresses in films."[20] That same article concludes by noting that she had no plans to ever act again, though she clearly decided it was worth trying one more time when she signed on for *Liquid Sky*.

Sheppard ended up getting married not long after her second film, and she's retreated from the limelight in favor of pursuing a happy family life.

## Niles McMaster (Dominick Spages)

Born: Date of birth unknown

Born in Chicago, Illinois, McMaster studied art at the University of Wisconsin, Madison. He appeared in two cult genre oddities in 1976—the other being the notorious *Bloodsucking Freaks*. He also appeared on one of the same TV shows which also guest starred Mildred Clinton, a soap called *The Edge of Night*.

Following *Alice, Sweet Alice*, he would continue to appear sporadically in the odd film (*Windy City*, 1984) and TV show (including a 1979 two-parter on *Barnaby Jones*), and he also did a good deal of commercial work for TV and radio, but he has been inactive on screen since the mid-80s.

Dominick (Niles McMaster) and Catherine (Linda Miller) try to figure out whether Alice (Paula Sheppard) is really a killer or not.

---

20. Chadwick, Bruce, "Out of 'Deep Sleep,' Into Wonderland of 'Alice,'" *Daily News*, November 4, 1977.

Since that time he has focused his energy on his art work; his paintings and drawings have made their way into various public and private collections.

## Jane Lowry (Annie DeLorenze)

Born: 11 February, 1937, Minneapolis, Minnesota
Died: 15 November 2019, New York City, New York

Unless there are other unidentified roles out there awaiting rediscovery, Jane Lowry made her film debut with a bit part in the film *Believe in Me* (1971), which was filmed in New York. Her scenes ended up on the cutting room floor. *Alice* was her sophomore credit and it was destined to remain her only significant work for the big screen. She also did a few guest spots on TV shows like *McCloud* and *Ryan's Hope*.

Lowry enjoyed much more success on the stage, where she was a prolific presence through the 1960s, '70s, and '80s. She appeared in numerous productions both off-and-on Broadway, including *The Only Sense is Nonsense*

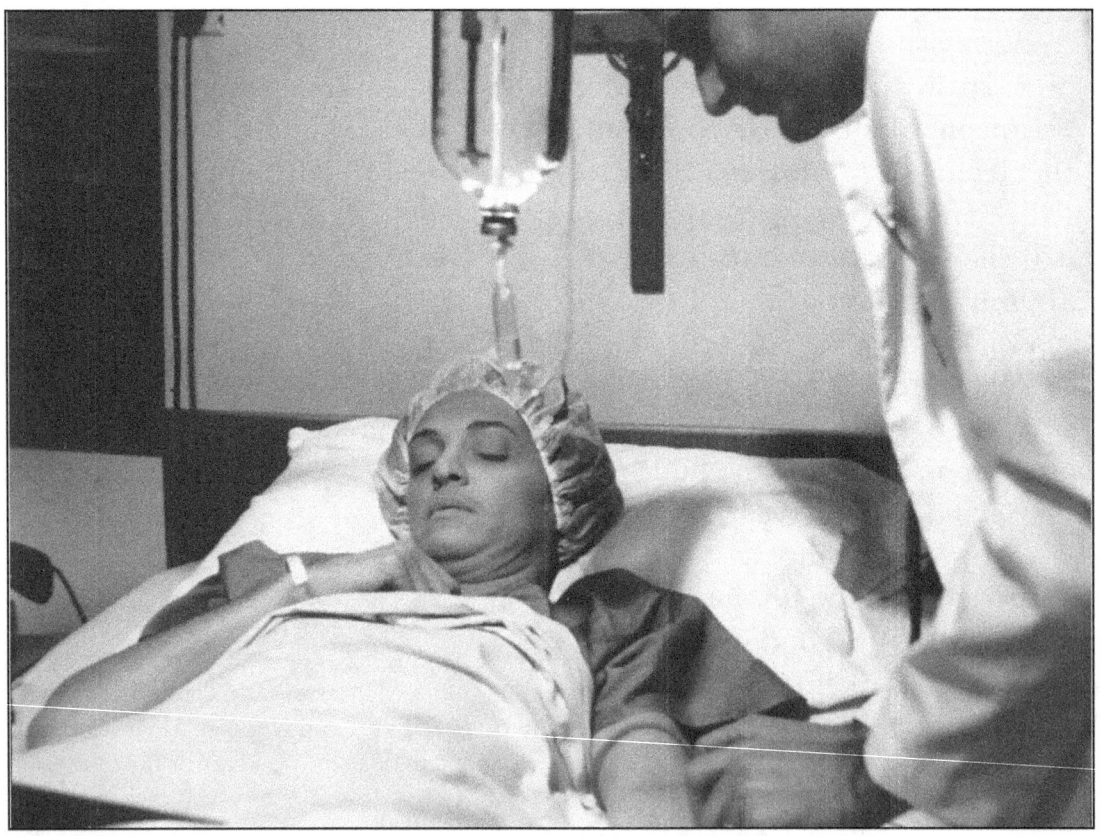

Annie (Jane Lowry) recuperates following her brush with death.

in 1961, *Poor Bitos* in 1964, *The Crucible* (as Elizabeth Proctor) in 1966, *The Time of Your Life* in 1967, *A Lovely Sunday for Creve Coeur* in 1979, and *The Summer People* in 1982.

Following her retirement from acting, Lowry devoted her energies to writing; her book of poetry, *Who Are We?*, was published in 2015.

## Rudolph Willrich (Father Tom)

Born: Date of birth unknown

Rudolph Willrich studied at the Royal Academy of Art in London. After graduating in 1967, he went on to enjoy a successful career, playing in everything from *Cactus Flower* and *Anna K* to *The Devil's Disciple*, a turn on Broadway in *Henry V* with Rex Harrison, and A *Midsummer Night's Dream*, in which he played Lysander.

He started appearing on the small and big screen in the early 1970s, making his film debut in *No Place to Hide*, also known as *Rebel*, which filmed in early

Father Tom (Rudolph Willrich) attempts to comfort Catherine (Linda Miller).

1970; it's best known today for being one of Sylvester Stallone's earliest credits. He was a familiar face on the small screen in the '70s, doing guest bits on such shows as *The Streets of San Francisco*, *Baretta*, *Kojak*, and *Police Story*.

He continued to rack up credits following *Alice, Sweet Alice*, appearing in such films as *9 ½ Weeks* (1986) and *The Shadow* (1994), as well as TV shows like *The Equalizer*, *Star Trek: The Next Generation*, *Star Trek: Enterprise*, and *The Practice*.

He has been inactive on screen since 2014.

## Michael Hardstark (Detective Spina)

Born: 16 February, 1943

Mostly seen on TV through the 1970s, Michael Hardstark only appeared in a few minor films, of which *Alice, Sweet Alice* is by far the best known.

He made his big screen debut with a small role in the very obscure Jules Dassin movie *The Rehearsal* (1974). Technically a Greek production, it was shot on location in New York and utilized local acting talent, though major names such as Melina Mercouri (who also produced), Laurence Olivier, Lillian Hellman, and Maximilian Schell all put in appearances, as well.

More typical of his credits are appearances on such TV shows as *The Many Loves of Dobie Gillis* (playing the semi-recurring role of Walter Funk), *Kojak*, and *Ironside*.

Father Tom (Rudolph Willrich) converses with Detective Spina (Michael Hardstark). Courtesy Nathaniel Thompson.

He was also active in the theater and did a national tour with the massively popular *Fiddler on the Roof*.

Hardstark has been inactive on screen since 1977.

## Alphonso DeNoble (Mr. Alphonso)

Born: 20 December, 1946, Paterson, New Jersey
Died: 17 November, 1978, Paterson, New Jersey

If anybody comes close to stealing *Alice, Sweet Alice* from Paula Sheppard, it's undoubtedly Alphonso DeNoble.

As Alfred Sole outlines elsewhere in this book, DeNoble was an eccentric character. He was prone to dressing up in priestly vestments and going to local graveyards, where he would take money from old ladies looking for his advice. He also worked as a bouncer at a gay bar in Paterson.

Perhaps appropriately, Sole first met DeNoble in a cemetery when Sole was visiting his father's grave. DeNoble was out doing his usual "priest" routine, and Sole struck up a conversation with him. DeNoble ended up getting cast in

Alphonso DeNoble makes an unforgettable impression as the disgusting landlord.

the lost *American Soap* before getting the showcase of his all-too-brief career as Mr. Alphonso. Oddly, his dialogue is clearly post-synched in the finished film; Sole told the author that it is DeNoble's own voice on the soundtrack, however.

The late director Joel M. Reed, who cast DeNoble in his only other film roles in *Bloodsucking Freaks* (1976, also featuring Niles McMaster) and *Night of the Zombies* (1981), revealed that DeNoble committed suicide by shotgun because he was so unhappy over his obesity. He was only thirty-one years old.

## Gary Allen (Jim DeLorenze)

Born: 4 September, 1942, Camden, Tennessee
Died: 6 June, 2020

Gary Allen got his start on television in the late '50s, appearing in guest spots on such shows as *Leave it to Beaver* and *The Jack Benny Program*.

He started appearing in low budget features circa 1968, but he hadn't amounted any significant credits by the time he appeared in *Alice, Sweet Alice*. Like most of his co-stars he did regional theater and popped up in various TV and radio advertisements.

He managed to snag small roles in some major films shot on location in New York, including Woody Allen's *Annie Hall* (1977), Michael Winner's *The Sentinel* (1979), and Billy Wilder's swansong *Buddy Buddy* (1981). He would

Jim (Gary Allen), Annie (Jane Lowry), and Catherine (Linda Miller) react to something suspicious. Courtesy Nathaniel Thompson.

reteam with Alfred Sole for *Pandemonium* (1982). Cult film buffs may also remember him in the slasher film *Don't Answer the Phone!* (1980).

On the small screen, he also popped up in everything from *Hart to Hart* and *Simon and Simon* to *Newhart* and *Mama's Family*.

He pretty much retired after playing a small role for the Coen Brothers in *The Hudsucker Proxy* (1994).

## Brooke Shields (Karen Spages)

Born: 31 May, 1965, New York City, New York

Whatever one makes of Brooke Shields' participation in *Alice, Sweet Alice*, there's no denying that her presence has helped to keep the film in the spotlight.

Karen (Brooke Shields) is a lamb to the slaughter.

Alfred Sole cast her in the small but important role of little, ill-fated Karen Spages, making this her big screen debut—but she'd been in the business since she was less than one year old thanks to the efforts of her mother, who was eager to make a star out of her.

Shields started off in modeling, then did a few minor appearances on television. Louis Malle's *Pretty Baby* (1978) generated plenty of controversy and helped to make her a star, and she cemented her popularity with such films as *The Blue Lagoon* (1980) and *Endless Love* (1981).

She would remain a pop culture fixture, thanks to a mix of acting, modeling, and spokesperson assignments, to say nothing of various activism causes, though the critical attitude towards her acting has remained mixed at best.

When Shields hit the big time thanks to *Pretty Baby* and *The Blue Lagoon*, *Alice* found itself being re-released—as the tone and tenor of some of the reviews gathered in this volume make clear, the misleading advertising, with Shields now promoted as the star of the picture, generated as much negative backlash as it no doubt reeled in unwitting patrons.

Shields has never gone out of her way to discuss *Alice, Sweet Alice*, and has refused overtures to do so, but she remains active in films and television.

54 • *Unholy Communion:* Alice, Sweet Alice

Louisa Horton as Dr. Whitman. Courtesy Nathaniel Thompson.

## **Louisa Horton** (Dr. Whitman)

Born: 10 September, 1920, Beijing, China (some sources say 1924)
Died: 25 January, 2008, Englewood, New Jersey

Born Louisa Fleetwood Horton, she was born in China to American parents and was brought up principally in the U.S. She started off on stage in the 1940s, and by 1948 she had made it to Broadway, starring in *The Voice of the Turtle*.

In 1951 she married future film director George Roy Hill, who helmed such hits as *Butch Cassidy and the Sundance Kid* (1969) and *The Sting* (1973, for which he won the Oscar as Best Director), with whom she had four children; they divorced in 1972.

She made her film debut in *All My Sons* (1948), appearing opposite Edward G. Robinson and Burt Lancaster, but her film career never really took off; just prior to *Alice*, she had appeared in the big budget *Swashbuckler* (1976), which was her first movie since the early 1950s. Horton enjoyed more success on TV, appearing in such programs as *Suspense, Omnibus, Inner Sanctum,* and *Lights Out*, but the stage remained her favorite milieu.

Prolific character actor Tom Signorelli appears as Detective Brennan.
Courtesy Nathaniel Thompson.

## Tom Signorelli (Detective Brennan)

Born: 19 October, 1935, Brooklyn, New York
Died: 6 July, 2010, New York, New York

A classic New York character actor if ever there was one, Tom Signorelli specialized in playing no-nonsense policemen and hoods.

After doing a variety of odd jobs, including working at the 21 Club in Manhattan, he made his debut on TV in an episode of *Wagon Train*. Later, he went on to appear in such popular programs as *Run for Your Life*, *The Fugitive*, *The Equalizer*, and *Law & Order*.

Signorelli was a familiar presence in such New York-based fare as Roman Polanski's *Rosemary's Baby* (1968, making a small appearance during the party sequence) and Sidney Lumet's *The Anderson Tapes* (1971) and *Serpico* (1973, also featuring Mildred Clinton). He also appeared for William Friedkin in *Sorcerer* (1977), Michael Mann in *Thief* (1981), Francis Ford Coppola in *The Cotton Club* (1984), and John Huston in *Prizzi's Honor* (1986). Signorelli also did a pair of films for Roger Corman in rapid succession: *The Trip* and *The St. Valentine's Day Massacre* (both 1967).

He retired from the screen in the mid-1990s.

Antonino Rocca, the legendary wrestler, makes his screen debut with a cameo appearance. Courtesy Nathaniel Thompson.

## Antonino Rocca (Funeral Director)

Born: 13 April, 1921, Treviso, Italy
Died: 15 March, 1977, New York City, New York

Antonino Rocca's cameo came about by chance. As Alfred Sole explained to the author, he was represented by the same agent who represented Lillian Roth. Since Sole was eager to cast Roth, he agreed to put Rocca in a small part, as well.

Born Angelino Biasetton in Italy, he moved with his family to Argentina while he was still in his teens. He eventually made his way to Texas in the late '40s, where he started a lengthy and very successful career in wrestling. Prior to that, the athletic young man had been an accomplished rugby player.

By 1962, his fame had risen to the degree that he was actually depicted on the cover of a *Superman* comic (#155) wrestling with the Man of Steel. His wrestling career was more-or-less finished circa 1967, but he stayed in the limelight by providing commentary on various wrestling programs into the 1970s.

He died in 1977 of complications following routine surgery; obituaries at the time listed him as being 49, but he was actually just a month shy of his 56th birthday. He was posthumously inducted into the WWF Hall of Fame. *Alice* was his only film credit.

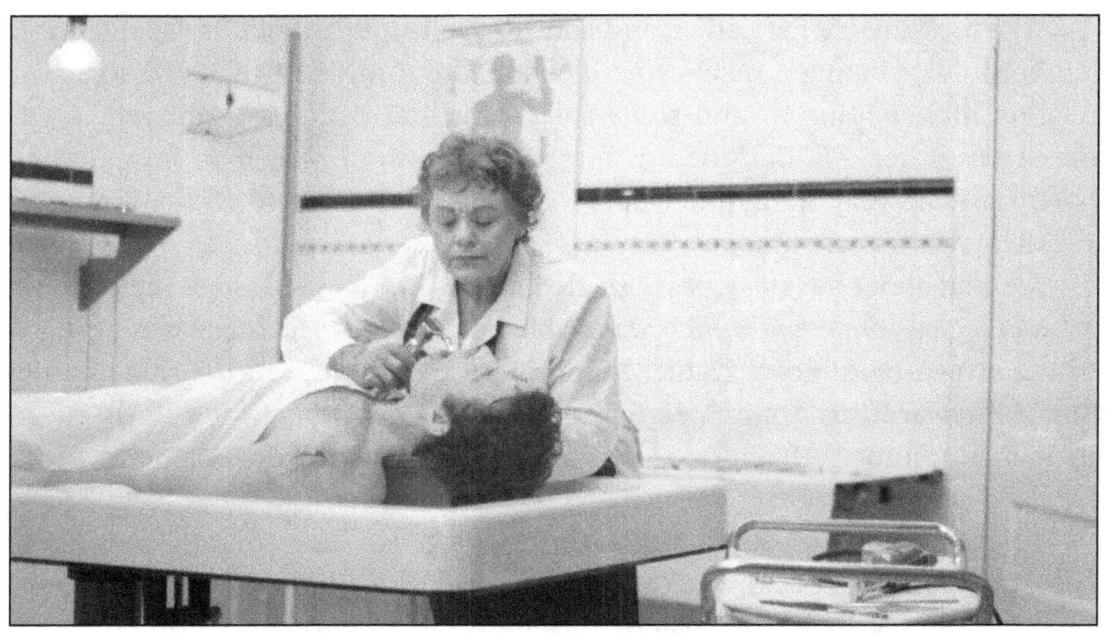

Lillian Roth makes her return to the screen in a cameo as the pathologist. Courtesy Nathaniel Thompson.

## Lillian Roth (Pathologist)

Born 13 December, 1910, Boston, Massachusetts
Died: 12 May, 1980, New York City, New York

Perhaps the most surprising piece of casting is Lillian Roth in the small role of the police pathologist. Sole did well to reach out to a very experienced actor, looking to give the role a bit of weight, and in the process Lillian Roth found herself on screen for the first time in several decades.

Interviewed by Marc Gunther in the July 21, 1975 edition of *The News*, Roth quipped, "I got this part just like the first ones I played. My agent pulled me into it just the way my mother used to drag me around town to audition for silent films back in the 1920s."[21]

Born Lillian Rutstein, she found fame on stage and on screen while still in her teens, though she had been pushed into performing from the age of 6. She and her sisters achieved fame on Broadway with a show called The Roth Sisters; this soon led to an invitation to go to Hollywood, where she ended up under contract at Paramount. Her films during this period included *The Love Parade* (1929), *The Vagabond King* (1930), *Animal Crackers* (1930), and *Madam Satan* (1930), the latter directed by Cecil B. DeMille.

---

21. Gunther, Marc, "For Lillian Roth, Paterson's An Upturn," *The News*, July 21, 1975.

The pressures of her career, and constant self-doubt about her appearance, led her to developing a reliance on alcohol. She threw herself into a string of relationships, hoping to find some solace, but her demons continued to get the better of her. All told, she was married 6 times—a couple of those unions barely lasted a year, though her final marriage in 1947 lasted all the way until she divorced one last time in 1963.

Candid about her struggles with alcoholism, she penned a moving memoir called *I'll Cry Tomorrow*, which was published in 1954. Her story was brought to the screen by director Daniel Mann in 1955, in a film of the same name; Susan Hayward was nominated for an Oscar for her portrayal of Roth. Roth, incidentally, joined Alcoholics Anonymous in 1946 and was a major advocate for the program.

Though film work had dried up in the late '30s, she continued to make sporadic appearances on TV through the 1950s. Roth remained a draw on Broadway and was even billed above up-and-coming Barbra Streisand in *I Can Get It For You Wholesale*, which ran from March through December of 1962, with Roth on board for the entire run.

Following her small role in *Alice, Sweet Alice*, Roth appeared in the low budget drama *Night-Flowers* (1979) and the higher-profile *Boardwalk* (1979), starring Lee Strasberg and Ruth Gordon.

She suffered a stroke in February of 1980 and passed away later that year in a nursing home in Manhattan.

## Patrick Gorman (Father Pat)

Born: 3 August, 1934, Visalia, California

After getting his start as a dancer for Judy Garland, Patrick Gorman settled into a prolific career as a stage and screen actor.

He came to films relatively late, in the mid-1970s, though he already had ample experience in a wide array of subjects in the theater. *Alice, Sweet Alice* was one of his earliest screen credits, along with Sydney Pollock's acclaimed thriller *Three Days of the Condor* (1975), in which he has a very small role.

Later, he would appear in such diverse big screen fare as *Airport '79* (1979), *The Nude Bomb* (1980), *In the Shadow of Kilimanjaro* (1986), *Gettysburg* (1993), *On Deadly Ground* (1994), and *Gods and Generals* (2003). He has always been much more prolific on television, however, appearing on such programs as *Happy Days*, *The Waltons*, *Eight is Enough*, and *MacGyver*.

Patrick Gorman (right) in the role of Father Pat. Courtesy Nathaniel Thompson.

Gorman never established a high profile as a "name attraction," but he has remained steadily employed in a tough profession well into his 80s—not everybody is so fortunate.

Dante Tomaselli and Michael Gingold; their passion for *Alice, Sweet Alice* lead them to collaborate on the screenplay for a proposed remake.

# Chapter 4
## The Locations of *Alice, Sweet Alice*
### By Michael Gingold

**In 1978-79,** the filmmakers behind a romantic drama called *Voices* claimed that their Hoboken-set production was the first movie to be shot entirely in New Jersey since the silent serial *The Perils of Pauline* back in 1914. However, at least one newspaper at the time noted that this was not true: Alfred Sole lensed *Alice, Sweet Alice*, under the title *Communion*, in and around Paterson, NJ a few years prior to *Voices*, over the course of 81 days during the summer of 1975. Paterson's *News* quoted Sole's co-scripter Rosemary Ritvo in April '78: "It seemed to be so ridiculous that so many people could say that 'Voices' would be the first full-length film produced in New Jersey in decades—something that is so taintly [sic] wrong."

Not only that, but the carefully chosen locations make Paterson as much of a presence in *Alice, Sweet Alice* as its varied and often eccentric human characters. The working-class/religious vibe that suffuses the film is evoked by its many well-chosen settings, with Sole's background in architecture and interior design giving him an appreciation for the aesthetics of building forms and dressings, and how to shoot them. He and Ritvo wrote the film with Paterson in mind, and with the latter serving as his production manager, the director spearheaded a true hometown production; Ritvo lived down the block from him, and across the street from her was the home of Sole's secretary, Marilyn Spages, who presumably inspired the name of *Alice*'s central family. The project employed a number of the city's residents—including a reported 700 extras—and resulted in $300,000 in local expenditures. Prior to the shoot, camera tests with the actors were undertaken at a soon-to-be-demolished house on Mill Street, and the production office, dressing rooms, kitchen, etc. were set up at the recently opened Paterson Mall on Fair Street.

(It was, in fact, not the only genre production to roll in Paterson at that time. In July '75, the *Paterson News* reported that fourth-year NYU film student Robert Sudol was shooting key scenes for his hour-long *Cwir's Keep* at Lambert's Castle. This horror/fantasy, in which a hunter mercy-kills a girl being burned at the stake for witchcraft and then encounters her spirit in an enchanted forest, starred Stephanie Soupios and Gunter Kleemann, the latter of whom would go on to play Andy in Meir Zarchi's notorious *I Spit on Your Grave*.)

As a longtime fan of movie location visits, and having directed and hosted a number of Blu-ray featurettes going back to the sites of classic and cult-fave horror films, I jumped at the opportunity to do so for *Alice, Sweet Alice* when Arrow Video was putting together its long-awaited special edition, released in August 2019. My co-producer/cameraman Glen Baisley and I spent a couple of chilly days in Paterson (assisted by local filmmaker Alan Rowe Kelly on the second of them) trekking around the city the previous winter, capturing the spots where the action happened…though finding them was not always

Passaic County Administration Building, the former site of the church and rectory. Courtesy Michael Gingold.

easy, due to certain misinformation about the locations that has turned up in numerous places on-line. In one case, it was a fortunate acquaintance that led us to one of the primary places.

Considering the notoriety Sole had engendered in the area due to *Deep Sleep*, he received a surprising amount of cooperation from Paterson residents and organizations. The fire department created artificial rain, the police department provided a polygraph for the scene in which Alice (Paula Sheppard) is given a lie-detector test, and local Charles Hannah provided vintage cars for the 1961-set film. In fact, the director's legal troubles indirectly paved the financial path for *Communion* to get off the ground. After initial funding for the film fell through, Richard K. Rosenberg, the lawyer who represented *Deep Sleep*'s producer—an accountant named Andrew Muskat—during the trial, raised replacement money in two weeks and became the movie's credited producer.

Even while Sole was being judged regarding *Deep Sleep* at the Passaic County Court House, he was able to use its parking lot to house equipment while he was filming the next street over. That site was the Third Presbyterian Church and the attached rectory at 64 Prince Street, where Father Tom (Rudolph Willrich) lives and is assisted by Mrs. Tredoni (Mildred Clinton). Finding a church or churches for a screen story in which they were crucial was one stumbling block faced by Sole and co.: A priest from the Diocese of Paterson read the script and forbade filming inside any of the city's houses of worship. Third Presbyterian had long been out of commission, however, and at the time of production was set to be razed to make way for a parking lot. Today, the massive and very modern Passaic County Administration Building stands in that space.

Perhaps it is for that reason that inaccuracies about where the church exteriors were lensed has been rife on the Internet. Look up *Alice, Sweet Alice* on-line, and some sources say they were shot at Paterson's First Presbyterian Church on Main Street, though even a casual glance at that building will reveal it's not the right place. Others have claimed that scenes were filmed at St. Michael's in Newark, though that building also doesn't match what's on screen, inside or out. As a result, I was stymied in trying to figure out where the onscreen church was…until I casually mentioned this dilemma during dinner one night with Jennifer Morrow, a longtime friend and former *Fangoria* writer, who had been a *Jeopardy!* contestant a few years earlier and has since become immersed in the on-line trivia world. She offered to query some of her friends in that realm, and send out a frame grab of the *Alice* church—and the very next day, one of them, Christine O'Donnell, replied. She dug up an old newspaper article that had eluded my research, in which Sole was interviewed while filming at Third Presbyterian. Mystery solved!

Washington Street offices, where the former Police Station once stood.
Courtesy Michael Gingold.

As for the interiors, Sole revealed in later interviews that those were filmed in the chapel of Paterson General Hospital, which was then located on Market Street. (A Paterson fire department station now stands in its place.) And for a brief shot of the steeple, St. John the Baptist Cathedral at 381 Grand Street was used. A postscript to this part of the travelogue: Despite Sole's *tsuris* with the Catholic Church, he was able to have the Rev. Gerard Greeley of St. Philomena's Monastery on board the production as religious advisor, and Greeley blessed the sets as well.

The religious settings aren't the only ones from *Alice, Sweet Alice* that no longer exist. In the film, Dom goes to speak with Detectives Brennan (Tom Signorelli) and Spina (Michael Hardstark) about Alice's case at the Paterson Police Station, which at the time was located at 111 Washington Street. After a fire in 1979, the precinct relocated and the building sat vacant for forty years; thanks to a helpful security guard, we were able to get into the gutted structure, which was then under renovation, to shoot footage for our doc. By November 2019, it reopened as an office building.

The sequence of Karen's funeral, attended by her grieving family including her newly returned father Dom (Niles McMaster) while the two detectives watch from across the street, was staged at the Cheek Funeral Home at 384 Broadway (aka Martin Luther King Jr. Way). Paterson police stopped traffic during filming of the drama outside the Home, but reportedly, none of the motorists who were held up honked their horns because they thought the service was real! In addition, the scene involving Lillian Roth as the pathologist performing the autopsy on Dom's body was filmed in Cheek's morgue. Coincidentally echoing the manner of Karen's demise, the Cheek Funeral Home also suffered a fire, burning down in a four-alarmer in 1991, and the space is a vacant lot to this day.

This house at James Street and Ryerson Avenue served as the location for the Spages' home. Courtesy Michael Gingold.

Among the locations that are still standing is one that has actually been standing for a long time: the John Ryle House at 9 Mill Street. Conjoined with the Daniel Thompson House (constructed in 1830, both are on the National Register of Historic Places), this was the home of the eponymous nineteenth century silk industry pioneer. Under Sole and his team, it became the dwelling of a less refined gentleman: perverted landlord Mr. Alphonso (Alphonso DeNoble, née Alphonso Nekros), whose filthy apartment was set up in the Ryle House, where some of the stairwell scenes were also shot. These set pieces match quite well with the exteriors of Alphonso's apartment house, where the Spages family lives and where Aunt Annie (Jane Lowry) crawls outside screaming after being stabbed. This building, at the intersection of James Street and Ryerson Avenue, is one of the easiest *Alice* sites to find: An early establishing shot includes a close-up of those paired street signs!

Like the police station, the abandoned warehouse where Dom pursues someone he believes to be Angela, only to be incapacitated and rolled to his death by the real killer, has undergone a significant transformation since '75. The expansive Thomas Rogers Building at 2 Market Street was once part of Rogers Locomotive and Machine Works, a key fabricator of steam trains during the nineteenth century. It now contains the Paterson Museum, which features numerous exhibits chronicling the city's history and industry, particularly pertaining to its manufacture of not only locomotives, but Colt firearms and submarines. (There's also a display honoring local boy and legendary comedian Lou Costello, who has a Memorial Park devoted to him not far away.) Dom's

The Paterson Museum in the Thomas Rogers Building, which provided the location for Dom's pursuit—and demise.

The former waterfall, which is now dried up. Courtesy Michael Gingold.

pursuit of the rain-coated figure begins by the nearby Ivanhoe Wheelhouse off Spruce Street, facing what was once an active waterfall, but has since run dry.

Still flowing, on a much bigger scale, is the nearby 77-foot Paterson Great Falls on the Passaic River, which is part of a National Historical Park surrounding it. This was also a filming site for an *Alice, Sweet Alice* scene—albeit one you can't actually see in the film. A dialogue exchange between Catherine and Dom was lensed here, and though it ultimately wasn't used in the final cut, a shot from it was circulated as a still and lobby card. From that image, we were able to deduce its setting and feature it in the doc. And thanks to a copy of the original screenplay provided by Sole's cousin, filmmaker Dante Tomaselli (with whom this writer—full disclosure—is working on an *Alice* remake), we were able to include a reading of the missing scene performed by actors Jude Pucillo and Sandy Oppedisano Rooney.

Other key locations included Public School No. 2 at 22 Passaic Street, which stood in for the Sara Reed Children's Shelter, where Alice is taken after she becomes a suspect in the murder spree; a pavilion at Westside Park (114 Totowa Avenue), where Dom and Father Tom discuss her situation; and Paterson's train station, where Dom arrives before reuniting with his estranged family. News stories from the time indicate a pretty smooth shoot that attracted a lot of curious and cooperative crowds. There was a small hiccup reported: At one point, some props were stolen from the production, and an ad ran in the

Public School No. 2, which stood in for the Sara Reed Children's Center.
Courtesy Michael Gingold.

The Paterson Train Station, where Dom makes his return to the community.
Courtesy Michael Gingold.

Paterson *News* offering a $1 thousand reward for their return. Sole noted in a later letter to the paper that the items were quickly recovered.

The director had high hopes for his first step into the horror world, and said at one point during the shoot that American International Pictures and ABC had made commitments to release and air the movie (the latter of which likely led the Paterson *News* to describe it as a "made-for-TV mystery" in a headline). Later, it was reported that Paramount or Universal would take on the distribution, before its ill-fated acquisition by Columbia Pictures. At the time, Sole was also quoted about a couple of follow-up projects he planned to make next. One was *Gray Rhapsody*, which he described as "a cross between *Klute* and *Taxi Driver*," to star Omar Sharif; another was a Paterson-set love story once again scripted by Sole and Ritvo, with DeNoble/Nekros as the intended leading man!

One more Paterson location played a key part in the movie's history: the former 3,000-plus-seat Fabian Theatre at 45 Church Street, where it had a gala premiere under the *Communion* title on Saturday, November 13, 1976 (though

The prop chalice which figures into the finale of the film.

it had actually screened the night before at the Chicago Film Festival). Costello and comedy partner Bud Abbott also premiered a number of their vehicles at the Fabian during the 1940s and '50s; the Fabian became a multiplex in 1977, hosted the premiere of *Lean on Me* (starring Morgan Freeman as Joe Clark, famed principal of Paterson's Eastside High School) in 1989, and closed in 1993. The $15-a-ticket *Communion* screening, preceded by a champagne reception, was a benefit for the Great Falls Development Corporation (for whom Sole had previously designed sets for fundraising auctions), with the proceeds going to restore nineteenth century factory buildings in Paterson's historic district, including those in the Great Falls Park. It was attended by the cast, crew, Paterson mayor Lawrence "Pat" Kramer, and numerous other city officials.

Afterward, the Paterson *News* ran a review of the movie by local Barbara Klein that was overall quite positive: "… the flawless set-up of the film's most moving scenes sent me slightly out of my seat," she wrote. "A particularly impressive performance is delivered by Paula Sheppard… It's a film that begins simply and builds into an intriguing climax." Yet it ran alongside another article, also by Klein, in which she impugned the movie's presentation of its setting. "The truth of the matter is, the film depicts Paterson as the next to the last place anyone would want to go. Alfred Sole focused on decrepit factories, garbage clogged waterways, empty liquor bottles, roaches, a rat and old, unattractive housing… Sole's choices of locations speak well of his talent as a filmmaker. Unfortunately, they don't give Paterson one ounce of positive exposure." She even took a swipe at the conditions in the Fabian: "Most of the long-stemmed plastic cups, several champagne bottles and some cookies cluttered the floor of the theater even before the movie began."

This inspired a series of angry rebuttals by attendees of the premiere in the *News*' subsequent letters pages, including one from Sole himself: "I was flabbergasted to read film reviewer Barbara Klein's immature, bird-brained attack on the [premiere]… I love Paterson. That's why I live here, why I made my film here… Mrs. Klein's 'old, unattractive housing' is an insult to me as a Patersonian. Thousands of fine people live proudly in neat, well-maintained homes such as that occupied by the principal family in 'Communion.' "

A more positive write-up appeared in the *Daily News*, written by Bruce Chadwick, who noted that the upbeat mood around the premiere was amplified by word that the movie had won an award at the Chicago Film Festival. And there was a bit of positive irony about the event, as Chadwick noted: "Members of the Passaic County Prosecutor's Office, the same office that arrested Sole and other actors for 'Deep Sleep,' were at the party sipping champagne," helping celebrate the director's achievement. And Ritvo told the journalist, "I'm just happy for Alfred. He's gone through a very bad time and now that's over."

# Chapter 5

## The Script

**The following screenplay** is reproduced with the written consent of its co-author, Alfred Sole. Mr. Sole has our thanks for his kindness in allowing us to make this valuable historical document available for public consumption.

As is so often the case, the differences between what is on the page can make for interesting comparison to that which ends up on screen. We are presenting the screenplay unaltered and without commentary so that you, the reader, can see where practical reality sometimes dictated changes during the making of the picture.

COMMUNION

Original Screenplay by

Rosemary Puglia Ritvo

Alfred Sole

Copyright Alfred Sole Productions, Inc.

1

Time:  March 1961

FADE IN

1A.  EXT   DAY   STREET
          It is late Thursday afternoon of a March day; it
has been raining intermittently.  A little girl in a blue-
hooded school coat lettered on the back in white, Holy
Family, bounces a rubber ball under her legs.

                    LITTLE GIRL
                 (chanting as she bounces)
            K my name is Karen, my mother's
            name is Catherine.  (she giggles)
            We live in (emphasizing) Paterson
            and my mother is a secretary.

1B.  INT   DAY   KITCHEN   SPAGES APARTMENT
          The apartment is old.  It consists of a kitchen,
a living room and two bedrooms.  The rooms are clean and
modestly furnished.  Catherine Spages, 36 years old, a
brunette with hair rather washed out, but neatly combed, is
in a hurry.  Dressed in her coat, she is doing some last
minute dinner preparations, so that her family can eat as
soon as she returns from an errand.

2.   INT   DAY   BEDROOM
          CLOSE UP of a face hidden in a clear plastic
mask.  The mask has the look of someone's warped idea of
beauty, that idea of beauty consummated by manufacturers
who supply America's five-and-dime stores.  Because it is
clear plastic it absorbs the flesh tones of the person
wearing it, and, with the recessed movement of the wearer's
eyes, seems like the face of an animated corpse.  The camera
pulls back to reveal a young girl.  In her hand is a box of
wooden matches.  Not finding what she wants, the young girl
moves at some point to the other side of the room.  The

(2 continued)

decoration of the room makes it clear that it is shared by two young girls. The girl stops at a doll carriage. She picks up and discards a doll, vengefully messing up the carefully set-up carriage; it is obvious that she has not found what she is searching for.

Hearing a noise from the kitchen, she looks toward the door. Perhaps Catherine's voice can be heard calling "Alice." She quickly makes her way to a bureau, stuffing the box of matches into the pocket of her school coat. The hooded blue coat bears the name Holy Family embroidered in white over a school emblem. She begins to go through the drawers. On the bureau in addition to children's items is a large photograph of a smiling priest. Triumphantly she finds the small box she is seeking, opens it, and pulls a porcelain doll in a white dress from under the tissue wrapping. The doll is smiling, but when the girl twists its head we discover the strange doll has three faces. The girl's hand stops twisting at the face that is crying. She is thrilled with the opportunity to treat the doll's head with roughness. Intercepted by the sound of her mother's voice calling her again from the kitchen, she stuffs the doll into the other pocket of her coat. She walks quietly over to the door, cracks it and listens. Pulling the mask off her face, she tiptoes out the door.

3. INT DAY HALL AND KITCHEN

Coming from the bedroom 12-year-old Alice Spages, a pale-haired, dark-eyed child, cases the kitchen, determining that her mother will not see her. She slips past her mother and out the door.

Mrs. Spages' face records that she has heard the door click. She looks up, thinks perhaps she has imagined it, and then, as if remembering, calls out:

> CATHERINE
> (with some annoyance)
> Alice, didn't you hear me call you?

Getting no answer, she moves toward the bedroom.

> CATHERINE
> (with exasperation)
> Why do I always have to call you a dozen times? You know I have to get to Sella's before it closes.
>
> (This line is completed as she reaches the bedroom.)

4. INT DAY BEDROOM

Catherine, realizing that Alice has gone, glances back toward the kitchen. She now knows the meaning

(4 continued) 3

of that door clicking. (Sound of a child crying.) She moves to the window which opens onto the front of the three-family house, and pushes aside the white ninon curtains in time to see Alice's back as she walks away down the street. The camera focuses on a frustrated Catherine trying to get Alice's attention by hammering on the large bedroom window, which, in her anger, she has failed to get open. Seeing Karen move toward the front steps, Catherine gives up at the window, and moves quickly out of the room.

5.  INT   DAY   HALLWAY
        Karen, a pretty blonde seven-year-old with skin not unlike her porcelain doll's, is on her way up the stairs in tears. She meets her mother in the hallway.

> KAREN
> (calling out)
> Mommy, Mommy...

> CATHERINE
> (in a rush of words)
> What is it, baby? What is it?
> What did she do to you now?
> Are you hurt?

> KAREN
> (almost simultaneously
> and between sobs)
> Mommy, she took it; she's going
> to break it. I had it all
> wrapped up and she took it.

> CATHERINE
> What did she take? Don't cry.
> You know I can't understand
> you when you cry.

> KAREN
> She took my doll, the doll
> Daddy sent me. She's going to
> break it--I know she is.

> CATHERINE
> No she won't. She won't break
> it. I promise. Calm down.
> I'll take care of her. Look,
> I have to get to Sella's
> before they close.

Karen's tears begin to subside.

> CATHERINE
> (wiping off her face)
> That's my girl. Mommy has to

(5 continued)                                                              4

>                    hurry. You want me to get
>                    your dress, don't you?

    Firmly taking Karen's arm, she leads her down the stairs.

6.  EXT  DAY  STREET
    Catherine and Karen come out of the front door of the apartment.

>                         KAREN
>                       (nervously)
>              But what if she won't come?
>
>                       CATHERINE
>              Don't you worry; she'll come.
>              You just tell her what I said.
>              (With firmness)  She knows I
>              have to be at school by 7:15.
>              Don't you worry she's going to
>              get it for what she did.  She
>              knows better than to leave
>              the house when I need her.
>              (These lines are delivered
>              almost to herself; Catherine
>              is not nearly so firm as she
>              sounds to Karen.)

    Mother and daughter separate. Karen gets on her bike, which is resting by the side of the front stoop.

7.  EXT  DAY  STREET
    LONG SHOT neighborhood from the roof of a two-story apartment. The streets are dry in patches. The neighborhood is a shabby area of nicely kept two-family houses and some apartments. The homes do not necessarily reflect the wealth of the owners. This is clearly a community, and many who could afford better stayed for that reason.

    Alice is walking in the background. Camera is on the street dollying with her, photographing her through parked cars. Alice is lighting matches and throwing them at car windows; occasionally she stops and aims one into an open window; fortunately her haste and the air snuff the match before it can cause fire.

    The camera pans with Alice and stops on an approaching pedestrian. With no guilt but with an annoyed pragmatism, Alice shoves the box of matches back into her coat pocket, leaving her hand in the pocket as a kind of cover. Innocently she nears the street corner and attracted by the display, walks over to look in the window of the local candy store. Hanging on a string strung across the window is an assortment of cheap toys, comic books and

(7 continued)                                                      5

two or three masks similar to the one Alice has been seen
wearing. Alice walks into the store. Through the store
window she is seen removing a "Jackie Kennedy" mask from
the string.

        CLOSE UP Karen riding her bicycle. As she sees
Alice leave the store, she yells and pedals faster toward
her. At the sound of her sister's voice Alice disappears
around the corner. When Karen approaches Alice, she slows
the bike, taking care to keep a respectful distance behind
her. Alice is ignoring her sister.

> KAREN
> Alice, Mommy said for me to
> get you. You are to come right
> home this instant. You have to
> set the table, Alice.

(The child gets no response whatsoever.)

> KAREN
> (with increasing loudness)
> You better listen to me because
> you're gonna get it when you
> get home. (pause) Where are
> you going anyway? (pause)
> What did you do with my doll?
> Did you break it?

        Alice begins to walk faster giving Karen no
choice but to keep following. Fighting hard to keep back
the tears, Karen clings to her naive idea of justice.

> KAREN
> (as if trying to work out
>   her sister's attitude in
>   her own mind)
> You really are mean, you know.
> I never did anything to you, did
> I? Did I? What did I ever do
> to you? Mommy will fix you.
> She knows...

        Alice turns suddenly; she startles and
frightens Karen, forcing her to turn her bike aside.

> ALICE
> (controlled and
>   with menace)
> Didn't I tell you never to
> follow me? If you don't obey
> me I have ways of punishing you.
> (measured) You're never gonna
> see that doll again.

(7 continued)                                                    6

> KAREN
> (abruptly with complete
> change)
> 'Sides I don't have your doll.
> What makes you think I have
> your doll anyway?

Camera is inside one of the buildings. Thunder and rain are beginning. The girls can be seen through the building window.

> KAREN
> (backing off and
> confused)
> You do too have it. I saw it.

(Sounds of thunder)

> KAREN
> (getting back on
> her bike)
> Anyway I'm not gonna get wet.
> I'm gonna go try on my dress--
> <u>and</u> my veil. (These last lines
> are tossed over her shoulder
> as she pedals off)

It begins to rain harder. CAMERA DOLLIES IN closer toward Alice, who is watching her sister. Her face is cold, but her eyes are reflecting something. She runs out of the frame in the same direction as her sister. The CAMERA DOLLIES close to the window as the rain pours hard on the glass.

TITLES
(Sound of rain-street noises)

DISSOLVE TO

8. INT   EVENING   SPAGES APT.
EXTREME CLOSE UP of water being poured into a tea kettle. CAMERA PANS with the kettle as it is placed on the stove. The gas flares up and is adjusted.

CAMERA DOLLIES BACK as Catherine goes over to the kitchen table and begins to open a box on the table. As Catherine pulls out a white veil from one of the boxes, sounds of Karen can be heard coming from the hall. Karen comes bursting through the door, wet from the rain.

CLOSE UP of Catherine looking at Karen; sound of the tea kettle beginning to boil.

> CATHERINE
> (annoyed)
> You're soaked. Where's your sister?

(8 continued)

                   KAREN
           (taking off her coat)
    She's coming, Mommy. I told
    her to come straight home.
    (spots the dress) My dress!
    (excited, she moves to pick
    it up)

With that Alice enters; she is good and wet.

                   CATHERINE
           (annoyed)
    Well, Miss Independence, it's
    a good thing you decided to
    come home. Don't think you're
    going to get away with this.

The incessant whistling of the tea kettle demands her attention. She turns to the stove.

                   CATHERINE
           (her back toward
             the girls)
    Get those wet clothes off.
    I want the table set
    immediately.

Alice ignores her mother's directions; instead she takes Karen's veil and walks out of the frame. Karen who is busy fussing with her dress does not notice that Alice has her veil.

CLOSE UP Catherine working at the stove. She continues mother-type criticisms; they've all been said before.

CLOSE UP Alice trying on Karen's veil before the mirror.

                   CATHERINE (V.O.)
           (occupied by what
             she's doing)
    I don't like this new habit of
    yours--disappearing when you're
    told to do something. You're old
    enough to know better. (angry)
    Sometimes I think you don't care
    about anyone but yourself. Karen
    be careful of that box, I want
    to save it.

When Catherine turns to look in Karen's direction, she becomes aware of Alice at the mirror. Alice is not listening to her.

(8 continued)

   CLOSE UP Alice looking in the mirror; she looks like an ugly bride, and her expression reflects the fact that she knows it.

> KAREN
> She's wetting my veil. Make her take it off.

> CATHERINE
> (simultaneously; with extreme exaggeration)
> You better listen to me young lady. Take your sister's veil off and get out of those wet clothes. One of these days you're going to go too far.

   CLOSE UP Catherine looking at Alice, thinking. Alice's defiance reminds her of other recent incidents which have indicated a change in her daughter.

   CLOSE UP Alice looking at her mother coldly. (Possibly the veil can be over her face)

> KAREN (V.O.)
> (weakly)
> Make her take it off Mommy.

> CATHERINE
> (V.O.; thinking back)
> (warning)
> Where have you been going? Don't think you can keep things from me, Alice. You're not too big for...

Alice doesn't give her a chance to finish.

> ALICE
> (wanting to hurt and trying something to ease her own agony)
> Why should you care where I go? I'm not Karen.

   Catherine is confused. She cannot answer this. It is a preposterous statement--except that it tells us a lot about Alice.

   With that Alice, having perhaps said too much, pulls off the veil and throws it as she runs from the room.

> ALICE
> (saying, yelling, crying in a rage)
> Take your old veil. Who wants the

(8 continued)                                                           9

> stupid thing anyway. I can't
> stand you, I can't stand you
> or anybody...

                  CATHERINE
             (moving toward door
               to hall)
    What is wrong with you, Alice?
    That's your sister. Sometimes
    I don't know what to do with you.

We hear the bedroom door slam and hear muffled words like "I hate her, she's not my sister," etc. Catherine stands helplessly staring at the closed door. This has happened lately, and she really doesn't know how to handle it.

In the interim Karen has picked up her veil and tries to smooth it out. She has moved out of the frame over to the kitchen table. We may see her form in the background, out of focus. She is absorbed in sadness. She is crying softly. She is _not_ crying about her veil. She is crying because once again her sister has made her day miserable.

At some point Catherine hears the quiet tears. Looking and seeing tears where there should be joy, she is swept with tenderness and pity. Karen always makes her want to scoop her up and cuddle her, even when she isn't crying. Wanting to comfort her, to make it all better, she goes over to the table and with soft sounds begins the healing. She has clearly forgotten all about Alice. Perhaps she cuddles her or strokes her hair. She would say things like:

                  CATHERINE
             (softly)
    Come on, don't cry; it's
    all right.

To distract Karen, Catherine takes the veil, and begins to arrange it on Karen. She continues talking and coaxing.

                  CATHERINE
    I can fix it. See nothing
    happened to it. You look
    beautiful. You look just
    like a little bride.

Karen is beautiful; she looks strikingly different from the way Alice looked when she modeled the veil earlier. Karen begins to smile, taken by the reflection of her own prettiness in her mother's face.

(8 continued)

                         CATHERINE
                      (continuing)
                 There, that's it. Smile. I
                 could just squeeze you to death.
                 You know, I think you're going to
                 be the prettiest girl there.
                 Wait 'til Father Tom sees you.

                         KAREN
                      (aware of her beauty)
                 I just love this veil; I think
                 I love the veil best of all.
                 I wish I could wear it all the
                 time. I can't wait 'til Sunday.

9A.  EXT  DAY  CHURCH
          LONG SHOT Catherine, Karen and Alice coming out
of the church. It is Saturday just after lunch. Karen with
the rest of the First Communion class has made her first
confession. Alice wanting to go in a different direction,
is forced by Catherine to follow.

9B.  EXT  DAY  RECTORY
          From a first floor window an old man watches the
threesome approach the door to the rectory. Catherine rings
the doorbell, and as she turns to say something to an
obviously annoyed Alice, Karen, with the excitement of a
seven-year-old, opens the front door and walks in.

                         CATHERINE
                 Karen, wait...

10.  INT  DAY  HALLWAY
          Father Tom, an attractive man in his late
thirties with an ascetic face that has known suffering and
learned to deal with it, has been eagerly awaiting the
Spages' visit. He appears in the doorway separating the
dining room from the hallway.

                         FATHER TOM
                      (in the distance)
                 I'll get it, Mrs. Tredoni.

          Meanwhile all three have entered the vestibule;
Karen is, of course, first. Catherine holds back, waiting
for the formal invitation. Alice, who is behind her
mother, is effectively closed out of the picture due to the
narrowness of the vestibule and her own holding back.

                         FATHER TOM
                 Come in, come right in. I'm
                 so glad you're here.

          The exuberance of Karen allows for no
formalities; she knows she has come to receive a present,

(10 continued)                                                  11

and as Father Tom has been like a father in more ways than one, this is an important moment for Karen. She can barely contain herself.

                        KAREN
            Hi, Father Tom. Mommy said you
            have--you wanted to see me.

                    FATHER TOM
                   (teasing)
            Oh, did I now? Why would I
            want to see you?

                        KAREN
                 (with sudden shyness)
            I don't know.

                    FATHER TOM
                 (with mock seriousness)
            Did you make a good confession?

                        KAREN
                 (shaking head and perhaps
                 a little breathlessly,
                 awed at the thought of
                 someone not making a
                 good confession)
            Oh, yes, Father.

They play a waiting game. She fidgets, wiggles from the tension of containing all the energy. Finally she breaks:

                        KAREN
            Mommy said--Do you have a
            present for me?

CAMERA DOLLIES with them as Father Tom leads them into the dining room.

                    FATHER TOM
                 (mischievously)
            Of course I do--Some of Mrs.
            Tredoni's delicious cookies.

11. INT   DAY   DINING ROOM
        The dining room is furnished with old-oak furniture. There are examples everywhere of someone's skill in embroidery and crochet. The table, covered with the remains of Father's lunch, has a crocheted cloth on it, but the cloth is covered with clear plastic.

        When the three come into the dining room, Karen takes the proffered cookie, but Alice begins to roam around the room. She is planning something, and will eventually

(11 continued)

disappear into the kitchen; the camera will pick up her exit.

>                    FATHER TOM
>           Sit down, sit down. (to
>           Catherine) Would you like
>           some coffee? How about a
>           cookie, Alice?

Alice ignores him and something in her, an antagonism or isolation, warns Tom, who makes a mental note not to call too much attention to Alice. It could precipitate some ugliness, and he doesn't want to deal with that today.

>                    CATHERINE
>              (eating a cookie)
>           Umm..these are delicious.
>           How about you?

>                    FATHER TOM
>              (declining)
>           It's always a battle to keep
>           my weight down with Mrs.
>           Tredoni's cooking.

>                    CATHERINE
>              (mockingly)
>           You've gotta have faith, Tom.
>           How many times have I told
>           you faith can do anything.

In the meantime Alice has disappeared into the hallway.

11B.  INT  DAY  HALLWAY
      Alice stares into a sun parlor where a white-haired old man sits, his back to her, in a wheelchair.

>                    FATHER TOM (V.O.)
>           Sure...It's easy for you to
>           say, but I don't want to be
>           the mountain that faith moves...

Reaching into her pocket Alice pulls out her Jackie Kennedy mask and puts it on. The old man turns, glaring at her.

12.  INT  DAY  KITCHEN
      The kitchen is old-fashioned, large and very clean. The floor is covered by an ugly old linoleum, the kind that requires constant attention and obviously gets it. The camera is on Mrs. Tredoni's shoulders and head as she scrubs vigorously. She is clearly listening to what is going on in the dining room. Absorbed in scrubbing and

(12 continued)

listening, she does not see Alice.

Father Tom's teasing voice may be heard saying something like:

> FATHER TOM (V.O.)
> A little bird told me, Karen, that you're the prettiest girl in the first grade. All those handsome boys talking about you. I thought I was your best beau.

> KAREN (V.O.)
> Oh, Father, etc.

As Mrs. Tredoni turns to rinse the scrub rag, her ear catches the sounds of laughter in the dining room. Mrs. Tredoni's disapproving face looks up and sees Alice's feet.

> MRS. TREDONI
> (frightened)
> Ooooh. You horrid child. Get out of my kitchen.

CLOSE UP Alice is wearing her mask.

13. INT  DAY  DINING ROOM
Catherine jumps up and moves toward the kitchen saying:

> CATHERINE
> Alice, where are you? Get in here. Who told you you could roam?

Alice appears at the hall between the kitchen and the dining room. She is still wearing her mask.

> CATHERINE
> Take that thing off your face.
> (yelling into the kitchen) I'm sorry, Mrs. Tredoni. (back to Alice) Stay in here with us and try to remember you're a young lady. What will Father Tom think of you?

CLOSE UP Alice takes off the mask; she moves to a corner of the room sullenly.

> CATHERINE (V.O.)
> You probably frightened Mrs. Tredoni half to death.

(13 continued)

Father Tom wants to avert the ugly scene he had anticipated earlier. He puts his hand in the pocket of his cassock as he turns to Karen who has become sober and quiet.

> FATHER TOM
> (smiling)
> Karen, look what I've found here
> --I guess there is something
> more for you than Mrs. Tredoni's
> cookies.

Karen brightens immediately, but holds back. Father hands her the wrapped box.

> FATHER TOM
> (coaxing)
> Go on, take it; it's got to
> be yours. There's no other
> Karen Spages around here,
> is there?

The child eagerly takes the gift, hesitating.

> FATHER TOM
> (encouraging her)
> Open it--we all want to see
> what it is.

Karen rips off the wrapping quickly and clumsily. Inside the red velvet box is an antique gold cross on a heavy worked chain. She holds it up, showing it to her mother. Karen's face is shining with joy.

> FATHER TOM
> (looking at Catherine)
> It belonged to my mother.

> CATHERINE
> Tom, you shouldn't have..what
> if she loses it?

> FATHER TOM
> Who else would I give it to,
> Kay?

While this exchange is taking place, Alice is sitting in the corner on a chair, playing nervously with the edge of a doily on a small table. On the table are various cheap knickknacks. CLOSE UP of Alice's hands playing with the doily and of the knickknacks slowly being drawn toward the edge of the table.

> CATHERINE
> (covering her embarrassment)
> What do you say to Father Tom?

(13 continued)                                                    15

                          FATHER TOM
                She doesn't have to say anything,
                but she can give me a great big
                kiss.

         Karen rushes over to Father and throws herself
into his arms.

                          KAREN
                I love you, Father Tom.  I
                really love you.

                          FATHER TOM
                     (pleased, tenderly
                      strokes the child's
                      hair)
                I know you'll take good care
                of it.

         During this exchange the camera is on Tom's and
Karen's and Catherine's beaming faces.  Tom is awkward in
his stroking of the child.

         The camera picks up Alice, and the tension
increases as it becomes apparent that the knickknacks will
soon be on the floor.  The camera may even pick up Mrs.
Tredoni, still scrubbing, recording a surprised disapproval
of the unpriestly intimacies which she hears in the next
room.

         Camera is on Tom, Karen and Catherine.  Suddenly
the expected crash is heard.  Catherine, horrified, turns
to Alice.

                          CATHERINE
                What have you--

                          ALICE
                     (like a much
                      younger child)
                I didn't mean it, Mommy.  I
                couldn't help it.  I didn't
                mean it.

14.  INT  DAY  HALLWAY APARTMENT
         Alice comes out of the apartment door.

                          CATHERINE (V.O.)
                     (happily, calling out)
                Button your coat.  Make sure
                you meet me in front of the
                church.

         Alice closes the door and begins to walk down
the stairs.  She is buttoning her school coat.

(14 continued)                                                              16

            The door on the second floor opens.  Someone is
peeking out of the door watching Alice.  As she reaches the
landing from which she is being watched, the door slowly
widens and a massive form appears.

(Sounds of opera music can be heard.)

                        ALPHONSO
                   (with a lewd whine)
                Where are you going?

                        ALICE
                   (startled by him,
                    but knowing she can
                    treat him with
                    contempt)
                None of your business, Fatso.

            Alice turns and continues to walk down the
stairs.  Alphonso extends his head out further.

                        ALPHONSO
                   (pleading)
                I'll give you a dollar if you
                go to the store for me.

            Alice pauses and gives Alphonso one of those
cold calculating stares she has given earlier to Catherine.
She continues to walk, ignoring Alphonso.  He is still
talking as she walks out of the frame.

                        ALPHONSO
                   (in panic, voice
                    getting louder)
                I'm not feeling well.  The
                stores don't deliver on Sunday.
                Please...Please.

            Alice can be heard going out the door.

15.   INT   DAY   ALPHONSO'S APARTMENT
            Alphonso weighs 450 pounds.  His hands, head and
feet look grotesquely small next to his bulk.  His world is
centered in one-room of a small apartment.  The room is
dirty, cluttered with junk and empty food cans.  His only
friends are his six cats.  He is about 35 years old; because
of his weight, his breathing is strained.  His only
communion with the world has been in fantasy.

            Alphonso slams the apartment door.  He is
wearing an old faded silk bathrobe stained with urine.

                        ALPHONSO
                   (whining to the cats)
                The little bitch.  I'll fix her.

(15 continued)                                                    17

                    See, my little pussies, I told
                    you she doesn't like us. But
                    she ought to. (pensively and
                    chewing his lip) I'll show
                    her...(voice trailing off)

        As he is talking, he may pick up a cat and begin
fondling it sensuously. He walks, holding it, over to a
table and grabs a box of cookies, takes the last one,
crumbles the box as if it were an empty pack of cigarettes
and throws it down. He then lies down on his bed, with the
cat on this chest...still stroking he begins to sing to the
crescendo of the music. The CAMERA PANS from Alphonso to
the window and DOLLIES to an EXTREME CLOSE UP of a cat
sitting on a window ledge watching him.

16. INT DAY CHURCH
        The church is a fair-sized cathedral in the
traditional "t" shape with some side altars. There is a
wall separating the church proper from a long entrance-type
room containing, among other things, the baptismal font,
and two confessionals. This room is entered by a center
door and two side doors. The choir can be heard singing.
It is Sunday morning.

        CLOSE UP candles being lighted with a
candlelighter. Flame flares.

        CAMERA DOLLIES BACK and we see the altar boy
lighting candles. Under the candles there is a statue of
St. Michael the Archangel with his sword raised.

        The CAMERA PANS with the boy as he joins two
priests and another boy on the altar.

17. EXT DAY CHURCH
(Sound of choir singing)

        Catherine is standing alone in front of the
church. A few people are entering. A little girl,
wearing her communion dress under her school coat, hurries
by with her mother. Two boys wearing blue communion suits
run inside the church. Karen comes out of the church
wearing a white communion dress; her face is marred with
nervousness. She doesn't want to do anything wrong today,
anything different from the other kids. She runs toward
her mother.

                        KAREN
                    (excited)
                    She isn't inside and they're
                    starting mass. I'm going to
                    be late.

(17 continued)

Angela, Catherine's teenage niece, comes running from the church.

                    ANGELA
                (breathlessly)
        Aunt Catherine, Sister Felicia
        is looking for Karen.

                    CATHERINE
                (trying to be calm)
        O.K. Go inside and join your
        group. You'll catch cold.

                    KAREN
        But,...

                    CATHERINE
        Don't worry. I'll be right
        there; I won't miss anything.
        (She straightens Karen's veil.)

Angela takes Karen's hand.

                    ANGELA
                (the little mother)
        Come on, Karen, come on.

They walk out of the frame toward the church.

CLOSE UP Catherine nervously looking for Alice.

18. INT DAY CHURCH
Father Tom at the altar is saying Mass.

The choir is singing. The camera follows Catherine as she enters from under the balcony. She walks to a pew near the front of the church and sits in the last seat on the side aisle. People smile and move over to give her some room.

In the next row back, her older sister, Annie, is trying to get her attention. She hands Catherine Karen's coat and scarf. Annie, in her early 40's, is definitely a matron who is used to bossing everyone. She is seated between her balding husband, Jim, and her son, Robert, an awkward 15-year-old who takes after his father.

Annie is trying to determine why Alice is not with Catherine. Catherine shrugs. Her worries increase now that she has Annie to contend with. She turns to the Mass, keeping her eyes on the altar. She sits frozen with an attempt to still her obvious anxiety.

In the rear of the church two nuns are lining up the children. Several of them are carrying large candles.

(18 continued) 19

They are restless, and the nuns are playing their usual role of repressing their youthful energy. The girls and boys are separated in two lines. There are more girls than boys.

      NUN
  Shh. Quiet. Thomas stand up
  straight. Listen for the music.
  (She begins to light the candles.)
  No talking.

The other nun is more or less inspecting the group, speaking reprovingly to this one and that. She might say, "No talking," "Hold your candles straight," etc. It is their show and they want it to be good, which means perfectly ordered, solemn, and with the restraint of adulthood.

Father Tom turns and faces the congregation and gives them a blessing. He nods his head which signals the choir to begin. He is holding a chalice. One nun starts the communion class singing. The second nun begins the procession. The procedure for the march down the aisle is boy and girl, boy and girl. They walk as in a wedding. As each pair reaches the foot of the altar, they genuflect in unison.

      NUN
    (pointing)
  One, two, step, one, two,
  step...

The nun counts the rhythm for five or six of the children. She moves with them toward the beginning of the pews at the back of the church. The second nun checks the posture, etc. of the remaining children and cuts away down the side aisle with a mock pretense at keeping out of the picture; actually she wants nothing more than to be the "Big Cheese."

The people are looking at the rear of the church. As the first of the youngsters move down the aisle, we might hear or see mouths saying, "aren't they cute"; parents are straining to see which is theirs--under the veils. Some parents are taking pictures.

LONG SHOT camera is on the balcony. The camera follows the nun and children walking up the center aisle. The last of the group is still bunched in the back. We lose sight of them for they are beyond the wall dividing the church from the entrance room.

In the rear of the church, Karen and the last of the girls are waiting their turn. Karen is the last one on line, holding one of the large candles. The veils are covering their faces and the mood is solemn. Each child leaves the frame as it is his turn to go down the aisle.

(18 continued)

    Camera is on the side aisle of the church. Children can be seen walking past the people in the pews.

    As Karen waits for her turn, two hands come from behind and quickly pull the candle against Karen's throat. The hands are covered with white communion gloves.

    CLOSE UP Karen's face. She is being choked to death. The person who is choking her is wearing a blue coat.

    Karen panics, choking. As she struggles, she rips off her veil.

    CLOSE UP children. The camera is on the side of the altar railing. You see the faces in profile and the priest's hand giving the Communion Host. The hand moves from the chalice toward the camera. Each child receives the Host, then leaves the frame. In the rear of the church, Karen's feet can be seen as she is being dragged away. They are pulled past the opening to the center aisle in full sight of the totally oblivious parishioners.

        FATHER TOM
      (repeating as he gives
      each child the Host)
    Corpus Domini Jesu Christi...
    (mumbling the rest rapidly)
    custodiat animam tuam in
    vitam aeternam. Amen.

    In the rear of the church, beyond the range of the congregation, the confessional door is open. Karen is propped up inside the cubicle with her arms wrapped around the candle. Hands reach in, strike a match, and relight the candle. The flame scorches the wall, and the wax drips on her dress. The gloved hand reaches out and yanks the gold cross from Karen's neck. The person closes the confessional door.

    The last of the children are leaving the altar, taking their places with the rest of the group in the front pews. Due to her position in the pew, it is difficult for Catherine to notice which of the girls is her daughter. As she strains to see from her kneeling position, someone in the row ahead stands to take a picture completely blocking her view.

    The choir is still singing.

    EXTREME CLOSE UP choir member singing. The CAMERA PANS down from her face past the balcony to the center aisle where Alice is walking to the altar. Karen's veil is slightly visible hanging out of the pocket of Alice's coat. The CAMERA DOLLIES down the aisle with her.

(18 continued)                                                  21

    Father Tom is standing on the altar. The last child leaves the altar as Alice walks up to Father Tom and kneels to receive Holy Communion.

    Catherine, straining to find Karen, sees Alice at the altar. Disbelief and confusion register on her face. Aunt Annie leans forward shocked. She is tugging at her sister's shoulder.

> AUNT ANNIE
> (in a low strained voice)
> What is she doing? She's got no
> business being up there. For
> God's sake, go get her.

    Father Tom, covering his surprise, bends to give the Host to Alice; his eyes become fixed on the rear of the church.

    Alice in profile, eyes closed tightly, mouth open with tongue extended to receive the Host. Father Tom's hand stops. There is a pause. He is still looking at the rear of the church. Alice opens her eyes to look at Father Tom. She has a questioning look; she clearly wants to receive Communion.

    Father Tom is staring at the rear of the church.

    Smoke is beginning to filter in. People in the last row are looking to the back of the church. An old woman begins to scream in Italian.

> OLD WOMAN
> (in panic)
> Fuoko, fuoko.

    Father Tom thrusts the chalice into the hands of the altar boy, and runs down the aisle. Those close to the altar are unaware of what is happening in the back and are shocked by the priest's action. People begin to follow the priest. They want to see what is happening; some of the more cautious ones are preparing to protect their own. Once again we hear someone yell "Fire." Alice remains at the altar kneeling; bewildered, she looks in the direction of the excitement.

> AUNT ANNIE
> (looking to the rear)
> My God, where's Angela? (Forgetting
> her sister, she starts for the
> rear of the church, followed by a
> confused Jim and Robert)

(18 continued)                                           22

        Catherine's attention is toward Alice and the little girls in white communion dresses. She pushes her way toward Alice clutching Karen's coat and scarf.

> CATHERINE
> (shocked)
> What are you doing up here?
> Where were you?
>
> ALICE
> (frightened and confused)
> I wanted to go to Communion, Mommy. But Father Tom didn't give me the Host. I didn't get the Host.
>
> CATHERINE
> (who is looking for Karen, ignores the answer; cutting in, she grabs her)
> I don't see Karen. Come on, we've got to find her and get out of here.

        Catherine sees a veil hanging out of Alice's pocket; she grabs the veil.

(Sounds of commotion getting louder.)

> CATHERINE
> (voice rising with the commotion)
> Where did you get this? Is this Karen's veil? Where is she?
>
> ALICE
> (excited, talking simultaneously)
> I found it on the floor when I came in. I thought maybe Karen dropped it. (defensively) I was going to give it to her.

        In the rear of the church loud noises are heard. A woman screams. The church doors are open; strong sunlight filters through and silhouettes the crowd. A man with a fire extinguisher is making his way through the crowd into the Baptistry.

> MAN (V.O.)
> Someone call an ambulance.
>
> ANNIE
> (screaming and pleading)
> Let me go to her! Let me go!

(18 continued)                                                          23

        Hearing her sister's voice, Catherine begins to realize that what is happening concerns her.

>                    CATHERINE
>                (grabbing Alice)
>            Come on!
>
>                    ALICE
>                (sensing danger, holding
>                 her back)
>            No, Mommy! I don't want to!

(Sounds of fire extinguisher spraying.)

        In the confessional Karen's body is in the same position that we saw it in earlier, but amid the damage of the fire and the foam of the fire extinguisher, she is barely recognizable. Annie breaks away from those holding her, pushing her way through the crowd toward her sister, who is pulling Alice with her down the aisle. There is a wild look on Annie's face. Catherine turns toward her.

>                    ANNIE
>                (agonizing, grabs hold
>                 of her sister)
>            Catherine! Catherine! Don't go
>            back! Don't go back!
>
>                    CATHERINE
>                (fighting to get free)
>            Let me go, Anna! What's wrong?
>            Where's Karen?

        In the struggle Catherine drops the veil.

        Father Tom is seen coming through the crowd. As the crowd breaks, some people follow him; others, confused, are blocking his way. Some are staring in the direction of Catherine. They want to see, are shocked; some are frankly curious, others embarrassed. It is the usual varied reaction of people drawn to view human disaster.

>                    MAN'S VOICE
>                (firmly)
>            Stand back! Let Father through!

        Some of the men begin to guide the crowd out.

(Sounds of a siren can be heard in the distance.)

        Upon seeing Father Tom, Annie gives up the struggle and steps aside.

(18 continued) 24

> ANNIE
> (crying and chanting)
> E morte!  E morte!

Turning toward Father Tom and seeing the reality on his face, Catherine holds out her hand to halt his approach. She is clinging to Karen's coat. She is beginning to call up something from the depths, something which will enable her to cope. She rocks ever so slightly, a dazed look on her face. She is saying:

> CATHERINE
> No, Tom! No! No! No!

Alice, staring bewildered, notices the veil. She moves numbly, picks up the veil, and stuffs it in her pocket. sitting in a nearby pew.

Annie's eyes follow Alice. An idea is forming in her head, and the horror of it shocks her into stillness. She remains staring, disbelieving.

19. INT  DAY  CONFERENCE ROOM-LIBRARY

The room is a large, contemporary executive conference room with the walls lined with books. The floor-to-ceiling windows indicate that the room is on a high floor in a skyscraper overlooking a modern American city. The room is dominated by a large rosewood table and some ten leather chairs. At the end of the table is a dark-haired rugged-looking man. His Brooks Brothers shirt and tie flatter his tanned athletic appearance. His confident yet casual air reveals a man who is comfortable with power. He is looking through one of several folders on the table, possibly making notes on the pad. There is a buzz on the phone nearest to him, its red light flickering. He presses a button on the phone and leans back, stretching in the plush swivel chair; he is glad for the interruption.

> MAN
> (calling out)
> Yes?

> FEMALE VOICE
> (heard through the room)
> There's a call on your private line.

> MAN
> Who is it?

> FEMALE VOICE
> It's a Father Tom Hale.

The man's face registers surprise.

(19 continued)                                                    25

                              MAN
                    Ask him to hold on. I'll take it
                    in my office.

          He leans forward, pushes the button on the phone,
gets up and leaves.

20.   EXT   DAY   AIRPORT
                    Plane preparing to land at Newark Airport. Plane
lands and taxies down the runway and comes to a stop. The
dark-haired man, wearing a brown-striped Brooks Brothers suit,
disembarks from the First-Class section of the plane.

21.   EXT   DAY   OUTSIDE TERMINAL
                    The dark-haired man is seen coming out of an
airport door, suitcase in hand. He hails a cab, gets in, and
the cab takes off.

22.   EXT   DAY   FUNERAL HOME
                    EXTREME CLOSE UP of wreaths bouncing. The CAMERA
PANS with the wreaths and pulls back to reveal the attendants
as they toss the flowers hurriedly on the flower car. There
is no ceremony to this; it is a job like any other job. There
are two limousines and several other cars lined up for the
funeral procession.

          The attendants carry out a tiny white coffin.
The coffin gleams in the brilliant morning sun. It is a
deceptive sun, contrasting strongly to the frosty breaths of
the pall-bearers. The air is quite cold.

          A group of mourners come out and slowly head for
the cars parked at the curb. The faces are strained and
somber. Among the mourners are a chicly dressed woman and her
husband, perhaps cousins of Catherine. With them is an old
woman, short and on the heavy side. She is dressed in black
even to her Oxfords and has on a typical round-shouldered coat
coat. There is a woman alone, somewhat like Catherine,
perhaps a friend who lives on the block. A group of women
with whom she works when volunteering at the school or
around the church are there also.

          Catherine and Annie come out. Although it really
isn't necessary, Annie is holding Catherine by her shoulders;
thus effectively putting a barrier around Catherine. This
forces Alice to walk at a little distance from her mother,
somewhat like a lonely end. Father Tom is following them.
Behind him is Jim, who forms a very loose group with Angela
and his son, Robert, who seem quite ill at ease.

          Annie assists Catherine into the first car. Alice
hangs back. Annie turns to Alice and motions her into the
car; she is telling the child to get on the other side of her

(22 continued)

mother. After Catherine and Alice are settled, Annie surveys the scene to be sure everything is to her liking. She notices that her daughter, Angela, is standing confused midway between the two limousines.

                    ANNIE
                (sharply)
        Go, (she gestures) go with your
        father.

23A  INT  DAY  POLICE CAR

The unmarked car is parked at a respectable distance; the two men have been taking telephoto shots unobtrusively in the hope of finding some clues to the case. Their camera seems to linger on Robert and Angela. It studies his face and his hands, which are small, slender and bony.

As the procession is about to depart, a cab pulls up.

The dark-haired man gets out. It is obvious he has stopped somewhere to change his clothes for he is dressed in a black suit and is carrying a raincoat.

                DETECTIVE TAKING PICTURES (V.O.)
        Who's that?

                SECOND DETECTIVE (V.O.)
        The father.

23B.  INT OF THE FIRST LIMOUSINE.

Father Tom has gotten out of the car and is greeting his friend, who is paying the cab driver.

                    ANNIE
                (with sarcasm to the
                group)
        Well, at least he managed to get
        here before they put her in the
        ground.

                    CATHERINE
                (reproving)
        Annie!

Inside the car all attention is directed toward the newcomer. Father Tom shakes Dom's hand and directs him toward the first car. Catherine meanwhile gets out of the car. She lets the door close loosely behind her. She and Dom meet near the car door. They embrace.

                    CATHERINE
                (trying hard to control
                herself)
        I'm so glad you're here.

(23B continued)                                                                    27

>    This action is seen from the point of view of Alice and Annie through the car window. Annie, showing signs of impatience, reaches over and pushes the automatic button which rolls the window down.

> ANNIE
> (curtly but with restraint)
> I don't want to rush you, but mass begins at 9:00. (They quickly break apart.)

CLOSE UP Dom's face peeking through the window.

> DOM
> (warm but reserved)
> Hello Alice. (The child remains silent; then crisply to Annie) Hello, Ann.

>    He pulls the door open and simultaneously Annie pushes the button to raise the automatic window. Catherine gets into the car and Annie moves to the center of the seat to make room for her sister and Dom.

> ANNIE
> (motioning)
> Sit on the fold-up Alice.

> ALICE
> (with a frightened firmness)
> I want to sit by my mother.

> ANNIE
> (firmly)
> Please do what you're told.

> CATHERINE
> Annie, please; there's plenty of room. (firmly) I want Alice next to me.

> DOM
> (at the door)
> I can sit on the fold-up. There's no problem.

> ANNIE
> (rising, and like a martyr)
> Never mind. I'll sit in the second car.

As Annie gets out of the car:

(23B continued) 28

                    FATHER TOM (V.O.)
           There's room up here, Annie.

24. EXT  DAY  FUNERAL HOME
          LONG SHOT Annie getting into the second car. The procession begins.

25. INT  DAY  POLICE CAR
          The tail-end of the procession can be seen passing through the window of the police car. The sound of the police radio is heard continually. There are two policemen in the car. Detective Raymond Beame, who is in the front seat, is a man in his early fifties. A veteran detective, his nondescript face belies the action he has seen. His assistant, Detective Michael Spina, is in his early thirties, brash and quite unlike his boss. Spina is sitting in the back seat unloading film from his camera.

                    SPINA
           The fat one didn't show up.

                    BEAME
                 (thinking)
           Where was the girl?

                    SPINA
           The mother said she was helping
           the nuns.

                    BEAME
           Did you talk to any of them?

                    SPINA
           No, not yet.

                    BEAME
           Find out exactly where she was.
           (knows it won't be easy) Well,
           let's get some coffee. (As he
           starts the car) I want to talk
           to that Alphonso character before
           they get back from the grave.

26. INT  DAY  APARTMENT
          CLOSE UP Jim as he takes a last quick drag of his cigarette and furtively looks around before dousing it in his coffee cup. CAMERA PANS with the cup as he stretches forward to drop it on a littered table. CAMERA PANS over trays of half-eaten food, piled-up used paper plates and plastic forks, and paper coffee cups. The funeral feast has come to an end. Annie can be heard with the last guest at the door.

                    GUEST (V.O.)
           Please don't hesitate to call--
           we want to do something. It's
           such a tragedy.

(26 continued)

                  ANNIE
              (firmly)
Thank you, there's nothing anyone can do. I'll be staying with my sister as long as she needs me.

During this exchange the CAMERA continues to PAN past Alice, at the table, who stiffens at Annie's words. The CAMERA STOPS at the door and DOLLIES back as the door is closing to reveal the whole apartment.

Jim and Robert are on the couch. Robert is biting his nails. Angela is intent on a Life magazine. Catherine and Dom are at the table. Annie walks toward the table ready to roll up her sleeves and clean up.

                  CATHERINE
              (to Annie)
You don't have to stay. After all, you're only ten minutes away.
              (weakly) Jim and the kids need you.

                  ANNIE
              (doesn't realize Catherine
              doesn't want her)
Please, Catherine, (as if to say, "don't say anymore") Jim wants me to stay. My Angela can take care of everything.

                  DOM
              (aware of Catherine's and
              Alice's feelings, tries
              his hand)
I've made arrangements to stay in town for a few days, so I'll be here if you need me.

                  CATHERINE
Thanks, Dom, but I'm sure you have to get back home.

                  DOM
              (seriously and gently)
Look, Kay, maybe this is a bad time to bring it up but...there are things we have to talk about.

                  ANNIE
              (lapsing into Italian,
              and nodding toward the
              kids)
Guarda...les ragazzi.

(26 continued)

>                    DOM
>               (ignoring her)
>          This is no ordinary situation.
>
>                    ANNIE
>          Stasita.
>
>                    DOM
>          Well, ask them to leave...there
>          are some things I want to know.
>
>                    CATHERINE
>               (understand, rises)
>          There's so much cake left over.
>          It's a shame to let it go to
>          waste. Alice, take this box
>          down to Mr. Alphonso.
>
>                    ALICE
>          Okay.

Alice obediently goes over to her mother.

>                    ANNIE
>               (to her kids)
>          Go with her. You can play in the
>          backyard.

Angela and Robert hide their annoyance at her directions.

>                    ANNIE
>               (as they leave)
>          Don't disappear--keep the noise
>          down.

27. INT DAY HALLWAY

Alice knocks on Alphonso's door boldly while Robert and Angela hang back, curious but a little scared. Alphonso opens the door quickly; he obviously has heard them coming and can't wait.

>                    ALPHONSO
>               (with his breathy whine)
>          I heard everyone leave. It's all
>          over, huh? You die and they put you
>          in the ground and it's over. Such a
>          pretty girl too. Such a shame, so
>          little...too pretty to wind up in a
>          box.

As Alphonso is talking, Alice stands in defiant mockery. Robert, clearly nervous, draws back away from the door. Angela, unafraid, thoroughly enjoys Alice's confrontation.

(27 continued)

> ALICE
> (ignoring him, thrusts
> out the box of cake and
> says with a sneer)
> My mother thought you could use
> some cake, Fatty.

Alphonso takes the cake and, replying to her dig, looks directly into Alice's eyes.

> ALPHONSO
> (with venom)
> God always takes the pretty ones.
> Thank your mother. Such a lovely
> lady. (He closes the door.)

> ANGELA
> Wow! His stomach is so fat I bet
> if someone stuck him with a knife
> he'd burst.

> ROBERT
> He scares me.

> ALICE
> (aware of Alphonso's
> implication)
> Him? (hard) That ugly bastard
> doesn't scare me.

Robert grins with a snort; he is excited by his cousin's boldness.

> ANGELA
> Come on, Alice; let's get out of
> here before my mother hears us.

They laugh as they leave the FRAME, followed by Robert. At the bottom of the hallway Angela stops abruptly, turning toward her brother.

> ANGELA
> Where are you going? We don't
> want you with us.

Angela takes Alice possessively by the arm. From above muffled noises of arguing voices can be heard. Robert looks up.

28. INT DAY APARTMENT

> DOM
> (yelling)
> Goddammit, Annie. The child was
> murdered. Don't you understand

(28 continued)

what that means? It takes a screwed-up guy to do a job like that. Aren't you afraid? He could come after Alice or Angela. (Everybody looks at everyone else. Even Jim looks up from the couch. Dom throws his hands up, exasperated) What's the matter with you people? Aren't you listening to me?

     ANNIE
   (angry)
You don't know half of what we've been through. You barely made it to the funeral.

     CATHERINE
   (warning)
Annie, please don't start.

     DOM
   (ignores the implication)
I understand what you're going through. She is my daughter after all.

     ANNIE
   (with intense implication)
You have no idea what I'm talking about.

     DOM
   (looking at her, and
    receiving no answer,
    he looks at Catherine)
What's she trying to say?

Catherine waves her hand in disgust. Annie's face remains rigid. Dom turns to Jim.

     DOM
   (to Jim)
What's this all about?

     JIM
   (blurting it out)
Alice was the last one in the church. (Jim gets up and walks toward the table to cover his embarrassment.)

     DOM
   (to Jim)
So? What's that supposed to mean?

(28 continued)

      CATHERINE
     (cries out)
Stop it! I won't listen to this
again.

      DOM
     (beginning to understand)
Are you trying to imply Alice had
something to do with the murder?

      ANNIE
I'm not saying anything of the kind.
My God, don't I love that child?
She's like one of my own. (with a
cut at Dom) I practically raised her.

      DOM
     (sarcastically)
I know all about that, Annie.

      ANNIE
     (angry)
You don't know all about anything.
All you know is to send a check
once a month.

      CATHERINE
Annie, please, not now.

      ANNIE
     (hurt)
It would never occur to you that
I'm trying to protect her, would it?

      DOM
Protect her? From what?

      CATHERINE
     (rising; coldly through
      her tears)
Are you so sure you're trying to
protect her? (There is a shocked
silence.) If you don't mind, I'm
going to lie down.

Catherine leaves the room. Everyone remains
silent. Sound of the bedroom door closing softly can be heard.
The long silence is broken by Annie, as she awkwardly fusses
with things on the table.

      ANNIE
     (whispering defensively)
You saw the photographers at the
church. The police do investigate
a murder, you know.

(28 continued)

> DOM
> (whispering)
> I still don't understand what that has to do with Alice.

> ANNIE
> (whispering)
> Everyone knew she was the last one in the church. They want to talk to her. They think she may have seen someone. What if the police find out about the veil?

> DOM
> What about the veil?

> ANNIE
> She had Karen's veil in her pocket.

> DOM
> (looks at her, puzzled; then realizing the implication, stands up, whispering)
> Jesus Christ, she probably picked the veil up from the floor. Did you bother to ask her where she got it from?

CLOSE UP Annie not answering. With that Dom goes to console Catherine, leaving Annie and Jim with their suspicions.

29. INT DAY POLICE STATION
The door of the police station opens and Dominic enters. The CAMERA DOLLIES with him as he glances around and, catching sight of the reception area, walks purposefully over to it.

This is the reception area of a 19th Century building. The duty officers are stationed on a high platform behind a five-foot panelled walnut bar, which is distinguished by an oversized brass railing--of the kind commonly seen in old saloons..whose magnificence has been dimmed by years of tarnish. The elevated position of the police adds a sense of aloofness which contributes to the insecurity of those who must do business here. Dominic obviously does not have this problem.

> DOM
> (to the officer)
> I have an appointment with Detective Captain Beame.

(29 continued)

       OFFICER
     (pointing)
  Take the elevator over there
  to the second floor. Go to your
  right. You'll pass some lockers
  and you'll see the room. There's
  a sign on the door.

CAMERA FOLLOWS Dominic to the elevator. The doors open and he and another police officer enter.

30. INT DAY ELEVATOR
  On the elevator is a short, skinny policewoman whose fiftyish face lights up at the sight of the policeman.

       POLICEWOMAN
  How's it goin', Joe?

       JOE
  Okay, Mary.

       MARY
     (calling out)
  Floor?

       DOM
  Second, please.

The doors have closed and the elevator has started to move.

       MARY
     (realizing they are
     descending)
  Oops! (laughing) Hey, I just
  came from the basement.

The elevator stops. The doors open on a basement room with a gray concrete floor, exposed plumbing, and abandoned desks. Two elderly janitors are engrossed in what seems to them an important conversation.

       FIRST MAN
  Why the hell are they holding an
  auction for four bikes? Hi Mary.
  Before that happens I'm gonna
  steal the red one.

They all laugh.

       MARY
  No, yyou don't--I've got my bid in
  for that one.

(30 continued)                                                    36

They all laugh and then become silent.

                    SECOND MAN
                  (meekly)
            Mary, what do you hear about the
            Spages case?

     The aloof amusement fades from Dom's face when
this question about his daughter is asked.

                    MARY
                  (soberly)
            They know as much about that as they
            know about those bikes. I can tell
            you this much. I sat in on the
            line-up yesterday. There is no
            encouragement there. (importantly)
            I could have told them that pulling
            in the regulars was a waste of
            time. If you want my opinion...

     Mary is interrupted by the opening of the doors.
Intent on eavesdropping, Dom ironically fails to notice that
the doors have opened for his floor. The doors begin to
close.

                    MARY
                  (pressing the hold
                   button to prevent
                   the doors from
                   closing)
            Hey, you wanted the second floor,
            didn't you?

                    DOM
            Oh, yes, thanks.

     Dom leaves reluctantly. The CAMERA FOLLOWS with
Dom as he goes to the right, past the lockers toward a door.

31.  INT  DAY  OFFICE
          Detective Beame's office is a small overcrowded
room nestled deep within the building. In an area able to
accommodate one desk comfortably, we find two desks one of
which is piled high with papers. There are a couple of
bookcases and some bulletin boards. There is a calendar with
a picture of President Kennedy on it over Spina's desk.

          Beame's desk is noticeably clear, except for his
lunch which has been carefully laid out on the desk. Beame,
carrying a cup of tea, sits down at his desk and unfolds a
napkin, placing it across his lap. He unwraps a neatly-
wrapped sandwich centering it on the wax paper. He picks
up half of the sandwich, sniffs at it and takes a bite.

(31 continued)                                                              37

He chews, making a face. Taking the top piece of bread from his sandwich, he shakes his head in disgust. There is a knock at the door.

>           BEAME
>           (preoccupied with the
>            sandwich, reaching
>            for a spoon)
> Come in.

Dom enters and hesitates.

>           DOM
> Raymond Beame?

>           BEAME
>           (scraping mayonnaise
>            from the bread)
> That's me.

Beame becomes aware of Dom staring at him. He holds up his spoon which contains very little mayonnaise.

>           BEAME
>           (quietly explaining)
> I've been telling her for twenty-
> two years--not too much mayonnaise.
> (carefully wiping the mayonnaise
> from the spoon with a napkin) Sit
> down.

As Dom sits down unbuttoning his coat, Beame takes another bite from the sandwich and chews with obvious pleasure. CLOSE UP Dom, looking at Beame with impatience.

>           BEAME
>           (meaning it)
> Sorry about your daughter. (He
> takes a sip of tea; realizing his
> manners) Like some coffee? How
> about tea? (As he asks, he
> removes the teabag from his own cup)

Dom shakes his head no.

>           BEAME
> How about a sandwich? (Shaking
> his head) She always packs two
> but I never eat the second.

>           DOM
>           (formally; wants to
>            get on with it)
> No thank you.

(31 continued)                                                              38

                    BEAME
               (wiping his mouth
                with a new napkin)
          You must have a lot of questions.

                    DOM
          You're goddamned right I do.  I
          was hoping you'd have some leads.

                    BEAME
               (vaguely, waving his
                hand)
          We're checking on a few things.
          (taking another bite of his
          sandwich)  As a matter-of-fact
          someone is down in your neighborhood
          doing legwork right now.  (He
          reaches into his drawer for the
          salt shaker.)

                    DOM
               (annoyed)
          Are you doing anything to protect
          Catherine...and my daughter?

                    BEAME
               (pausing with the
                salt shaker in his
                hand and looking
                sharply at Dom)
          What makes you think they'll be
          another attack on your family?

                    DOM
               (knows nothing)
          I don't know.  I couldn't imagine
          anybody killing Karen.

                    BEAME
               (salting the meat)
          Most murders are committed by
          someone who knows the victim.

                    DOM
               (puzzled)
          If it's someone who knew Karen,
          why did he pick the church?  It
          seems pretty stupid to take a
          chance in front of all those
          people.

(31 continued)

> BEAME
> (leaning back in his
> chair)
> Yes, I've been thinking about that myself.

Sounds of brakes squeaking outside draw Beame's attention to the window. Leaning closer he studies the scene below. Several policemen are getting into a police car with its dome flashing.

> BEAME
> (as if to himself)
> ...in the midst of a crowded church he drags the body across the floor and carefully props it up in the confessional. (Sounds of a siren fading in the distance; staring absently at Dom) Very deliberate, wouldn't you say?

> DOM
> (trying to get
> Beame's attention)
> Why did he try to set fire to the church?

> BEAME
> (impatiently)
> He didn't try to set fire to the church. (finishing his sandwich) Do you mind if I talk to Alice today?

> DOM
> Where's that going to get you?

> BEAME
> Alice was the last one to come into the church. She might have seen something—something that means nothing to her but that will set us in the right direction. For example, like exactly where she found that veil.

At this point, the door opens and Mike Spina comes in.

> BEAME
> (turning to clear
> away his lunch)
> Mike, this is Dominic Spages. I've just been asking his permission to talk with Alice.

(31 continued)

                SPINA
            (friendly)
I was just down in your neighborhood. Sorry about your trouble. (He smiles warmly; getting no response, he takes off his coat) Boy, it's raw out there. (To Beame) Jesus Christ, the defroster still isn't working. (Getting no response, Spina goes over to the coffee) Any coffee left? Would you like a cup, Mr. Spages?

                DOM
           (brushing him aside)
No thanks. (To Beame quickly) About that veil--(firmly) it's obvious to me that Alice came in just after the murder. (Beame looks at him questioningly) I spoke with her and she said it was on the floor when she came in. Karen must have dropped it in the struggle.

                SPINA
           (trying to assert
             his authority)
Mr. Spages, how did Alice know it was Karen's veil? (turning to his boss with triumph) I checked. They're all alike. They're all purchased from the same store.

                DOM
           (surprised and defensive)
Alice never said it was Karen's veil. (Trying to remember, he shrugs) Everyone just assumed it was.

                SPINA
           (coming close to
             implying Dom is lying)
According to your sister-in-law, Alice said it was Karen's veil.

                DOM
You don't know Annie. She's always jumping to conclusions--especially where Alice is concerned.

                SPINA
           (pushing it further)
But your wife didn't disagree with her.

(31 continued)

> DOM
> My wife has been under a lot of strain.
>
> BEAME
> (musing)
> Does your sister-in-law dislike your daughter?
>
> DOM
> Yes, (pauses) but I think it's more accurate to say she doesn't like me.
>
> SPINA
> (contemptuously)
> Do you really think your sister-in-law dislikes you that much--that she'd want to implicate your daughter in a murder?
>
> DOM
> (cutting him off angrily)
> I don't like the way you're questioning me. You really must be desperate to start on a 12 year old child. (standing up) On second through, I don't think it's a good idea for you to talk to Alice. She's been through enough hell.

Dom turns to leave, then turns back.

> DOM
> (disgusted)
> I came down here to see if there was anything I could do to help.
>
> BEAME
> (calmly to Dom)
> Do you really think I'm looking to pin a murder on a 12 year old girl?

The question goes unanswered as Dom, looking from Beame to Spina to Beame, realizes the difference between the two men.

> BEAME
> (referring back to Dom's offer)
> I need to talk to Alice. Can you help me with that?

(31 continued)

42

                    DOM
            (looks at him thinking,
            then decisively)
        I think it would be best if I
        prepared Catherine first. I'll
        call you later.

Dom turns to leave.

                    BEAME
        Would you be able to get back to us
        by, say, three o'clock?

                    DOM
            (nodding his head)
        I'll try.

As soon as Dom is out of earshot, Beame turns to Spina and looks at him thoughtfully.

                    BEAME
            (quietly)
        Sella's has been supplying Holy
        Family with veils ever since I can
        remember.

Turning back to his desk, Beame picks up the phone. Spina looks at Beame as if to say, "Okay you smart-ass bastard." He moves quickly to his coat, pulls out a rolled-up manila envelope, and throws it on Beame's desk. CLOSE UP of manila envelope, with a printed return address that reads Holy Family School.

32. INT DAY POLICE STATION
        Dom gets off the elevator, walks over to a phone booth, and dials.

33. INT DAY RECTORY
        Father Tom is sitting at a neatly set table. It is obvious he has just started lunch. He looks up at the sound of the phone ringing.

        CAMERA PANS from Tom across the room into the hallway and DOLLIES to an open door marked office. Nothing can be seen in the room, but an oak table. Just outside and to the left of the door is a poor reproduction of the Pieta, which is resting on an embroidered doily.

                    MRS. TREDONI (V.O.)
            (coming from the room)
        Holy Family Rectory. (pause) I'm
        sorry he's having lunch right now.
        (pause, then firmly) I'm sorry
        Father does not like to be disturbed
        at meal times.

(33 continued)

CLOSE UP Father Tom, aware of the conversation. He puts down his fork and quietly moves to a phone in the hallway. He cautiously picks up the phone and, placing his hand over the mouthpiece, listens in.

During this action Mrs. Tredoni's voice can be heard.

              MRS. TREDONI (V.O.)
            (continuing)
If you give me your number, I can have him call you. (pause) I don't care who it is. Don't raise your voice to me. I'm just following the rules. (pause) If I gave in everytime someone told me that, he'd never eat a meal without an interruption.

Tom recognizes Dom's voice.

              FATHER TOM
            (into the phone)
It's okay, Mrs. Tredoni.

Sounds of the phone clicking to a disapproving "humph."

              FATHER TOM
Sorry, Dom. (pause) I know. (pause) She's just doing it for my own good. This does happen more often than not. I told her to put you through but I guess she forgot. Where are you?

All of Dom's replies in the following conversation are indistinguishable.

              DOM
            (barely audible)
I'm at the police station.

              FATHER TOM
Did they mention anything about the school?

              DOM
            (barely audible)
No. What about the school?

              FATHER TOM
Well, they came and took Alice's records. I couldn't stop them.

(33 continued)

>                    DOM
>              (barely audible)
>         I don't believe those sons-of-
>         bitches. Do you realize what
>         they're trying to do?
>
>                    FATHER TOM
>         Take it easy; I know Beame; he's
>         not that kind of guy.
>
>                    DOM
>              (barely audible)
>         Yeah, well the bastards want to
>         talk to Alice.
>
>                    FATHER TOM
>         Have you called Catherine?
>
>                    DOM
>              (barely audible)
>         Yes, I told her we were coming
>         over.
>
>                    FATHER TOM
>         All right, hold on. Before we go
>         I want to talk to you alone.
>         I've got some things to tell you,
>         but we just haven't had a chance.
>         I'm leaving right now. Be there
>         in ten minutes.

Father Tom hangs up the phone and the CAMERA FOLLOWS him as he takes his raincoat from the closet.

>                    FATHER TOM
>              (leaving; calling out)
>         I'll be gone for a couple of hours,
>         Mrs. Tredoni.
>
>                    MRS. TREDONI (V.O.)
>         Will you be home for dinner?
>              (realizing he is gone, she starts
>              talking out loud to herself) I
>         know his couple of hours. Humph.
>         I knew that was going to happen.
>         That's precisely why I hate to
>         interrupt his meals. There is a
>         good reason for every rule.

As she speaks, the CAMERA PANS across the hallway and into the dining room to a SHOT of the dining room table with its abandoned lunch.

34. INT   DAY   APARTMENT BEDROOM
Catherine is on her knees going through Karen's dresser drawers. She is looking for something important to her. As she goes through the clothes, she is visibly upset. Her hands caress some of the garments. She might pick one up and linger over it lovingly. She might even bury her face in one of the garments.

>                   ANNIE (V.O.)
>               (from the kitchen)
>           Alice, put that knife down;
>           (pause) that's too heavy, be
>           careful.

Catherine, needing this time to be alone with her grief, looks up with pain; she has had enough of the tension between Annie and Alice.

35. INT   DAY   KITCHEN
CLOSE UP of a gallon of milk as it crashes to the floor. The bottle shatters in many pieces and the milk splatters over Alice's shoes and socks, the floor, refrigerator, table, etc.

>                   ANNIE
>               (yelling; she goes
>                 to shake her)
>           What did I tell you?

>                   ALICE
>               (pulling away)
>           Don't hit me, don't hit me.
>           (She shoves her aunt) I didn't
>           mean it.

>                   CATHERINE
>               (simultaneously
>                 running into the
>                 room)
>           What's the matter? What happened?
>           Oh, my God, what a mess.

>                   ANNIE
>               (still fighting with
>                 Alice; clenching her
>                 fists)
>           I'm not going to hit you. Stay
>           still. Have I ever hit you?
>           What you need is a few good smacks.

>                   ALICE
>               (furious, is moving back)
>           You liar, you were too.

(35 continued)

> CATHERINE
> (simultaneously)
> Alive, don't move; you're walking on the glass.

> ANNIE
> (continuing to Alice)
> She called me a liar. (going toward her) By God, now I am going to hit you.

> CATHERINE
> Annie!

> ALICE
> (walking toward her mother)
> You see she is going to hit me. It was an accident.

> CATHERINE
> (desperate)
> Stay still; you'll cut yourself.

> ANNIE
> (getting hold of herself)
> You see this mess and I just finished cleaning. Didn't I tell her to be careful. She never listens to me.

> CATHERINE
> (trying to control her anger)
> Annie, it was an accident. She's sorry. (to Alice) Tell your aunt you're sorry.

(Alice turns her back.)

> ANNIE
> It's always an accident. Accidents don't happen when you use the stick. (Annie gets a mop.)

> ALICE
> (turning)
> You hate me. I didn't do it on purpose.

Alice moves angrily stepping hard on the glass.

(35 continued)

      CATHERINE
Alice, shut up! I want you to
stand still. Be careful of that
glass.

      ANNIE
Now she's tracking it all over
the place. (continues mopping)

      CATHERINE
Go over to the table and stay put
while we clean this mess up.

      ANNIE
I told her it was too heavy. And
she goes right ahead and does it
anyway. What kind of an idiot
carries a gallon of milk and a
plate at the same time? (turning
with an "I-told-you-so" to
Catherine) This is why she should
be back in school.

      ALICE
    (furious)
I'm not going back to school.
I'm never going back. (begging
to Catherine) I want to stay
with you.

      ANNIE
Your mother doesn't need you here.
I'm here. You belong in school.

      ALICE
    (enraged)
She does too. She does too.
I'm not going. I won't go.

      CATHERINE
    (pleading)
Anna, why must you keep insisting
about this school business?

      ANNIE
With the trouble she's been having,
she can't afford to miss a single
day.

Alice looks sharply at her aunt.

      CATHERINE
I spoke with Father Tom and we
agreed that Monday is soon enough.

(35 continued)

>        Alice looks at her mother.
>
>                    ALICE
>           Not Monday, Ma, please.
>
>                    ANNIE
>           Have it your way, Catherine.
>           Just remember what I've said.
>                (looking pointedly at Alice)
>                (In Italian) "The devil makes
>           work for idle hands." (looking
>           pointedly at Alice) The child
>           belongs in school. Angela's
>           heard Sister say plenty about
>           questa ragazza.
>
>                    ALICE
>                (interrupting; furious
>                 that Annie is talking
>                 about her)
>           This is my house. You won't be
>           here forever. (harder) I can't
>           wait 'til you're gone.
>
>                    CATHERINE
>                (calmly)
>           Alice, I forbid you to talk that
>           way to your Aunt Annie.
>
>                    ALICE
>                (suddenly submissive
>                 to Catherine)
>           Mommy, I'm sorry I dropped my
>           sandwich. She makes me so nervous
>           that I do everything wrong.
>
>                    CATHERINE
>                (has to be firm)
>           You don't mean what you're saying
>           Aunt Annie loves you. She only does
>           things for your own good. (voice
>           softening and becoming reasonable)
>           If you had listened to her, you
>           wouldn't have dropped the milk.
>
>        Alice is pouting, furious that her mother is
> siding with Annie.
>
>                    ALICE
>           Why is she always right? You always
>           take her side.

(35 continued)

> CATHERINE
> (firmly)
> That's enough. (then concerned)
> Now come this way. Are your socks
> wet?

> ALICE
> (walking over)
> No.

Catherine looks her over, kneeling to inspect her legs. Alice looks gloatingly in Annie's direction. Catherine is cleaning her shoes with the rag.

> CATHERINE
> Mommy does need you dear.
> (rubbing the shoes, then
> firmly) But you must realize
> Aunt Annie is very generous
> to stay with us.

> ALICE
> (not convinced)
> Yeh...

> CATHERINE
> And I don't want to hear anymore
> about not going to school. You
> must go back. (tenderly) We both
> have to get back to our usual lives.
> (looking up at her) I know how
> much you miss Karen. So do I.
> (Catching her tears, she goes back
> to the shoes, pretending to
> examine them closely.)

Alice reaches down as if to comfort her kneeling mother.

> ALICE
> I'll be your...

Catherine hastily rises, accidentally pushing Alice away.

Alice moves back, stung by what she thinks is a rejection.

(35 continued)

> CATHERINE
> (realizing what she
> has done)
> Oops, I'm sorry. (Catherine reaches out to smooth the child's hair aside.)

Alice keeps her distance.

> CATHERINE
> (trying to make up)
> You're my big girl, right?

> ALICE
> (changing so as to
> cover what she almost
> revealed)
> I guess so.

> CATHERINE
> Well, then you can help me.

> ALICE
> (a little angrily)
> What can I do?

> CATHERINE
> (moving to the counter-
> top where bills are kept)
> You can take the rent check down to Mr. Alphonso.

Alice takes the envelope.

> CATHERINE
> (continuing)
> Now that will really help me--and Aunt Annie. Play in the yard for awhile and as soon as this mess is cleaned up, we'll call you. And you know what?

> ALICE
> What?

> CATHERINE
> (talking as if to Karen)
> I'll make you a new sandwich. I'll make your favorite--I'll make you a peanut butter and jelly.

> ALICE
> (hurt, quietly, looks
> away)
> Okay, but...

(35 continued)

>                    CATHERINE
>                    (understands)
>          Oh, that's right. I'm sorry. I
>          meant grilled cheese. Open-
>          faced grilled cheese--and I'll
>          put the tomato on it the way you
>          like it.
>
>                    ALICE
>                    (turning to leave)
>          Okay, thanks. (Alice grabs her
>          blue coat from the hook on the
>          door and leaves the apartment)

Catherine looks sadly after her. She becomes conscious of the sounds of Annie cleaning behind her. She turns to Annie, eyes flashing a bit. She is filled with mixed emotions, to apologize to Annie, to criticize her, to thank her, to ask her to leave. She doesn't know how to begin. Annie becomes aware of Catherine's eyes on her.

>                    ANNIE
>                    (interpreting)
>          Kay, we're never going to agree
>          on how to handle that child.
>                    (sternly) But your methods
>          haven't seemed to work very well.
>
>                    CATHERINE
>                    (defensively)
>          Annie, she's going through a lot.
>          My God, this is a bad time. She
>          really loved her sister.

As Annie roughly rinses and wrings the rag, her firm-set lips express what she would not put in words. Suddenly she switches the subject.

>                    ANNIE
>                    (anxiously)
>          Did you find it?
>
>                    CATHERINE
>                    (sighs)
>          No, I went through all her
>          clothes. I'm sure it was lost
>          at the church. I just allowed
>          myself to hope a little (feigning
>          optimism) Don't worry, when Vinnie
>          gets around to sweeping, I'm sure
>          he'll find it.
>
>                    ANNIE
>                    (bluntly)
>          Well, it's not in Alice's drawers.

(35 continued)

>           CATHERINE
>      (shocked and angry)
> Annie, why did you do that? I
> told you I would ask her. Why
> don't you trust her?
>
>           ANNIE
> I know how important that cross
> is to you, Kay. I never can do
> anything right anymore...maybe I
> should leave like Alice said.
>
>           CATHERINE
> You know I want you here. (too
> emphatically) And so does Alice.
> But...maybe it would be better if
> we were alone for awhile.

36. INT DAY ALPHONSO'S APARTMENT

Alphonso is seated in an overstuffed armchair with his feet propped up on an ottoman. Dressed in his silk bathrobe, he is listening to opera music. On his huge belly sits one of his cats which he is stroking. His eyes move sharply toward the door. Studying it for a second, he returns to his music and the cat.

A second time he looks to the door; this time sure of his suspicion.

>           ALPHONSO
> Come in, Alice.

He looks away, pretending to be absorbed in the music. He feigns indifference. Finally he realizes that the girl is not coming in.

>           ALPHONSO
>      (turning in irritation
>       toward the door)
> You heard me. What's the matter?
> Are you afraid? I know you're there.
> Alice.

The door slowly opens and Alice peers around boldly.

>           ALPHONSO
>      (without looking at her)
> You can come in. I won't bite you.

He pretends to be intent on the music; perhaps he begins to nod his head in time to the movement.

Alice is curious. Emboldened by his lack of notice, she steps further into the room.

(36 continued)                                                  53

                    ALICE
                  (sharply)
             How did you know it was me?

                    ALPHONSO
                  (looks meaningfully at
                    her)
             I know everything about Alice.
             Shh. (taking his stubby finger
             from his lips, he begins to move
             it in time to the music.)

                    ALICE
                  (staring at him)
             I have the rent check.  I was
             going to slide it under the door.

     He ignores her continuing to move his finger
to the music.  The cat on his belly begins to follow Alphonso's
finger.

                    ALICE
                  (waving the envelope)
             Where do you want me to put this?
             (looking around with distaste)
             There's so much junk around this
             filthy place.  I bet you never
             clean it.  It smells of cat's pee.

                    ALPHONSO
                  (ignoring her; riled and
                    holding out his hand)
             Didn't your mother tell you to <u>give</u>
             me the check?

                    ALICE
             What's the matter, Fatty?  Stuck
             in the chair?

                    ALPHONSO
             What did you break, Clumsy?

             (She doesn't answer.)

             You don't like your Aunt, do you?

                    ALICE
             I don't like you.

                    ALPHONSO
             You know why you don't like us?
             Your aunt and I are two very
             perceptive people.  We know what

(36 continued)

>           you did at the church. I
>           can't wait to tell your father
>           all I know about you. (He
>           quickly turns up the volume on
>           the record player to cut off
>           her answer.)
>
>                     ALICE
>                (competing with the
>                 music)
>           What have you got to tell?

Alphonso ignores her.

>                     ALICE
>                (continuing more
>                 loudly)
>           Who's gonna believe you anyway?
>           What the hell do you know? (Alice
>           sticks the rent check into a nearby
>           bowl of cat food and turns to leave.)

Alphonso quickly gets up and puts the cat on his shoulders as if it were a baby.

>                     ALPHONSO
>                (taunting)
>           I know what you have downstairs.
>
>                     ALICE
>                (turning quickly)
>           Have you been snooping through
>           my things?
>
>                     ALPHONSO
>                (with a mocking laugh,
>                 stepping closer)
>           Your things? They're not yours.

Alice notices Alphonso moving closer, but intent on hearing what he has to say remains motionless.

>                     ALPHONSO
>                (continuing)
>                (wanting to frighten
>                 her)
>           The dead have ways. The dead
>           don't rest easy. Karen will come
>           for them. (Alphonso moves as if
>           he wants to get the envelope
>           saying as a cover) Look what
>           you've done to the check.

(36 continued)                                                55

        With incredible agility he grabs her hand, and with his massive belly maneuvers her against the wall. (sounds of the ended record going round and round)

                ALICE
             (engulfed in his
              massive flesh)
       You better let me out because
       I'll scream and my mother will
       call the police.

              ALPHONSO
             (laughing)
       The police were already here
       today, and if they come back,
       I'm going to take them downstairs.

        Alphonso shoves her harder against the wall with his belly.

                ALICE
             (pushing back)
       You better let me go, you weirdo.

              ALPHONSO
             (simultaneously and
              pushing Alice more)
       Go ahead and cry out, you thief.

        Alice, from the intensity of her hatred, suddenly works one of her hands free and grabs the cat by the throat.

                ALICE
       Get away from me, you bastard,
       or I'll kill your cat.

        The cat struggles. With that Alphonso, beaten, backs away, forced to let her have his pet.

              ALPHONSO
             (whining and pleading)
       Don't hurt kitty. Please don't
       hurt my Princess.

        Alice, with her hands outstretched, dangles the choking cat by the neck as a barrier between them as she makes her way to the door.

                ALICE
       You pushed up against me once
       before, you disgusting slob.
       You'll never do that again.

(36 continued)

She throws the cat down and runs out the door. The cat, terrified, runs under the bed. Alphonso, torn with anxiety, goes to the bed, and on his hands and knees, tries to entice the cat to him. He might be saying:

>                    ALPHONSO
>           Oh my poor beauty. Come to
>           Daddy. Did she hurt you? That
>           bitch. I'd like to kill her.

37. INT  DAY  HALL
Alice runs down the steps, jumping the last three to the basement door.

38. INT  DAY  BASEMENT
In the darkness Alice can be seen working her way to the light cord. She switches on a dim bulb, stopping to catch her breath. The scanty light reveals a dusty old basement with plumbing pipes and electrical wires exposed. There is a converted coal burner, an abandoned wine press, some barrels, lots of boxes and an old ironing board. At one end of the basement is a laundry area. On a clothesline sheets and other laundry are hanging. Steps leading to the outside cellar door are visible.

The camera follows Alice across the basement to the more remote of two slatted coal bins.

39. INT  DAY  COAL BIN
Alice enters the bin leaving the door open to allow some of the light to penetrate the dark recess. It is clear that the room has been abandoned to the storage of long-forgotten, useless items. Alice makes her way to a small niche which is secluded by a large abandoned wardrobe.

In her hiding place there is an old spindly-legged table with one drawer. Alice opens the drawer, fumbling for a box of matches. CLOSE UP of the match being struck. CAMERA PANS with the match as Alice lights a white candle lopsided in an old jar. As the candlelight flames, it brings into view Karen's doll which has been carefully propped up. Its sleeping face is visible. Among the few other items is an old photograph of Alice and her father who is dressed in a cap and gown, a jar of cockroaches with air holes punched in the lid, an old white child's prayer book and an ice pick.

Having enough light, she reaches under the table and pulls out a water-stained cardboard suitcase, sliding it to the side. Opening it, she checks to be sure that her treasures have not been disturbed. Inside the suitcase, resting on top of a white communion dress, are a veil, a pair of white shoes, Alice's mask, and Karen's red velvet box. Satisfied that no one has been in the suitcase, Alice

(39 continued)

reaches into her pocket and pulls out a napkin. She opens the napkin carefully to a tiny, tiny piece of cheese. She puts the napkin and cheese on the table. Tapping the lid of the jar to force the bugs to the bottom, she loosens the lid. EXTREME CLOSE UP of Alice's hand as she thrusts the cheese into the jar slamming the lid back on.

40. EXT DAY STREET

LONG SHOT Tom's car coming to a stop at a red light. People are hurrying through a heavy rain. A young couple in jeans and pea jackets run laughing, reveling in the rain. They separate around an old couple, huddling together under a large black umbrella. A lonely old man with his coat around his ears is walking slowly, trying unsuccessfully to protect himself. Two ladies in raincoats and plastic tie caps are heading for a bus stop, clutching their shopping bags. As the light changes, Father Tom's car moves through the intersection. CLOSE UP through the windshield wipers of Dom and Father Tom. The soundless movement of their mouths indicates that they are involved in a serious conversation. The rain beats heavily on the windows.

41. INT DAY CAR

>               DOM
>           (looking away)
>       I guess I'll always feel a
>       little guilty.
>
>               FATHER TOM
>       What for?
>
>               DOM
>       It seems I've forced you into
>       the role of father.
>
>               FATHER TOM
>           (interrupting and
>            turning him off)
>       Nobody forced me into anything.
>       You should know better. I'm
>       involved because I want to be.

There is a silence in the car during which Dom studies Tom's face.

>               DOM
>           (plunging)
>       You know when you called, Tom,
>       I really didn't want to come.
>       I can't help it. I feel I don't
>       belong here anymore.

(41 continued)

>FATHER TOM
>That's understandable.

>DOM
>Julia understood it too. (pause) But it was obvious that she felt I should come. (sighs) I guess a part of me will always be here... with Catherine (pause)...and the kids. (troubled) Alice is my...

>FATHER TOM
>   (interrupts with no
>   rancor)
>Julia was right. You have a responsibility here. (changing the subject) How is she?

>DOM
>   (thinking about some-
>   thing else)
>Fine.

>FATHER TOM
>When is the baby due?

>DOM
>It's a goddamned shame. She should have a husband to share this grief with.

CLOSE UP Father Tom doesn't want to talk about this subject.

>DOM
>It's strange how things work out.

>FATHER TOM
>How so?

>DOM
>I remember when we were in high school---you were the one always goofing off. (smiling) I spent half my time getting you out of trouble. (pause) Now the roles seem to be reversed. (reminiscing) Remember the prom? I'm dancing in close to Catherine and you yell out over the mike--"Hey, Dom, leave six inches for the Holy Ghost." (they laugh)

(41 continued)

As the laughter dies away the click-click of the windshield wipers dominates the silence.

> DOM
> (soberly)
> Still, Tom, I don't see why you didn't tell Catherine. If things were so bad at school she should have been the first to know.

> FATHER TOM
> It wasn't that serious until recently. Anyway they weren't really sure exactly what should be blamed on Alice. She has a knack for making things look like accidents. I thought I could handle things quietly. She used to talk with me a lot, but lately she's set up a barrier.

> DOM
> (thinking)
> Do you think she should see a psychiatrist?

> FATHER TOM
> I wanted to talk to Kay about that...

> DOM
> (nodding)
> It's a hell of a time...Poor Alice! Can you imagine what Annie would do with that?

> FATHER TOM
> Don't worry.

> DOM
> (looking at him, surprised)
> I've seen what Annie can do.

> FATHER TOM
> (with a smile)
> Kay can handle her.

CLOSE UP Dom's face. He is surprised at Father Tom's assurance.

42. INT  DAY  HALLWAY
    LONG SHOT. A small figure wearing a blue coat, which inadequately covers a white dress, cautiously opens the basement door. CLOSE UP. The camera follows her little white shoes as they move softly to the front door of the apartment. The door opens slightly.

43. EXT  DAY  FRONT DOOR OF THE SPAGES' HOUSE
    A small white-gloved hand reaches out feeling for the doorbell. Fingers count up from the bottom and, finding the third button, press it in, holding.

44. INT  DAY  KITCHEN
    CLOSE UP of bell box ringing. Catherine and Annie are in the kitchen. Catherine moves to the kitchen window and opens it.

>           CATHERINE
>           (calling out)
>     Who is it?

The bell rings insistently.

>           CATHERINE
>           (annoyed)
>     It must be Alice. I guess she
>     locked herself out.

45. EXT  DAY  KITCHEN WINDOW
    MEDIUM CLOSE UP Catherine peering out of the window.

>           CATHERINE
>           (loudly)
>     If that's you, Alice, stop pushing
>     that button.

The bell continues sounding.

46. INT  DAY  KITCHEN
    Annie, near the door, reaches for her coat.

>           ANNIE
>           (impatiently)
>     I'll get it. (The bell stops
>     ringing.) Do you need anything
>     else besides the milk?

>           CATHERINE
>     No. If it's Alice, her sandwich
>     is ready.

47. INT  DAY  HALLWAY
    The hooded girl gently closes the front door and, glancing at the stairs, tiptoes to a concealed angle beside the stairway.

(47 continued)

   Annie can be heard coming from the apartment.

48. INT DAY STAIRWAY
   Annie pauses at the top of the stairs, and, selfishly delaying, takes time to tie on her rain cap, button the top button of her coat, and place her pocketbook on the crook of her left arm.

49. INT DAY FIRST FLOOR LANDING
   The masked girl remains motionless. With Annie's first step sounding down the stairs, the white-gloved hand reaches under the coat.

   CLOSE UP of Annie's feet descending. She pauses to smooth her stocking.

   MEDIUM SHOT of the masked girl crouching close to the bannister. As Annie's legs appear through the spindles, with unleashed fury the small hand strikes, slashing with a large kitchen knife at Annie's ankle, calf, knee. Annie screams. Wildly attempting to escape the animal attacking from behind its spindly cage, she pulls her body back against the farther wall, trying to use her pocketbook as a kind of barrier. The knife hits the pocketbook, and, then at its farthest reach, slips to the soft flesh of Annie's thigh.

   Annie's terrified screams orchestrate with the sounds of Alphonso lumbering out of his apartment. Instinctively she reaches to protect her bleeding legs; her knees buckle, catapulting her onto the landing.

        ALPHONSO
       (from above)
    What's going on? What's going
    on?

   Catherine can be heard running out into the hall.

        CATHERINE
    Annie! Annie!

   Annie on her side turns, facing the hovering figure with its knife raised.

        ANNIE
       (screaming)
    Alice, no...no!

   The assailant hesitates, abandoning her intent.

  62

         In an attempt to get away, Annie's hands connect
with her fallen pocketbook which she hurls toward the assailant, who is lowering her knife. With the strength of terror
Annie in one motion rises, brushing the killer in her haste.
She staggers toward the front door, prepared at any moment
to be attacked by her assailant, who has, in fact, fled into
the darkness of the basement.

         Catherine, reaching the second floor, is blocked
by a frozen Alphonso, who is yelling directly into her face:

                         ALPHONSO
              Alice! Alice! She's killing Annie.

                         CATHERINE
                         (enraged)
              Move! Move!

50.  EXT  DAY  RAINY STREET
         As Annie stumbles down the front steps falling on
the ground, Catherine comes from the door nearly slipping on
the rainy concrete. Reaching her sister, who is trying to
crawl away from the house, Catherine bends to envelope her
with sobs of:

                         CATHERINE
              Anna! Anna! My God, what happened!

         Annie, believing she is still being attacked,
wildly punches at her sister.

                         ANNIE
                         (screaming)
              Alice, get away from me! No,
              Alice! No!

         Catherine, stunned, draws back, avoiding the blows,
and slaps her sister across the face. Annie stops suddenly,
staring wide-eyed; then, moaning, she falls back and begins
sobbing convulsively.

                         CATHERINE
                         (reaching out to her sister)
              Anna, I'm sorry. I had to do...

         She sees the bleeding legs, and in one motion rips
the skirt from Annie's body and begins trying to stem the
flow of blood. Several neighbors have gathered.

                         CATHERINE
                         (completely in charge)
              Call the police! Someone get an
              ambulance!

51. INT   DAY   FATHER TOM'S CAR
The camera is in the rear of the car.  TWO SHOT Dom and Tom.  There is a clear view of the street ahead.

> FATHER TOM
> You can't expect to run people like you do a business. (pause) I think you're overreacting.

While Tom is speaking, the scene in front of the Spages' house comes into view.

> DOM
> (interrupting)
> What the hell's going on?  Something's happened.

52. EXT   DAY   RAINY STREET
Tom steers the car sharply around the corner, diagonally across the street, and stops at an angle as close to Annie and Catherine as he can.  The two jump from the car and run toward Catherine, who has stood up and is looking at them, perhaps taking a step toward them.

> CATHERINE
> (relieved)
> Oh, thank God!  I can't stop the bleeding.

> DOM
> Did anyone call an ambulance?

> FATHER TOM (to Dom)
> Let's get her into the car.

They lift Annie.  Tom takes the head and shoulders and Catherine helps by holding the injured legs.  They move to the car.

> DOM
> Jesus Christ, what happened?

> CATHERINE
> Someone attacked her in the hallway.

> DOM
> Has anyone called the police?

> CATHERINE
> (tersely)
> I don't know.

Annie moans.

(52 continued)

>FATHER TOM
>Easy, easy.

>CATHERINE
>Be careful with her legs.

All attention is directed to the difficulties of getting the injured Annie into the back seat. Tom backs into the car, supporting the body. When he climbs out the other door, he yells across the car to Dom.

>FATHER TOM
>Stay here. Tell the police I'm taking her to St. Michael's.

>ANNIE
>(moaning)
>Jim. I want Jim.

>FATHER TOM
>(closing car door)
>Don't worry, Annie. I'll call Jim.

Catherine squeezes in with Annie trying to steady her legs on her lap. The car begins to pull away. Catherine can be seen tapping Tom on the shoulder saying "Stop." The car jerks to a stop.

>CATHERINE
>(rolling down the window, a shrill note in her voice)
>Dom, find Alice! Make sure you find her.

LONG SHOT as the car drives away leaving Dom standing in the street. As he walks out of frame the CAMERA PANS up to the second story window. Alphonso can be seen watching from behind the curtains.

53. EXT   DAY   BACKYARD
Dom comes around the corner of the house.

>DOM
>(calling out)
>Alice.

Looking around the yard, he observes that the cellar doors are open.

>DOM
>(calling down the steps)
>Alice!

(53 continued)

        Dom cautiously starts down the steps into the darkness of the basement. He pauses at the bottom, blinded by the sudden passage from the sunlight outside. Eyes acclimated, he looks around. Spying a piece of two-by-four, he picks it up against the possibility of needing protection. He moves into the basement, quietly checking each hidden blind spot as he comes up to it. He passes under the clothesline. A damp towel slides from the line and plops on the floor. The tiny sound echoes in the silence. Dom stands still. He senses the presence of someone, though there is no real movement or explicit noise. Looking around, his eyes catch a flicker of light coming from the coal bin. Clutching the wood tighter and raising it in preparation, he walks toward the bin as if on eggshells. The door to the bin is slightly open. He pauses, listening. Someone is inside. Dom raises the board and simultaneously jerks open the door, throwing it back and neatly stepping in the opposite direction. A terrified voice screams out.

                      ALICE
            Don't take me! I swear to God
            I didn't steal it!

        Recognizing the child's voice, Dom lowers the board and follows the sound to the recesses of the bin.

                      ALICE
                (hearing Dom's approach,
                  thrusting out the doll)
            I was saving it for you, Karen.
            You can have it. (louder) You
            can have it!

                      DOM
                (simultaneously)
            Alice, it's Daddy. It's Daddy.

                      ALICE
                (wide-eyed, then
                  sobbing)
            Oh Daddy, Daddy, help me, please
            help me.

Rising, she throws herself into her father's arms.

                      DOM
                (holding her tight)
            Alice, no one's going to hurt you.
            It's okay, Ally, it's okay.

(53 continued)

                    ALICE
              (simultaneously)
      I saw Karen! I saw Karen!
      (crying harder) Oh, Daddy, I
      never meant for her to die.

54. INT  DAY  HOSPITAL
      Catherine is talking inside a phone booth; her strained face belies the encouraging words she is speaking. Father Tom is standing outside, trying to listen.

      EXTREME CLOSE UP of Father Tom watching her anxiously.

55. INT  DAY  PHONE BOOTH

                    CATHERINE
      You mustn't be upset, Alice. (pause;
      softly) I don't know. (assuringly)
      But I do know we'll figure it out.
      Tell Daddy I'll be home very soon.

      CLOSE UP of Catherine replacing the receiver on the book of the pay phone, hanging onto it for a moment. Father Tom waits patiently. She turns and opens the door.

56. INT  DAY  HOSPITAL

                    FATHER TOM
       (softly)
     Is she all right?

                    CATHERINE
     Yes...(slowly) she was so frightened.
     (suddenly helpless) Oh, Tom, what am
     I going to do? Everything's happening
     so fast. (eyes reveal her confused
     thinking) Dom said whoever did it must
     have scared her half to death.

                    FATHER TOM
     Was she down there the whole time?

                    CATHERINE
     She must have been. (suddenly) Oh,
     Tom, who's doing this to me?
     Haven't I had enough?

                    FATHER TOM
       (quietly)
     Catherine, you must hold yourself
     together.

(56 continued)

     CATHERINE
    (softly)
Yes...(looking at him, holding
back something, eyes filling)
Alphonso told the police it was
Alice. (tensely) They're on
their way.

     FATHER TOM
    (shocked)
Did he see her, Kay?

     CATHERINE
    (angry)
Of course not. How could he?
He's just repeating what he
heard Annie scream. Don't you
see?--people believe what they
want to believe.

     FATHER TOM
Catherine, what's important is
how the police will look at
these things.

     CATHERINE
    (looking away)
They don't know her. No one
knows her like I do. (frightened,
she turns back) What if Annie
tells them...(voice trailing)...
what she told me?

     FATHER TOM
    (quietly)
We have to wait and see what
happens.

     CATHERINE
    (frightened)
What can they do, Tom? Can they
take her away? I won't let them
do that. She's no murderer.
She'd never hurt anyone.

     FATHER TOM
    (gently trying to
     prepare her)
Look, Catherine, if the police
have good enough reasons, they'll
take her in for questioning.
Once they talk to Annie, you've
got to be prepared for that.

(56 continued)

> CATHERINE
> (looking at him, thinking,
> then quickly)
> I'll tell them she was hysterical.
> She didn't even know me. (grasping)
> Annie would never say such a thing
> if she were herself.

Simultaneously Beame can be seen coming through the elevator doors.

> FATHER TOM
> (calmly)
> Catherine, Captain Beame's here.

> CATHERINE
> (freezes, then quickly)
> Tom, I've got to talk to Annie.
> Give me a minute.

She walks away, leaving Father Tom no choice but to stall Beame. Camera follows Father Tom as he walks toward Beame.

57. INT DAY EMERGENCY WARD
Catherine moves down the large ward, footsteps echoing in the near-emptiness. CLOSE UP of the only other patient, an old woman whose eyes hopefully seek the sound of Catherine's footsteps. Catherine continues past her to the curtains encircling Annie's bed. Annie's eyes move in the direction of the approaching footsteps. Catherine pauses at the curtain. As she slowly draws back the curtain, Annie, glimpsing her sister, closes her eyes, feigning sleep. Catherine pretends not to notice.

> CATHERINE
> (whispering)
> Annie. (pause; them more
> urgently) Annie.

Catherine moves close to the bed, staring down at her sister.

> CATHERINE
> (firmly)
> I want to talk to you, Annie.
> (no answer; then hopefully) I
> know you won't do this to me.
> (still no answer; ready to for-
> give, if that's the problem) You
> didn't realize what you were
> saying. How could you? You
> were so upset.

(57 continued)

  Annie's eyes open; tears run down her face. Pitying her sister, she turns away in anguish.

       CATHERINE
      (getting angry)
   Don't turn away like that. (pause)
   What's wrong with you? Have you
   gone crazy? Am I some stranger?

  Catherine stares at her sister's averted head. She realizes that Annie is not going to speak.

       CATHERINE
   Pray to Momma, Annie (shaking
   her head, with pain)...I'll
   never forgive you.

  The doors of the ward are heard opening. Catherine turns from Annie. Father Tom and Captain Beame, with a nurse in the lead, enter the ward. Catherine moves nearer to the bed.

       CATHERINE
      (tightly)
   They're here.

  The nurse arrives first, pulling the curtains from around the bed.

       NURSE
      (winding up the bed)
   How are you feeling, Mrs. Lorenzi?
   Dr. Barnet says it's okay for you
   to talk to Captain Beame.

       ANNIE
      (seeing Father Tom)
   Where's Jim? Did you call him?

       FATHER TOM
      (reasurring)
   He's on his way; he'll be here
   any minute.

  Beame, acknowledging Catherine's presence, turns toward Annie.

       BEAME
   I won't keep you long. (looking
   at her) You know I have to talk
   to you. (She nods, tears in her
   eyes) Do you think you can tell
   us what happened?

(57 continued)

   Annie turns to Catherine; she remains silent, eyes frozen on her sister; CLOSE UP of Beame looking at Catherine; then gently, trying to gain Annie's attention.

      BEAME
   It's important for you to tell
   me exactly what you saw.

She still does not speak.

      BEAME
    (sensing)
   Father, do you mind, could you
   and Mrs. Spages please go out
   for a few minutes?

Tom looks at Kay, who hesitates.

      CATHERINE
   I'm her sister. After all, I
   was there too.

      BEAME
   Of course, Mrs. Spages. And I
   want to hear anything you can
   tell me. (firmly, dismissing her)
   I'll be with you in a few minutes.

   Tom turns to escort Catherine out. Catherine, having no choice, begins to leave. The doors can be heard opening; Jim is seen entering the ward.

      JIM
    (to himself, as he
    moves with increasing
    speed toward the group)
   Annie, Annie...(to the group)
   What happened?

      ANNIE
    (sitting up)
   Jim? Oh, Jimmy.

      JIM
    (reaching her quickly)
   I was so worried. Someone said
   that someone tried to kill you.

      ANNIE
    (without pause)
   Oh my God, Jimmy, it was awful;
   she stabbed and stabbed. (touching
   her legs) My legs...

(57 continued)

                    JIM
Who, Annie? Who?

                CATHERINE
             (simultaneously)
Annie, don't—I warned you!

                  ANNIE
             (continuing)
She tried to kill me! (crying)
Oh my God, I don't believe it.
(She repeats this line in
Italian.)

Beame's eyes dart to all faces, recording.

                CATHERINE
Annie...shut up!

                    JIM
For Christ's sake, Kay, let her
talk. What's going on here?

                  ANNIE
             (hysterically, looking
              at Catherine)
She's like my own. I love her,
Catherine.

                CATHERINE
You do not; you hate her because
I had to get married.

                  ANNIE
             (shocked)
How can you say such a thing?
(to Father Tom) May God strike
me dead if I'm lying!

                    JIM
Annie, don't. What are you saying?

                CATHERINE
             (drowns him out, furious)
Lie, lie, you're all liars! Face
it, Anna, you want to believe it
was her. (to Beame) Why not Angela?
She wasn't in the church. (There
is a shocked silence. Catherine is
wild now.) You see! you see! (to
Tom, who is moving to calm her)
Oh, Tom, what are they trying to
do?

(57 continued)                                                    72

        Annie turns to Jim simultaneously, dividing the room:

                      ANNIE
                (wildly pleading)
        As God is my witness, I'm not
        lying! I'm not lying! (She
        breaks into sobs.)

        As the last few lines are said, the CAMERA DOLLIES into a CLOSE UP of Beame surveying the scene. Beame moves to a bedside phone.

                      BEAME
        Outside line, please.

58. EXT   DAY   STREET
        Camera follows an unmarked car as it passes in front of the police station and disappears around the corner.

59. INT   DAY   INTERROGATION ROOM

                      BEAME
                (on the phone)
        Jesus Christ, where the hell is
        he? They'll be here any minute.
        Send him up as soon as he gets
        here. (pause) Yeah, well, I don't
        want them changing their minds.

60. EXT   DAY   BACK OF POLICE STATION
        Dom, Kay and Alice get out of the unmarked car and start toward the building.

61. EXT   DAY   FRONT OF POLICE STATION
        LONG SHOT a police car with light flashing pulls up. A small, nondescript man in a gray coat, carrying a black attache case, gets out of the car and moves hastily up the steps.

62. INT   DAY   BEAME'S OFFICE
        CLOSE UP Karen's red velvet box. Someone is rhythmically opening and closing it. Camera pulls back to Spina, who looks up as the small man in gray unceremoniously bursts into the office.

                      SPINA
                (placing the box in
                Alice's suitcase.
                Alice's school jacket
                is visible)
        Where the hell were you?

(62 continued)

> CRANSTON
> (annoyed)
> Ray knows it's my day off.
> (taking off his coat to reveal a conservative gray suit; looking at Spina) What the hell's going on? It was like flies greeting shit when I came in.

> SPINA
> I hope you're prepared to test a twelve-year-old girl.

> CRANSTON
> Who?

> SPINA
> Karen Spages' sister. (looking at him wryly) She tried to stick a butcher knife in her aunt this afternoon.

> CRANSTON
> Then what the hell do you need me for?

> SPINA
> (disgustedly)
> Beame won't book her 'til he's absolutely sure. (with a sarcastic smile) Pappa Beame's got a soft spot for little girls. (taking out a typed page) Here's a list of the questions they agreed to. Let's get the hell up there before he blows a fuse.

63. INT DAY OBSERVATION ROOM

The room is a plain office with a large one-way window used to observe polygraph tests and interrogations in the adjacent room. A speaker in the corner of the room makes it possible to listen in on conversations in the Interrogation Room. Its drabness is accentuated by some cheap metal office furniture.

Through the one-way mirrored window Alice is seen sitting in the next room at a long table. Standing over the polygraph equipment is Captain Beame. He is explaining the operation of the machine to Alice and her parents who are seated at the other end of the table. At Cranston's entrance Beame turns to the door. Introductions are made.

64. INT   DAY   INTERROGATION ROOM
CLOSE UP Alice sizing Cranston up. Cranston, wasting no time, moves to the chair next to Alice and sets his briefcase on the table.

>            CRANSTON
>      (trying unsuccessfully to
>       conceal his impatience)
>   I guess Captain Beame explained
>   how everything works. (opening
>   his briefcase, he takes out a
>   pack of blue cards and puts the,
>   on the table. CLOSE UP cards:
>   printed on the back of the cards
>   are white square letters which
>   spell "Flinch.")

Dom and Kay move to leave the room. As they pass behind Alice, Kay leans to kiss her unresponsive face.

>            DOM
>      (patting her shoulder
>       and whispering)
>   We'll be right next door.

>            CATHERINE
>   Do exactly as Captain Beame told
>   you. Don't worry. Everything's
>   going to be fine.

They start for the door.

>            CRANSTON
>      (waiting for them to
>       leave, picking up the
>       pliable tube and mov-
>       ing toward her)
>   Just lift up your arms. This
>   won't hurt.

>            ALICE
>      (harshly to cover
>       embarrassment and
>       shrinking back in
>       distaste as if to
>       protect herself from
>       his familiarity)
>   I know all about it! Anyway, I'm
>   not afraid.

65. INT   DAY   OBSERVATION ROOM
Beame enters the room with Catherine and Dom. Spina, alone in the room, is standing against the glass. Through the glass Cranston is seen handing five cards to

(65 continued)

Alice. Seeing them enter, Spina leans over and raises the volume. Catherine and Dom are drawn toward the one-way window. Cranston can be seen setting the cards down.

                CRANSTON
            (V.O. amplified)
Now remember, you're to say no to every card. I want you to lie. (pause) Is it the three?

                ALICE
No.

                CRANSTON
Is it the six?

                ALICE
No.

                CATHERINE
            (simultaneously to Beame,
            as Cranston continues ask-
            ing Alice about three more
            cards)
Why does he want her to lie?

                SPINA
            (interrupting)
That's how they test the machine.

66. INT DAY INTERROGATION ROOM

                CRANSTON
            (folding the cards)
Thank you. (matter-of-factly) It was the three, wasn't it?

CLOSE UP Alice; her eyes widen with surprise.

                ALICE
            (softly)
Yes.

                CRANSTON (V.O.)
Now we know it's working.

Alice's eyes slide to the machine. She hastily covers a flicker of fright.

                CRANSTON
Let's get to those questions. (pause) Okay, Alice? (pause) Do you intend to answer truthfully to every question?

(66 continued)                                                                76

          CLOSE UP Alice hesitating.  CLOSE UP Cranston prodding.

>                    CRANSTON
>         Please answer yes or no.

>                    ALICE
>              (looking at the machine;
>               CLOSE UP machine, point-
>               of-view Alice)
>         Yes.

>                    CRANSTON
>         Do you know for sure who stabbed
>         your aunt?

>                    ALICE
>              (hesitates, then firmly)
>         No.

          CLOSE UP of the machine indicating a lie. (Point-of-view Alice)

>                    CRANSTON
>         Did you stab your aunt?

67.  INT   DAY   OBSERVATION ROOM
          Catherine leans foward watching Alice.  CLOSE UP speaker.  Alice's voice is heard:

>                    ALICE
>              (firmly)
>         No.

Catherine leans back.  Dom, standing behind her, pats her shoulder.  From the window of the observation room:

>                    CRANSTON
>              (voice amplified)
>         During your entire life did you
>         ever deliberately hurt someone
>         who trusted you?

Through the window CLOSE UP Alice thinking.  She turns her head toward the mirror, appearing to be looking at the group watching her.

          Alice looks at the machine, then at Cranston who blinks impassively.

>                    ALICE
>              (almost inaudibly)
>         I...I...put Debbie's coat in the
>         toilet. (talking to the machine)
>         But I didn't lie!

(67 continued)

        MEDIUM CLOSE UP group watching.

                ALICE (V.O.)
           I told Sister I did it.

Surprised, Catherine's knuckles whiten as she grips the arm of the chair. Dom, behind her, rhythmically squeezes her shoulder.

68. INT DAY INTERROGATION ROOM

                CRANSTON
           (gently, V.O.)
        In the suitcase found in the
        basement were a white dress
        and a mask. Are they yours?

                ALICE
   Yes.

CLOSE UP Alice staring at Cranston defiantly.

                CRANSTON (V.O.)
        Did you at noon today stab
        (Alice's eyes flicker, then
        glaze) your aunt with a knife?

                ALICE
           (eyes glazed)
   No.

TWO SHOT of Alice and Cranston from their reflection in the one-way mirror.

                CRANSTON
        Are you deliberately withholding
        any information about the attack
        on your aunt?

                ALICE
   No.

The camera moves in closer to the reflection.

                CRANSTON
        Do you know who stabbed your
        aunt?

                ALICE
   No.

CLOSE UP machine as it indicates a lie.

(68 continued)

>                    CRANSTON
>                  (repeating)
>          Do you know who stabbed your
>          aunt?
>
>                    ALICE
>                  (lashing out)
>          Yes! yes! I told them it was
>          Karen. (turning toward the
>          mirror with a tortured look)
>          I told them it was Karen. No
>          one believes me.

CLOSE UP machine; the tape continues to move indicating the truth.

>                    CRANSTON
>          Thank you. I'll take those
>          things off you.

69. INT  DAY  OBSERVATION ROOM

>                    BEAME
>          They're finished. Why don't
>          you go to her. I'll be with
>          you in a few minutes.

Spina and Beame keep silent as Dom escorts Catherine to the door.

>                    BEAME
>                  (quietly waiting for
>                   the door to close)
>          Any word from the boys?
>
>                    SPINA
>          They're still working over
>          the grounds.
>
>                    BEAME
>          I wish they could find that
>          knife. (pause) Did you bring
>          her coat down to the lab?

They look up as Cranston comes in.

>                    CRANSTON
>          Look, I don't know what to
>          tell you.
>
>                    SPINA
>          Well, for Christ's sake, did
>          she fail or didn't she?

(69 continued)

                CRANSTON
            (hedging)
      Technically I guess she failed.

Spina looks triumphant; Beame wants to know more.

                CRANSTON
            (in answer to Beame's
             look)
      Look, I asked if she knew who
      stabbed her aunt. She lied.
      She said no. Then I asked her
      again. She said it was her
      sister. And she wasn't lying.
      But her sister's dead. So what
      the hell do you want from me?
      The kid is off the wall.

Beame turns away, wanting to think.

                SPINA
            (persuading)
      You've got to hold her, Ray.
      If not for the murder, for the
      stabbing of her aunt. (pause)
      Let the psychiatrist give us
      some answers.

                BEAME
            (making up his mind)
      Call Mary to stay with her while
      I talk to them in my office.

As Beame leaves, Spina goes to the phone and pushes a button.

                SPINA
      Have Mary come to the Interrogation
      Room.

Cranston has walked over to the window and is watching Alice.

                CRANSTON (V.O.)
      She's a weird little girl. Did
      you notice her tits? (turning to
      Spina) When I went to put the
      tube around her, she looked at
      me as if I was going to feel her
      up.

CLOSE UP through the window of Alice staring at the mirror as her hands tentatively and almost involuntarily inch the polygraph machine toward the edge of the table.

(69 continued)                                                          80

EXTREME CLOSE UP of her fingers pushing the machine.  CLOSE
UP Spina as he catches Alice's action.

                        SPINA
                Hey--that little bitch is dump-
                ing your machine.

He bolts for the door as Cranston, turning, starts pounding
on the glass as if he could be seen.

                        CRANSTON
                    (impotently)
                Hey!  Hey!  Hey!  Stop it, damn
                you, stop it!

70.   INT   DAY   INTERROGATION ROOM
        Cranston's pounding resounds in the room; Spina's
footsteps echo in the hall.

        MEDIUM CLOSE UP Alice looking calmly at the mirror.
Then as if seeing Cranston, she sweeps her arm forcefully
across the table.

        EXTREME CLOSE UP of machine crashing to the floor.

71.   INT   DAY   MONSIGNOR'S BEDROOM
        CLOSE UP of an old man's face turning sharply.
His eyes open in frightened anger.  MEDIUM CLOSE UP of door
opening.  The camera moves from the point-of-view of the
intruder toward an EXTREME CLOSE UP of the old man's con-
torted face.

                        MONSIGNOR
                    (commanding as of old)
                I don't want you in my room.

        MEDIUM LONG SHOT of a priest turning the Monsignor's
wooden wheelchair in the direction of the door.

                        FATHER PAT
                    (gently)
                It's time for lunch, Monsignor.
                Mrs. Tredoni wants you to eat
                with us today.

        The camera pans with the two priests as they pass
an alcove in the bedroom dominated by a large statue of St.
Michael the Archangel with his sword raised.  Monsignor, the
titular pastor of Holy Family, submits to the excursion to
the dining room.

72.   INT   DAY   DINING ROOM
        Father Pat wheels Monsignor to the head of the
dining room table.  The table is set for three.  Mrs. Tredoni

(72 continued)                                                              81

is cutting the meat on one plate into tiny bite-size pieces.
As Father Pat takes one of the places, Mrs. Tredoni puts the
child's portion in front of Monsignor.

        MONSIGNOR
        (whining)
   I'm not feeling well. (snapping)
   Tell the children to stay out.

        MRS. TREDONI
        (harshly)
   You know I don't let any children
   in the house. (impatiently) Do you
   want me to feed you or can you
   manage by yourself?

        MONSIGNOR
        (angry)
   I'm not dead yet.

  Mrs. Tredoni picks up Monsignor's fork and puts it
into his shaking hand.

        MONSIGNOR
        (snapping)
   Where's my Sanka?

        MRS. TREDONI
        (sarcastically)
   I have only two hands, Monsignor.
   (to Father Pat) Isn't Father
   coming to lunch?

73. EXT DAY RECTORY
   Father Tom and Dom pull up to the rectory and park
the car.

74. INT DAY CAR
   Father Tom hands Dom the keys.

        DOM
        (taking them)
   Are you sure you don't want to
   come to the Shelter with us?

        FATHER TOM
   No. She needs the two of you
   now. (getting out of the car)
   Come inside. I'll get the
   information you want.

75. INT DAY DINING ROOM
   Father Pat is preparing to leave the table as Mrs.
Tredoni appears with a second pot of coffee. She glances at

(75 continued)                                                    82

the empty chair and at Monsignor's half-eaten lunch.  Her
face betrays worry and annoyance.

                    MRS. TREDONI
                 (to Father Pat)
            More coffee?

Monsignor looks up expecting his cake.

                    FATHER PAT
            Not today, Mrs. Tredoni.  I've
            got to get over to the school.

Sounds of the front door opening.

                    FATHER PAT
            I bet that's Tom now.

                    MRS. TREDONI
            And everything's ice cold.

                    MONSIGNOR
                 (looking up from his
                  reverie, reprimanding)
            Cold?  Cold?  No, she's a good
            woman.  Tell him not to worry.

                    MRS. TREDONI
                 (turning to him as
                  Father Pat leaves
                  the room)
            You're not eating your lunch.

                    MONSIGNOR
                 (commanding)
            I want my cake now.

    Mrs. Tredoni ignores him and takes the fork from
the old man's hand.  The camera lingers on a CLOSE UP of
Mrs. Tredoni feeding the priest mechanically.  Listening to
the conversation of the three men in the hall, she shovels
the food into the Monsignor's mouth with increasing care-
lessness.

                    FATHER PAT (V.O.)
            How did it go?

                    DOM
            Just as we expected.  The judge
            ruled that she be held for
            psychiatric observation.

                    FATHER PAT
                 (encouragingly)
            Don't lose hope.  (pause) How's
            Catherine taking it?

(75 continued)

> DOM
> (proudly)
> Even the lawyer was amazed at her strength.

EXTREME CLOSE UP Monsignor choking. He looks with a wild hate at Mrs. Tredoni and spits the food out.

76. INT DAY HALLWAY

> FATHER PAT
> Ralph's a good man. From the way people talk you've got one of the best crininal lawyers around.

Father Pat finishes buttoning his coat and turns to leave.

> FATHER TOM
> (calling out)
> Thanks for covering for me this morning, Pat.

The sound of the door can be heard closing as Father Pat leaves.

77. INT DAY DINING ROOM
Father Tom precedes Dom into the dining room.

> MRS. TREDONI
> Do you want some lunch, Father?

> FATHER TOM
> No thank you, Mrs. Tredoni. (slowly and loud) Monsignor?

Monsignor turns and, seeing his favorite, gives Tom a beatific smile. Then, totally ignoring Dom, he continues to play with his food.

> FATHER TOM
> (continuing)
> Monsignor, you remember Dominick Spages. (He nods without hearing or seeing) (to Dom) Have a seat. (Dom looks at him, questioning.) He's not cogent at all anymore. He's been this way for some time now. (pause) Mrs. Tredoni, would you get Mr. Spages some coffee.

As Dom sits, Monsignor slowly becomes aware of the presence of a guest.

(77 continued)

>                    MONSIGNOR
>               (querulously to Mrs.
>                Tredoni)
>          I can't see anyone today.
>
>                    MRS. TREDONI
>               (loudly)
>          Monsignor, this is Mr. Spages;
>          he's waiting for Father Tom.
>
>                    MONSIGNOR
>          Spages. (to everyone)  A good
>          woman. (lapsing)  God bless all
>          the good women. (sharply to Dom)
>          Do you know her?
>
>                    MRS. TREDONI
>               (coldly)
>          He's her husband.

CLOSE UP Dom, his eyes revealing some surprise at the word "husband." He decides not to correct her.

>                    MRS. TREDONI
>               (continuing to Dom)
>          I offer my prayers for her...
>
>                    MONSIGNOR
>               (interrupting)
>          Prayers...yes...ask her to pray
>          for me...
>
>                    MRS. TREDONI
>          Do you want to go back to your
>          room?
>
>                    MONSIGNOR
>               (angrily)
>          Stay out of my room. (then as
>          if she were an idiot)  Can't
>          you see I have a visitor?
>
>                    MRS. TREDONI
>               (pouring Dom's coffee)
>          His mind is gone, but his heart's
>          as strong as ever.
>
>                    FATHER TOM
>               (speaking as he enters)
>          Here's the order sheet for the
>          coats.  I called Mother Superior
>          and told her you were on your way.
>          She has the names and addresses
>          of all those who purchased one.

(77 continued)

>
> DOM
> Angela has one of these coats, doesn't she?
>
> FATHER TOM
> (chastising gently)
> What are you groping for? Do you realize how many kids have these coats?
>
> DOM
> Alice said she saw Karen in her school coat. She must have seen someone and whoever it is might be on that list.
>
> FATHER TOM
> (gently)
> And if this lead doesn't work, how long will you stay around and play detective?
>
> DOM
> I'm staying until the murderer is found. (rising) It's getting late. I better go. Thanks for the car. I'll drop it off later.
>
> FATHER TOM
> (as they head for the door)
> Keep it as long as you need it.
>
> DOM
> (nodding thanks)
> I can rent one by tomorrow.

As Father Tom and Dom leave the room, Monsignor pushes the wheelchair back from the table.

> MONSIGNOR
> (to Mrs. Tredoni)
> Tomorrow? No. I don't want that girl in the house. She can't talk to St. Michael.

78. EXT DAY ROAD
MEDIUM LONG SHOT of a sign, "Sarah Reed Children's Shelter." The camera pans with Father Tom's car as it enters the wrought-iron gates and travels toward a large, multi-storied concrete building. Dom gets out of the car and goes around to open the door for Catherine. She is holding a stuffed shopping bag. From the back seat Dom takes a suitcase. They walk toward a door lettered in black, "Children's

(78 continued)                                                86

Division." Dom rings the doorbell, and they wait in silence. A few moments pass; the door is opened by a woman in a white uniform.

      DOM
    We're here to see Alice Spages.
    We're her parents.

      WOMAN
    Oh, yes, Mr. Spages. I was told
    to expect you. Dr. Whitman would
    like to see you for a few minutes.

79. INT DAY OFFICE OF STAFF PSYCHIATRIST
  EXTREME CLOSE UP of a grotesque figure with his hands outstretched. The CAMERA PANS across to a soldier gripping a broken sword and continues panning to a mother clutching her dead child. Camera slowly pulls back to reveal a cheap reproduction of Picasso's Guernica and continues panning across volume after volume of books devoted to the understanding of children.

      DR. WHITMAN
     (V.O. as camera pans)
    Subject: Alice Spages, 12 years,
    one month, normal physical develop-
    ment, no apparent physical defects.
    Subject is a hostile, suspicious
    adolescent. Overt antagonisms,
    especially toward a maternal aunt
    with whom she stayed during the
    birth of her sister. Subject
    represses hostilities toward her
    mother and estranged father.
    Jealousy of dead sister neutralized
    in role imitation. Strong indi-
    cations of a schizoid personality.

  The camera finishes its pan on a MEDIUM CLOSE UP of a petite, maternal-looking woman whose genial smile lines are deceptively disarming. Proudly displayed on the wall behind are framed proofs of her academic expertise.

      DR. WHITMAN
     (continuing into the
      dictaphone)
    Subject is capable of extremely
    violent action. Note cunning
    antisocial behavior as per school
    records. Product of a broken,
    (pauses slightly) yet orthodox
    Catholic home.

Sound of someone knocking on the door.

(79 continued) 87

> DR. WHITMAN
> (switching off the dicta-
> phone)
> Come in.

> WOMAN
> (entering)
> Dr. Whitman, Mr. and Mrs. Spages are here.

> DR. WHITMAN
> Yes, come in, sit down.

Catherine and Dom move toward the desk, which is cluttered with books and open folders. Catherine sits on one of two chairs. Dom gathers up a pile of books in the other.

> DR. WHITMAN
> Put them anywhere. (with well-trained cordiality) I had a session with Alice this morning. I thought I ought to talk with you before you see her.

> CATHERINE
> (worried)
> Is something the matter?

> DR. WHITMAN
> (deflecting the question)
> It's far too soon to be making judgments. (smiling as if to say, "You understand") As understaffed as we are, we strive to give the children as much time as they would get in private practice. I've diagnosed hundreds of children exactly like Alice, but to eliminate any possibility of error, one learns to suspend judgement (pause) until he has observed as much as he can.

> DOM
> (disliking her)
> I think you should know that my lawyer is doing all he can to get Alice back home with her mother.

> DR. WHITMAN
> That's what I wanted to warn you against. (shaking her head) I wouldn't encourage Alice to believe

(79 continued)

that you'll be taking her home soon. (smiling as if to cushion her words) Perhaps being home with her mother isn't the best thing.

          CATHERINE
        (really upset)
What do you mean?

          DR. WHITMAN
        (looking at Catherine)
Be prepared for hostility from Alice. At this point it's only natural for her to feel that you're responsible for her predicament. She is nursing an inordinate amount of anger and resentment which stems from a rather negative self-image. (kindly translating for the layman) You might say, like all of us, she blames others for her troubles.

          CATHERINE
        (bitterly)
Well, isn't that normal? A lot of people are responsible for her being here.

          DR. WHITMAN
        (as if to say, "don't
         fool yourself")
Alice has many deep-seated problems.

          CATHERINE
        (raging inside)
But she's no murderess!

          DR. WHITMAN
        (firmly)
She needs psychological help.

          DOM
        (cutting in and put-
         ting her in her
         place)
I assume there are no objections to our working with our own psychiatrist.

          DR. WHITMAN
        (pausing and looking,
         then very sweetly)
Not at all. (pushing the bell)

(79 continued)

                Alice should be in the living
                room now. (she rises, forcing
                them to rise) Let me remind
                you to be candid about the issue
                of coming home. (smiling) Be
                assured she'll get the best
                possible treatment here. (The
                nurse opens the door.) Take
                the Spages to the living room.
                (They begin to walk out.)
                (af if remembering) Oh, Mrs.
                Spages. Why would Alice conceal
                from you the fact that she's
                begun menstruating?

Stunned and embarrasssed, Catherine shakes her head as if to say, "I don't know."

                DR. WHITMAN
                (sweetly)
                It never ceases to amaze me how
                often parents don't know their
                children as well as they presume.

Not giving Catherine a chance to reply, Dom firmly takes her by the arm and steers her out of the office.

80. INT DAY HALL

                DOM
                (holding her close
                 and whispering)
                Jesus Christ, don't get upset.
                If she knew anything, she
                wouldn't be working in this
                place.

They follow the woman down a hallway to the right and stop before a door. To the right is a smaller room separated from the entrance by a wall, half of which is a large glass window. Inside a woman is sitting by a switchboard. Another woman in a striped uniform is talking to her. The guide unlocks a second door at the end of the entrance room and leads Dom and Catherine into a small living room.

81. INT DAY LIVING ROOM OF SHELTER

                WOMAN
                Alice should be finished with
                the testing by now. I'll go
                get her.

As the guide exits, the door clicks shut behind her.

(81 continued)

                     CATHERINE
                (giving vent to her
                fears)
        I don't trust that woman. All
        that stuff about taking her time.
        She's already made up her mind.

                     DOM
        For God's sake, trust me. Our
        psychiatrist will be here tomorrow.

Dom sets the suitcase down and looks around the living room which is simply furnished in rather drab Colonial-type furniture. The walls are scotch-taped with posters and yellowed cut-outs from magazines, which struggle to convince that they were arranged by happy children.

They separate, each wanting to investigate the room alone. Catherine moves tentatively still absorbed in thoughts about Dr. Whitman. She is still clutching the paper bag.

                     CATHERINE
                (looking around)
        I don't care what they do with
        the walls; they can never make
        it look like someone's living
        room.

The camera follows Dom as Catherine watches him make his way to one of two doors on the left wall. CLOSE UP Dom peering through a small window in the door. The camera picks up a neatly-furnished bedroom, decorated with more of the same cut-outs. The only personal touch is a doll propped against the pillows on the chenille-covered bed.

82. INT   DAY   BEDROOM
CUT TO the interior of an identical bedroom. Catherine's face appears at the window.

                     CATHERINE
                (through the window)
        This must be Alice's bedroom.
        Some of her things are on the
        bed.

Catherine's eyes widen, holding back tears.

83. INT   DAY   LIVING ROOM
As Catherine turns from the small window, she sees that Dom is trying the handle of the door on the opposite side of the room. He is surprised to find that the door is locked. They look at each other, and both look toward the entrance. Their faces register the realization that this small living room is in fact a prison.

(83 continued)

> DOM
> (trying to understand)
> I wonder how many kids they have here.

They are startled by the sound of a key opening the entrance door. Their eyes follow the door as it opens; Alice enters with the Woman. She stands sullenly just inside and to the right of the door.

> WOMAN
> (pointing to a small bell)
> When you're finished with your visit, just ring the bell.

The door clicks shut. Kay and Dom move toward Alice, but the child's hostile face keeps them at a distance.

> DOM
> We've seen your bedroom, Ally.

> CATHERINE
> (pointing)
> That's it, isn't it? (eager to be positive) It's really nice.

> ALICE
> (dismissing their attempts)
> Why did you bring the big suitcase? Aren't you taking me home?

> DOM
> Not until the doctor says you're ready.

Alice angrily walks over to the sofa, giving them no choice but to follow.

> CATHERINE
> (trying to break the silence)
> What did you and the doctor talk about?

> ALICE
> A lot of things.

> DOM
> (urging)
> Like what, Ally?

(83 continued)

>                ALICE
>          (provoking)
>     I told her Aunt Annie lies...
>     (coldly to her mother) and you
>     let her.
>
>                CATHERINE
>          (anguished)
>     That's not true.
>
>                ALICE
>          (cutting her)
>     What's in the bag?
>
>                CATHERINE
>     I thought you'd like some of
>     your things...
>
>                ALICE
>     Why? Don't you want me to come
>     home? You and Aunt Annie and
>     that slob Alphonso-- you just
>     want to keep me here.
>
>                DOM
>          (firmly but softly)
>     Alice, you're hurting your mother.
>     I don't want you to talk like that.
>
>                ALICE
>          (lashing out with a
>           hard laugh)
>     How would you like to hear what
>     Aunt Annie says about you?
>
>                DOM
>     Someday you'll learn to ignore
>     people like that.
>
>                CATHERINE
>          (taking courage from
>           Dom)
>     You don't have to worry. Daddy
>     will find out the truth.
>
>                ALICE
>          (pointedly)
>     How can he? He has to go home...
>     to his wife.
>
>                DOM
>          (putting a hand on
>           her shoulder)
>     I promise you, Ally, I'm going to
>     stay here until I find out who
>     was in that hall with your aunt.

(83 continued)

     ALICE
    (softening)
But I don't want to stay in this
place. Why can't I come home?

     DOM
You heard the judge. You have to
stay until your medical tests are
complete.

     ALICE
    (moving away in anger)
Medical tests? She's a psychiatrist. Everyone thinks I'm crazy
because I said it was Karen.
    (to Dom) And you don't believe
me either.

     DOM
    (moving his chair
     closer as if he's
     going to confide)
Can you understand that there
are two different reasons why
you're here? One of them is
because your Aunt was attacked
while you were in the basement.
(pause) We know you didn't do
it. And I'll find out who did.
Do you understand?

     ALICE
    (sulkily)
Yes, but...

     DOM
    (interrupting)
The other is because you saw
Karen. That can't be so---and
with the help of a doctor---a
psychiatrist---we'll straighten
that out too. But it may take
time.

     ALICE
    (stubbornly)
I did see Karen.

     DOM
Look, many times we think we
see something and later we
realize we were wrong. But
sometimes it's important to know
why...and that's where a
psychiatrist comes in.

(83 continued)

The sound of the key opening the door to the entrance attracts their attention. Alice's eyes dart to the door.

       WOMAN
      (from the door)
   I'm sorry, but the time is
   almost up. Dr. Whitman would
   like to see you for a few more
   minutes before she leaves.

       ALICE
      (trying to hold them)
   Someone has to take my suitcase
   into my room.

Dom starts toward the suitcase.

       CATHERINE
   You go ahead, Dom. I'll meet
   you outside. (he hesitates, and
   she says firmly) I can manage
   it.

       DOM
      (understanding, turns
      to Alice, putting his
      arms around her and
      hugging her)
   I know I can rely on you. (He
   squeezes her.)

MEDIUM LONG SHOT Dom and the Woman leaving the room. The CAMERA PANS with Catherine as she picks up the suitcase and moves toward the small bedroom. Alice follows carrying the paper bag.

84. INT DAY BEDROOM
   Catherine puts the suitcase on the bed. Alice, looking into the paper bag, takes out a hand puppet and begins to play with it, ignoring her mother.

       CATHERINE
      (opening the suitcase)
   Shall I help you put your things
   away?

       ALICE
   No. I want to leave...I'll do
   it later.

       CATHERINE
      (slowly closing it,
      stalling)
   I...I packed your heavy robe,
   in case...

(84 continued)

>                    ALICE
>               (coolly)
>          I don't need it.
>
>                    CATHERINE
>               (still stalling)
>          Oh, the little radio is in the
>          bag.  Now don't stay up all hours
>          listening to it.
>
>                    ALICE
>               (still cool)
>          I can't.  I'm not allowed.
>
>                    CATHERINE
>          I guess they want to be sure
>          you get your rest.

CLOSE UP Catherine looking at Alice, not wanting to leave.

>                    CATHERINE
>               (continuing)
>          I better go.  (pause) I'll be
>          back tomorrow.  (suddenly) Oh,
>          Alice, you know I love you,
>          don't you.
>
>                    ALICE
>               (not giving)
>          I suppose so.
>
>                    CATHERINE
>               (toing to her)
>          You'll be on my mind every
>          minute, dear.  (kissing her
>          and hugging her; Alice merely
>          submits.)

Catherine moves toward the door, trying to keep control.

>                    ALICE
>               (holding up the puppet)
>          Why'd you bring this?  You know
>          I don't play with it anymore.

Catherine turns, glad for the excuse.

>                    CATHERINE
>          I'll take it back.  I'm sorry.
>          I keep forgetting how old you
>          are.

(84 continued)

   She kisses Alice again, then forces herself to move toward the door.

85. INT DAY LIVING ROOM
   She pushes the bell, restraining herself from looking back. As she rings the bell the second time, Alice comes running into the room.

> ALICE
> (crying)
> Don't go, Mommy! Don't leave me! I'm frightened. I don't want to be alone. I need you.

   Catherine meets her halfway and sweeps her into her arms. She is crying. As she kisses, rocks, and cradles her:

> CATHERINE
> I need you. You're my whole world. I have no one but you.

> ALICE
> (simultaneously)
> I'm so awful. How can you love me?

> CATHERINE
> (rocking her)
> Oh Alice, Alice, don't ever say such a thing. You're everything to me. What would I ever do without you? (holding her face and looking into her eyes) Nobody will hurt us. You'll see, darling. Everything's going to be perfect again. Just you wait and see.

86. EXT DAY FALLS
   CLOSE UP of the bottom of a large waterfall. The spray and mist rising from the turbulence, accompanied by the incessant roar, create through their hypnotic repetition a sense of continuity. The CAMERA PANS up against the tumbling water to a LONG SHOT of Catherine, her small figure resting against the wooden rail of the suspension bridge. She seems engulfed in the crescendo of sound and motion. The CAMERA continues PANNING to Dom, who is sitting inside the car.

87. INT DAY CAR
   Dom's hand reaches to set a container of coffee on the dashboard. The steaming coffee mists the windshield, threatening to obliterate the image of Catherine. Frightened momentarily by the feeling she might jump, Dom gets out of the car.

88. EXT DAY FALLS
LONG SHOT of Catherine intent on the water, as Dom makes his way toward her.

>           DOM
>      (somewhat urgently)
> Catherine.

Her thoughts interrupted, she turns with a puzzled look, then smiles.

>           DOM
>      (continuing, to cover)
> Aren't you cold?

>         CATHERINE
>      (not hearing him and
>       talking simultaneously)
> It's beautiful, isn't it, Dom?

>           DOM
> You always liked this place...

They stand in appreciative silence. Dom, becoming aware of the cold, buttons the top of his coat.

>           DOM
>      (turning to Catherine,
>       and putting up the
>       collar of her coat)
> You must be freezing. (taking her arm) Let's go back.

They start walking, huddled against the cold.

>           DOM
>      (breaking into a
>       trot and smiling)
> Come on, slowpoke.

Running like children, they jump into the car, slamming the doors behind them.

89. INT DAY CAR

>         CATHERINE
>      (shivering)
> It's more like January than March.

>           DOM
>      (handing her the coffee)
> Here. Drink this. It'll warm you.

(89 continued)

    Catherine cradles the cup in an effort to warm her hands. Dom takes out a cigarette and begins looking for a match. He looks in each of his pockets. Catherine watches with amusement. Flustered with the frustration of not finding the matches, he suddenly realizes that she is watching him.

        CATHERINE
      (coyly)
    Try your shirt.

    Dom looks down at his shirt pocket, then reaches in and brings out the matches. He looks at her; they both smile, remembering.

        CATHERINE
      (breaking up the silence)
    Are you happy?

        DOM
      (knowing what she
       means)
    As happy as anyone can be, I
    guess. (pause) What about you?

    She ignores him.

        CATHERINE
    Did you talk to Julia today?

        DOM
      (brushing it aside)
    I spoke to her this morning.

        CATHERINE
    How is she?

        DOM
    Don't change the subject. I
    asked you, are you happy?

        CATHERINE
    I guess I've been content until
    now.

        DOM
    Are you seeing anyone?

        CATHERINE
    No one special.

The mood begins to change.

(89 continued)

> DOM
> (almost wishing
> she was)
> It must've been hard on you...
> and the kids.
>
> CATHERINE
> I keep wondering if Alice would
> have...(pause, then lightly) I
> haven't been so good as mother and
> father.
>
> DOM
> (silent, then wanting
> to take some of the
> blame)
> I should have visited more often.
>
> CATHERINE
> (generously)
> You were busy, Dom...with all the
> travelling and then Julia...you
> have...
>
> DOM
> Dammit, Kay, let's not fool each
> other. I stopped coming long before
> the divorce. I felt you wanted me
> to clear out.
>
> CATHERINE
> I guess I was selfish. I didn't
> realize how much Alice needed you.
>
> DOM
> I never understood what you were so
> afraid of. You put up an Iron Curtain.
>
> CATHERINE
> (ambivalently)
> Holding you back. (pause) You
> would have grown to resent me.
>
> DOM
> I loved you, Catherine. (She is
> silent, almost threatened by what
> he has said.) You made it so easy
> for me to leave--(hedging) almost
> as if you wanted it more than I did.
>
> CATHERINE
> (sadly)
> I could never have fit into the mold
> you had in mind.

(89 continued)

>                    DOM
>         You were afraid to try.
>
>                    CATHERINE
>              (looking at him,
>               realizing he has
>               never understood;
>               then quietly)
>         Perhaps...that's one way to look
>         at it.   (They are silent.)
>
>                    CATHERINE
>              (breaking the silence)
>         I bet you're starved.
>
>                    DOM
>              (smiles)
>         How did you guess?  Did you hear
>         my stomach growl?
>
>                    CATHERINE
>         Take me home.  I feel like cooking.

90.  INT  EVENING  CHURCH
          LONG SHOT a little girl in a hooded school coat passes the altar, genuflects, and walks to the side altar to light a candle before the statue of St. Michael.  CLOSE UP the candle catching fire.

91.  INT  EVENING  KITCHEN OF THE SPAGES APARTMENT
          Two fingers pinch out a low-burning candle on the kitchen table.  The CAMERA PULLS BACK to Dom taking a drag from a freshly-lit cigarette.

>                    DOM
>              (talking to Kay in
>               the other room)
>         It makes just as much sense.

     The CAMERA FOLLOWS him as he makes his way to the living room.

92.  INT  EVENING  LIVING ROOM

>                    DOM
>              (continuing as he
>               makes himself
>               comfortable on the
>               couch)
>         I can't believe she has any great
>         love for her mother.  (taking a
>         drag) I'll find out tomorrow if
>         she was in school yesterday.

(92 continued)

                CATHERINE
           (entering with a coat in
           her hands; her voice some-
           what strained)
This is the coat. It was packed away. (a little upset) You can see how much smaller than Alice's this is. Angela's would be bigger yet. (shaking her head) How could she confuse the two of them?

                DOM
It's dark down there, remember. She was so frightened she didn't even **recognize** me.

                CATHERINE
           (thinking about Angela)
I don't know, Dom.

                DOM
What do you mean you don't know. Everybody's saying it's your daughter, aren't they.

      Sound of the phone ringing. Catherine goes to the phone.

93. INT EVENING CHURCH BASEMENT
      The little girl is holding a receiver to her ear. The phone can be heard ringing.

                CATHERINE (V.O.)
Hello? (pause) Hello?

94. INT EVENING LIVING ROOM
      Getting no answer, Catherine hangs up somewhat annoyed.

                CATHERINE
I think it was Annie. What does she expect me to do? Call <u>her</u> up and forgive her?

                DOM
What makes you so sure it's her.

                CATHERINE
Last night Jim was here. (pause) The poor fool says she keeps dialing my number and hanging up. (sarcastically) My sister can't stand to be ignored.

                DOM
Maybe you should talk to her.

(94 continued)

                  CATHERINE
                  (surprised)
        I will... only when she admits
        that she lied.

                  DOM
        Don't be so hasty. It could be
        to our advantage. Maybe you'll
        find out something.

The phone begins to ring.

                  CATHERINE
                  (looking at Dom)
        I couldn't...(phone continues
        ringing) I can't.

                  DOM
                  (picking up the phone
                   and handing it to her,
                   whispering)
        Try...for Alice.

Catherine takes the phone.

95. INT  EVENING  CHURCH
    The little girl is holding the phone to her ear.

                  CATHERINE (V.O.)
                  (tentatively and
                   softly)
        Hello. (pause) Hello. Annie,
        is that you? I won't hang up.
        Talk to me. What do you...

96. INT  EVENING  LIVING ROOM

                  CATHERINE
                  (breaking down, thrusts
                   the phone at Dom)
        It's no use. I can't. I can't
        do it. There's too much hate
        inside. (She moves to the couch
        and begins to cry.)

                  DOM
                  (into the receiver)
        Hello, Ann...(sound of the phone
        clicking)

    Dom looks at the receiver, then hangs up.
Hesitating, he looks at Catherine, then makes his way to the couch.

(96 continued)

>           DOM
>         (softly)
> It's okay. (putting his arm
> around her) I shouldn't have
> asked you to. (Catherine puts
> her head on his shoulder; he
> rocks her, cuddling her; he lifts
> her chin so that their eyes meet;
> he smooths away the tears) We'll
> do it without her. (Unconsciously
> he begins to trace the lines in
> her face, rediscovering its
> beauty; Catherine takes his hand
> to stop him, but she does not
> remove it from her face.) I'll
> make everything all right.

>           CATHERINE
>         (caught up in his
>          sincerity)
> Can you? Can you?

He moves toward her and begins kissing her; she responds eagerly; both are caught in the possibility of yesterday.

The phone begins to ring. Catherine stiffens. Dom continues, wanting to shut it out.

>           CATHERINE
>         (gently pushing him
>          away)
> Let me.

>           DOM
>         (seeking her)
> Leave it. It's not important.

>           CATHERINE
>         (rising)
> Yes, I want to...I can handle
> her. (She moves to the phone,
> firm with purpose; she picks up
> the receiver.) Annie?

>           LONG DISTANCE OPERATOR
> I have a person-to-person call for
> Mr. Dominick Spages.

>           CATHERINE
>         (eyes widening with
>          surprise)
> Oh (embarrassed)...I'm sorry
> operator. Yes, he's here. Just
> a moment. (She hands Dom the phone.)

(96 continued)

>                    DOM
>               (taking the receiver)
>          This is Mr. Spages. Julia?
>          What's wrong?
>
>                    JULIA (V.O.)
>          I didn't mean to bother you, dear.
>          Is it all right? (Catherine watches
>          him with growing awareness of the
>          present.)
>
>                    DOM
>               (awkwardly)
>          What a silly question. Of course
>          it is. What's the matter?
>
>                    JULIA (V.O.)
>               (teasing)
>          Doctor says mother and baby are
>          fine.
>
>                    DOM
>               (misunderstanding)
>          You had...
>
>                    JULIA (V.O.)
>               (interrupting)
>          No, silly, not yet. We have a
>          little time. It's just that I'm
>          kind of lonely and Ginny's here,
>          and...
>
>                    DOM
>               (looking at Catherine
>                and turning slightly
>                to cover his embarrassment)
>          Look, I can't talk right now.
>          I'll call you back.
>
>                    JULIA (V.O.)
>               (pause)
>          I just called to tell you...
>          Ginny insists I stay with them.
>          I keep telling her I'm fine but
>          it is kind of close, and, well,
>          they want me there.
>
>                    DOM
>          That's a good idea.
>
>                    JULIA
>          I just didn't want you to worry.
>          I mean if you called and I didn't
>          answer. I'll be there until you
>          come home.

(96 continued)

> DOM
> All right. Fine. I'll call you there tonight.

> JULIA
> Okay. I miss you. (coyly) Can't wait 'til you get back.

> DOM
> (hesitant and
> embarrassed)
> Me too. Take care.

Dom hangs up the phone. Saying nothing, his eyes follow Catherine as she takes his coat from the closet.

> CATHERINE
> (cooly, to cover her
> hurt)
> Alice is right. (pause) Don't play detective, go home.

> DOM
> (caught between both
> worlds, defensively)
> Did it ever occur to you that home is here too?

> CATHERINE
> (wanting to hurt)
> Just because you want to play father doesn't mean you're entitled to play husband.

Dom takes the coat and puts it on.

> DOM
> (looking at her)
> Just for the record... I really meant it.

> CATHERINE
> It doesn't matter.

> DOM
> (angrily)
> Maybe if I were Tom... (he stops abruptly; Catherine is angered by this betrayal.) I'm sorry, Kay. I don't know why I said that. But I am a man and I can't help being jealous. (a little bitterly) I always felt if I had been more like Tom, we'd still be married.

(96 continued)

>					CATHERINE
>					(understanding her
>					own anger)
>			I'm sorry too. I wanted it as
>			much as you did. It would have
>			been good to have been held...
>				(softly) to pretend that it was
>			yesterday.
>
>					DOM
>			You're even more beautiful now,
>			you know.
>
>					CATHERINE
>					(beaming)
>			That was very nice. (she laughs)
>			We're both so foolish. Even if
>			there was a way of going back it
>			would start all over again.
>
>					DOM
>					(sadly)
>			I guess you're right.

He walks to her, kisses her cheek. Then he puts his head against her forehead.

>					TOM
>					(teasing)
>			I wonder what the church would
>			say about a ménage à trois?
>
>					CATHERINE
>					(pretending to be
>					shocked)
>			It sounds dirty. You better go.
>
>					DOM
>					(starting for the door)
>			I'll pick you up tomorrow. About
>			two?
>
>					CATHERINE
>			Dom, (hesitating) don't you think
>			you should go back? It's not fair.
>
>					DOM
>			Leave this decision to me. (firmly)
>			I owe this one to Alice.

97.  INT   DAY   HOTEL ROOM
     Strong sunlight filtering around the edges of the drapes indicates that it is morning. Dom is lying on the bed, face down. His one arm is hanging over the edge of the bed. On the night table nearby on top of the telephone book is the

(97 continued)

list of school coat purchasers. The short abrupt rings of the telephone interrupt his sleep like an annoying alarm clock. He picks up the phone.

>                    DOM
>               (groggily)
>          Hello.
>
>                    VOICE
>               (tearful)
>          Uncle Dom?
>
>                    DOM
>          Who is this?
>
>                    VOICE
>          Angela.
>
>                    DOM
>               (instantly alert)
>          Angela? (pause) What's wrong?
>
>                    VOICE
>          I ran away. I'm hiding. I've
>          got Karen's cross.
>
>                    DOM
>          Talk louder. I can't hear you.
>
>                    VOICE
>          I've got Karen's cross and Mommy
>          won't let me give it to you.
>
>                    DOM
>               (thinking fast)
>          Listen, honey, let me meet you.
>          We can talk about it.
>
>                    VOICE
>          You'll tell...
>
>                    DOM
>          You know better than that. Has
>          Uncle Dom ever done anything to
>          hurt you? (pause, trying to
>          convince her) I'll come alone.
>
>                    VOICE
>               (after a silence)
>          I'm at...I'm near the Ivanhoe
>          Building. (she breaks into tears)
>
>                    DOM
>          Stop crying. I'll be there in
>          fifteen minutes. (gently) There's
>          nothing to be afraid of.

98. EXT  DAY  HOTEL
         Dom comes out of the hotel and acclimates himself to the cold. Lighting a cigarette, he waits for the car. The boy pulls up with the car. LONG SHOT Dom gets in and pulls away.

99. INT  DAY  CAR
         Dom is absorbed in his thoughts. The car radio plays the news of March 10, 1961.

100. EXT  DAY  STREET
         The car makes its way through a once-prosperous industrial district, a ghost town of vacant factories, broken glass, and debris. Passing an old locomotive factory, Dom turns the corner and pulls into a dirt lot. Getting out of the car, he looks around, then crosses the street toward the Ivanhoe Building, an abandoned storage mill. He pauses on the stone bridge built over the creek which was once part of an elaborate canal system. The sound of the small falls in the back of the building mingles with the noise of traffic in the cold morning air. While he waits, his eyes absorb with distaste the waste-strewn banks and sullied waters. Standing near the top of the falls a little girl, half-hidden by the foliage, watches. Unaware, Dom lights a cigarette.

                         LITTLE GIRL
         Hisst.

Dom looks in the direction of the sound.

                         DOM
                    (calling out)
         Angela?

         His eyes move to the edge of the bridge trying to determine the source of the sound. Two rats scurrying along the bank disappear into the bushes. Thinking he was mistaken, he walks back along the bridge.

                         LITTLE GIRL
                    (louder)
         Hisst.

Dom looks up, catching sight of the motionless girl.

                         DOM
                    (making his way around
                     the bridge)
         Angela, what are you doing up
         there?  Come down.

         The little girl hesitates, then disappears into the bushes.

(100 continued)

> DOM
> (calling out)
> Where are you going?  Don't you
> want to talk?

The CAMERA PANS with Dom as he makes his way to the top of the falls.  From this position he can see the little girl come out of the lot, cross the street, and disappear through the wooden door of the old locomotive factory.  Annoyed, he quickly retraces his steps, following the figure to the factory door.

101.  INT  DAY  FACTORY HALLWAY

Dom opens the door and peers into a dimly-lit concrete hallway littered with broken glass from smashed windows.  Hesitating, he looks up the wooden stairway.

On the second floor landing the little girl takes a step cautiously, then stops abruptly as she crunches down on some broken glass.

> DOM
> (calling out)
> Angela, why are you running away?
> (as he ascends the stairs)  Be
> careful.  It's dangerous in here.
> You might get cut.

The little girl, hidden in the darkness, reaches into her shopping bag, pulling out a large kitchen knife.  She turns toward the direction of Dom.  As Dom reaches the top of the landing, the masked figure lunges toward him, her knife catching him in the arm.

> DOM
> (yelling in surprise)
> Jesus Christ, what are you doing?

He deftly grabs her wrist to ward off a second attack.  Viciously she kicks him between the legs.  Doubling over, he stumbles backward down the steps, wrenching her arm causing the knife to clatter down with him.  The little girl runs up the stairs.  Furious, Dom picks himself up, grabbing at the slash on his arm.

> DOM
> (looking up, yelling
> with rage)
> You little bitch.  Wait till I
> get hold of you.

Forgetting caution in his anger, he mounts the steps, quickly reaching the third floor landing.  The entrance

(101 continued)                                             110

to the third floor is barricaded. Absently touching the pain in his groin, he is distracted by the sound of feet moving across the floor above. Newly charged, he starts up the stairs, taking two at a time.

>                    DOM
>              (yelling as he reaches
>               the entrance way)
>        It's no use--I'm gonna get you.

From the fourth floor entrance two pigeons come flying out into the hall, forcing Dom to duck. One pigeon makes his way through a broken window; the other hits the glass and bounces off falling down the stairwell. Turning cautiously, he enters the doorway.

102.  INT   DAY   ASSEMBLY ROOM
Stretching before him is an immense room the size of a football field. Once the work area of the locomotive factory, the room is dotted with large columns supporting a sky-light roof. At the far end of the room two massive wooden doors which had received powerful machines are now closed.

Midway, half-hidden by one of the columns, the little girl, breathing heavily, waits.

>                    DOM
>              (afraid that she might
>               run, tries to reason
>               with her; walking slowly
>               toward her)
>        Don't run, Angela. I'm not mad
>        anymore. I want to help you.
>        You don't have to be afraid of
>        me. I'll...

Suddenly the figure whirls, aiming a brick at Dom, her smiling mask creating the bizarre illusion of a "Pie-in-the-face" comic routine. The brick smacks against his forehead, breaking in half. Dom falls unconscious.

Racing to get the brick and finish the job, the figure realizes its uselessness and begins rushing about to find another weapon. A pile of debris proves fruitless. Her eyes catch sight of a rope dangling from one of the skylight windows. She yanks at the rope; the metal handle gives; the rope snakes to the ground just missing her. She gathers it up and moves toward Dom. Working rapidly with the rope, she haphazardly begins to tie Dom into a web-like trap. Catching sight of the receiving doors, she pauses, then with a sudden surge, continues.

103.  EXT   DAY   END OF BUILDING
The two wooden receiving doors shove outward toward the CAMERA and flap back against the building. A square shaft

(103 continued)

of sunlight intrudes on the gloom. The CAMERA MOVES from the daylight to the edge of the door and waits for the little girl.

104. INT DAY ASSEMBLY ROOM
The little girl is trying to drag the tied-up body across the room. Tiring after a few feet, the girl changes her method: She begins to move the weighty body by lifting first one end, then the other. The slowness of the method frustrates her. Desperately she sits on the floor and begins kicking the side of the body toward the doors. Becoming conscious of pain in his side, Dom groans. The girl increases her efforts, breathing heavily. Within yards of the door, Dom becomes aware of what is happening.

> DOM
> (writhing in the ropes)
> Angela, don't do this to me!

The little girl ignores him and continues.

> DOM
> (looking at the open
> doors in desperation,
> screaming)
> Help! Help! (turning to Angela)
> You can't do this. (hoping to
> strike a chord) God will punish you.

The girls stops pushing. Dom watches as she crawls toward him. Karen's cross is visibly dangling from her neck.

> DOM
> (relieved)
> I knew you wouldn't...Untie me,
> and...

> GIRL
> (interrupting)
> You filthy pig! You and that whore!
> That's who God wants punished.
> (pulling off her mask) Father Tom
> belongs to the Church.

Dom's eyes register shock.

> DOM
> (struggling to free
> himself)
> Holy Christ...Mrs. Tredoni...my
> God...Why?

(104 continued)

> MRS. TREDONI
> (chanting, begins to
> shove him toward the
> edge)
> St. Michael the Archangel defend
> us in battle...

> DOM
> (simultaneously pleading)
> Mrs. Tredoni, don't do this...

> MRS. TREDONI
> (continuing)
> Be our protection against the
> snares of the devil...

Dom in a last effort lunges animal-like trying to bite her; he catches in his teeth Karen's cross which snaps from her neck.

> MRS. TREDONI
> (stopping abruptly and
> grabbing the chain from
> his mouth)
> Give me that! Give it to me!
> It's mine.

Realizing the cross could be his salvation, Dom lets it slip from his teeth into his mouth. With her hands she tries to force his mouth open. Dom moves his head and body as much as possible to thwart her.

Taking off her shoe, the insane woman tries to beat his lips, but his movement makes it difficult. Infuriated, she begins kicking him closer to the edge.

> MRS. TREDONI
> (chanting with a labored,
> trance-like voice)
> We humbly beseech God to command
> him. Do thou, O Prince of the
> heavenly host, by the divine power...

> DOM
> (simultaneously, almost
> choking on the cross)
> You're going to get caught. Tom
> will find you out.

> MRS. TREDONI
> (pushing his body close
> to the edge)
> ...thrust into hell Satan and the
> other evil spirits who roam this
> world seeking the ruin of souls.

(104 continued)                                                    113

          EXTREME CLOSE UP of Dom's last few images as he
falls to his death.

          From a CLOSE UP of Dom's face on the ground, the
CAMERA PULLS BACK to an EXTREME LONG SHOT of the factory and
the city with the spires of its churches etched against the
sky. The doll-like people go about their daily business.
Sounds of city noises.

105.  INT  DAY  CHURCH
          LONG SHOT the altar in darkness. In the sacristy
someone switches on a light and can be heard moving busily
about the room.

          The front doors of the church open, and Mrs.
Tredoni hurriedly enters. The CAMERA FOLLOWS her through the
shadows to the side aisle. Suddenly the altar is flooded with
light. Startled and in panic she retraces her steps keeping to
the shadows. The lights in the Church proper illuminate the
interior, forcing her to take refuge in a nearby confessional.
As the door closes, the red "in-use" button goes on over the
door of the occupied cubicle.

          From the sacristy Father Tom in his black cassock,
carrying a penitential stole, crosses the altar, genuflects,
and kneels to pray.

106.  INT  DAY  CONFESSIONAL
          Nervously Mrs. Tredoni removes her coat and pulls
from her shopping bag a patterned housedress. Sounds of
children can be heard echoing in the stillness of the church.
She stops surprised. Her eyes narrow in confusion.

                    VOICES
               Hello, Father Tom.

                    FATHER TOM
               Hi Jimmy.

                    VOICE
               Hello, Father.

                    FATHER TOM
               Hello.

                    SISTER'S VOICE
                    (clapping her hands)
               All right now. Let's get settled
               quickly. Don't keep Father waiting.
               Into the pews...

          Mrs. Tredoni slowly cracks open the confessional
door. From her point of view in the confessional Father Tom
is standing next to Sister as the last of the children take
their seats. She closes the door and begins struggling with
her dress.

107. INT DAY CHURCH

> FATHER TOM
> (to the children)
> This will be your last confession as a group. Think carefully about what you want to say. But remember I don't have to hear everything you've done since last Sunday.
> (pausing then dramatically) After all we don't want Sister to miss her lunch.

All the children begin to giggle. Father Tom turns smiling to Sister, who fails to appreciate the humor.

108. INT DAY CONFESSIONAL

From the crack in the door Mrs. Tredoni sees Father Tom walk away from Sister in the direction of the confessional. Closing the door, she struggles to put on her coat. Reaching in the shopping bag, she takes a black oxford and, removing the white shoe, puts it on.

> SISTER'S VOICE
> Everybody ready? Let's make a good act of contrition.

As the young voices are heard chanting the traditional prayer, Mrs. Tredoni reaches for the second shoe. Sounds of Father Tom entering the priest's box in the confessional. Mrs. Tredoni drops the oxford and freezes. The panel that divides the penitent from the priest abruptly opens. Mrs. Tredoni falls to her knees. Her eyes freeze on the aperture; through it the shadowed profile of the priest's head is visible.

> FATHER TOM
> (through the window)
> Is someone in here?

> MRS. TREDONI
> (in panic)
> Bless me, Father, for I have sinned...

> FATHER TOM
> We're only hearing the children this morning.

> MRS. TREDONI
> (whispering)
> Bless me, Father, for I have sinned...Father I need confession.

                    FATHER TOM
          Mrs. Tredoni, is that you?
          What's wrong?

                    MRS. TREDONI
          Please hear me, Father. (pause,
          nervously)  I'm troubled.

                    FATHER TOM
                    (reassuringly)
          Go ahead.  I have time.

                    MRS. TREDONI
                    (stalling)
          I...I lost my temper.  I got
          angry at Father Pat.  (As she
          recites she struggles to slip
          off the remaining white shoe
          and replace it with her oxford)
          I...I neglected my morning
          prayers.

                    FATHER TOM
                    (gently coaxing)
          This can't be the reason you
          wanted confession this morning.

                    MRS. TREDONI
                    (freezing with the shoe
                     in her hand)
          Oh, no, Father.  There is something.
          (silence)

                    FATHER TOM
                    (encouraging)
          Yes...(she is silent) I know you,
          Mrs. Tredoni. (She puts on her shoe.)
          You're a good woman.  It can't be
          as bad as you think.

                    MRS. TREDONI
                    (having found something,
                     blurts out)
          I'm losing my patience with
          Monsignor.  Sometimes I wish...
          Oh, Father, I remember when
          everyone respected him so...

                    FATHER TOM
          I understand.  It's not easy to
          see someone we love suffer.

(108 continued)

MRS. TREDONI
You don't understand. Sometimes I even think it would be better if God...(She stops, unable to say it; firmly) It's a sin to have such thoughts.

FATHER TOM
It's not a sin. You've devoted so much of yourself to us it's only natural that you would want God to spare us from pain.

MRS. TREDONI
(moved by the magic
of his voice)
Yes, Father.

FATHER TOM
(continuing)
You have great faith. It's because of this you can look to death as a resolution. There is no greater reward than to spend eternity with Our Lord.

MRS. TREDONI
(putting her clasped
hand to her chest in
a gesture of affirmation)
Oh, yes, Father.

FATHER TOM
I'm just sorry you didn't come to me sooner.

MRS. TREDONI
(unconsciously touching
her breast)
I am too, Father.

FATHER TOM
There's no need to go to confession for this. When you're upset come to me. I am your confessor, but I am also your friend.

MRS. TREDONI
(running her hand downward
across her belly)
Oh, thank you, Father.

109. EXT  DAY  CHURCH
Mrs. Tredoni, leaving the confessional elated, regally walks past the waiting line of children oblivious to their awed "Hello, Mrs. Tredoni's," which sound sequentially through the church. As she files by in her hooded coat, which matches theirs except for the insignia, she looks, but for a few inches, like one of them.

EXTREME LONG SHOT Mrs. Tredoni haughtily nods to Sister, walks down the aisle, ascends the steps to the altar, and, genuflecting, exits through the sacristy.

110. EXT  DAY  STREET
A city bus stops at a corner. Catherine Spages gets off the bus. She walks quickly down the street to the rectory of the church.

111. INT  DAY  KITCHEN
In a tiny work area, noticeably neat, Mrs. Tredoni contentedly dices vegetables with her kitchen knife. Sound of the doorbell ringing. Annoyed, she rinses her hands and leaves the kitchen.

112. INT  DAY  HALL
Catherine's figure is visible through the window of the door. With set lips Mrs. Tredoni opens the door.

> CATHERINE
> I'm sorry to bother you, Mrs. Tredoni.

> MRS. TREDONI
> (unsettled by Catherine's
> appearance)
> Father Tom's not here.

> CATHERINE
> I was looking for Mr. Spages. I know he had to drop off Father's car.

> MRS. TREDONI
> I haven't seen him. (There is a silence.) You'll have to excuse me I'm preparing supper.

> CATHERINE
> Do you mind if I wait? Maybe they're together; (looking at her) I'm a little concerned.

> MRS. TREDONI
> (opening the door and
> stepping back)
> Suit yourself. You can wait in the office. (hoping to dissuade her) He may be gone for some time.

(112 continued)                                               118

                    Catherine enters and follows Mrs. Tredoni to the
office.

                         CATHERINE
                    Do you think something could be
                    wrong with the phone? I called
                    several times, but there was
                    no answer.

                         MRS. TREDONI
                    I was out. You can turn on the
                    light. There are some magazines.

          Catherine sits down, then realizes that Mrs.
Tredoni is still standing, watching her.

                         CATHERINE
                         (uncomfortable, wanting
                          to fill the silence)
                    I'm sure they're together.

          Without answering Mrs. Tredoni walks away, leaving
Catherine to stare after her.

113.  INT   DAY   KITCHEN
                    Mrs. Tredoni enters the kitchen. Closing the
door, she leans against it, struggling for self-control. Her
hand searches absently the area of her throat for the missing
cross. Her eyes are mesmerized by the kitchen knife lying
amid the vegetables on the counter. Slowly she reaches out
toward it.

114.  INT   DAY   MORGUE
          CLOSE UP of Dom's face.

                         VOICE
                    There is a ten centimeter laceration
                    of the dorsum of the left forearm.

          The CAMERA PULLS BACK to reveal Dom's naked body
on a dissecting table. The doctor rests the arm by the side
of the body. He continues examining the body.

                         DOCTOR
                         (as he examines)
                    Right humerus is fractured.
                    Contusions and abrasions of the
                    thorax. Right clavicle is
                    fractured. (moving the head of
                    the corpse) It appears like the
                    cervicle spine is fractured.

          As the Doctor is speaking, the CAMERA PANS and
DOLLIES in close to an open door through which Father Tom and

(114 continued)

Captain Beame can be seen. Father Tom is hanging up the phone. The doctor's voice fades down.

                SPINA (V.O.)
        If the shelter says she left at
        2:30, she should be home by now.

                FATHER TOM
           (worried)
        She's not at the Rectory.

                BEAME
        I'm sure nothing's happened to
        her. (talking to Spina who is
        out of the frame) Close that door.

Spina walks into the FRAME and closes the door. CUT TO doctor who is forcing the jaw open.

                DOCTOR
        Hematomas of the lips.

He puts his finger in the bruised mouth to check the teeth. Noticing something, he reaches in further and grabs hold of a piece of chain. Pulling on it fails to dislodge it.

                DOCTOR
        Pass me the laryngoscope.

He inserts the laryngoscope which forces the mouth further open, enlarges the throat, and illuminates it. With a forceps he pulls out the gold cross. As it comes from the mouth, the cross gleams in the light from the laryngoscope.

                DOCTOR
           (dropping the cross
           into a tin pan, coolly)
        That's what I call taking your
        religion seriously.

115.   INT   DAY   OFFICE

                FATHER TOM
           (anguished)
        Dammit, why did he go down there?

                BEAME
        Did he give you any indication
        that he knew something?

                FATHER TOM
        Last time I saw him I gave him a
        list of families who bought school
           (MORE)

(115 continued)

> FATHER TOM (continued)
> coats. He was convinced Alice
> had confused Karen with someone
> else. Because of Annie, he suspected
> his niece, Angela.

> BEAME
> Can you get me a copy of that list?

> SPINA
> (to Beame)
> We never did find out where that
> kid was.

The door opens and the doctor enters.

> DOCTOR
> You won't believe this. (unfolding
> a piece of muslin and laying bare
> the cross) It was lodged in his
> throat.

> FATHER TOM
> Karen's cross!

They look. Beame takes the cross.

> DOCTOR
> It had to have been worn by the
> killer. (as they examine it)
> It wasn't forced down his throat.
> He bit down on it. (pointing)
> Look at the teeth marks.

> SPINA
> Is this all there was of the
> chain?

> DOCTOR
> We're checking the contents of
> the stomach now.

> BEAME
> (musing)
> This accounts for the bruises
> around his mouth.

> DOCTOR
> Whoever killed him wanted that
> cross badly.

They are silent.

(115 continued)

                    SPINA
              (going to the phone)
        I better have someone check where
        that kid was today.

                    DOCTOR
              (leaving)
        I'll let you know about the
        stomach as soon as I can.

                    FATHER TOM
              (waiting for the
                opportunity, soberly)
        Ray, when can Alice go home?

                    BEAME
              (looking at him; quietly)
        I'll make arrangements to have
        her released. (pause) Father, do
        you have a number where we can
        reach his family?

                    FATHER TOM
        It's just his wife. Let me make
        the call. I think it would be
        better if I tell her brother and
        have him break the news. (quietly)
        She's pregnant.

116.  INT DAY OFFICE
     Catherine sits staring into space, a Newsweek magazine unopened on her lap. Suddenly aware of being watched, she looks to the door. Mrs. Tredoni is standing in the doorway.

                    MRS. TREDONI
        I've made you some coffee.

     Catherine gets up and takes a few steps toward the door.

                    MRS. TREDONI
              (standing aside, so that
                Catherine precedes her)
        It's in the kitchen.

     Catherine goes out the door and starts down the hall.

117.  INT DAY HALL
     Catherine walks timidly. She would feel more comfortable if Mrs. Tredoni led the way. Mrs. Tredoni's tiny body seems to block out the form of Catherine as she follows her down the hall.

118. INT  DAY  KITCHEN
Catherine, ahead of Mrs. Tredoni, pauses awkwardly.

          MRS. TREDONI
Sit down.

Mrs. Tredoni stands over her; then, as if remembering, she goes to the stove and takes the coffee pot, turning off the flame. Walking up behind Catherine, she reaches over her shoulder and pours the coffee.

          CATHERINE
        (uncomfortable)
This is very nice of you. I didn't intend to put you to any trouble.

Mrs. Tredoni moves back to the stove with the pot.

          CATHERINE
        (being polite)
Aren't you having any?

          MRS. TREDONI
        (going to the refrigerator
         and taking out a paper bag)
I make it a rule not to have coffee after breakfast.

Mrs. Tredoni puts the bag on the table. She rips the bag open.

          CATHERINE
        (wishing she were home)
I guess this is silly of me. I should really go home. (Mrs. Tredoni has unwrapped a large fish, its head intact.) I don't know why I'm so worried. (Mrs. Tredoni cuts off the fish's head.) It's just that I can't understand where he could be. (The eye of the fish appears to be staring at Mrs. Tredoni.)

          MRS. TREDONI
        (looking at Catherine)
Maybe you're afraid God will send St. Michael to take another of your loved ones. (Catherine is silent, somewhat unnerved.) When St. Michael took my little girl, I thought only of how cruel God was.

(118 continued)

>                    CATHERINE
>                     (surprised)
>               I'm sorry, Mrs. Tredoni, I never
>               knew you had a little girl.
>
>                    MRS. TREDONI
>                     (moving toward her with
>                      the knife)
>               Don't you see. He wanted to teach
>               me. We pay for the sins of our
>               parents. (moving closer) I was
>               sent here to take care of Father
>               Tom.

They hear the front door open.

>                    FATHER TOM
>                     (calling from the hallway)
>               Mrs. Tredoni...
>
>                    CATHERINE
>                     (glad for the interruption)
>               It's Tom...

Catherine walks out of the kitchen, leaving Mrs. Tredoni staring, knife in hand.

119. INT DAY HALL
Catherine enters the hall.

>                    CATHERINE
>               Tom...I...
>
>                    FATHER TOM
>                     (simultaneously)
>               Catherine, what are you doing
>               here? I've been trying to find
>               you all afternoon.
>
>                    CATHERINE
>               Where's Dom? Is something wrong?
>
>                    FATHER TOM
>                     (taking her by the arm
>                      and walking out of the
>                      frame and into the living
>                      room)
>               There's been an accident.

120. INT DAY KITCHEN
Mrs. Tredoni stands listening at the kitchen door.

(120 continued)

       CATHERINE (V.O.)
      (screaming)
   Dominick! Dominick! Oh, Tom,
   help me! help me!

  Mrs. Tredoni closes the door, smothering Catherine's cries and Tom's gentle replies. Her hand again goes unconsciously to the unadorned area of her throat for the missing cross. CAMERA MOVES IN CLOSE to a face filled with hatred.

121. EXT DAY AIRPORT
  A door of a hearse is opened, and Dom's casket is lifted out and carried toward a waiting plane. In the distance, watching from behind a fence, are Catherine and Father Tom. They seem oblivious to the rain which accentuates the bleakness of the surroundings.

       FATHER TOM
      (taking her arm)
   We better go. She'll be
   waiting.

  The CAMERA PANS with them as they get into the limousine. As the limousine pulls away, through the rain-splattered window, Catherine can be seen looking back toward the runway.

122. EXT DAY RUNWAY
  The CAMERA FOLLOWS the plane as it takes off.

123. INT DAY LIMOUSINE
  They ride in silence. Karen's cross is visible around Catherine's neck.

       CATHERINE
      (in a low voice)
   I'm not going to tell her just
   yet. She's been without a father
   for a long time. I'm not going to
   take him away from her so soon.

Father Tom remains silent.

       CATHERINE
   I understand what he meant now--
   about being torn between two worlds.
   A part of me has gone with him.

  They continue riding in silence. Catherine turns to stare out of the window.

124. EXT  DAY  ROAD
CLOSE UP of Catherine looking out of the window. She is fingering the cross. From her point of view the CAMERA PICKS UP the traffic. The world is rain-drenched and muddy. Visible in the distance are rows of indistinguishable apartment buildings, inhabited by people who seem to Catherine secure in their anonymous dwellings.

125. INT  DAY  LIMOUSINE

          CATHERINE
        (turning from the
        window, upset by her
        thoughts)
I can't live with this feeling --why have I lost control of my life?

          FATHER TOM
        (trying to soothe her)
You haven't lost control. Death does this to people.

          CATHERINE
Haven't I had more than my share?

          FATHER TOM
        (gently)
There's no such thing as a share.

The two of them ride in silence, listening to the rhythm of the rain on the roof.

126. EXT  DAY  ROAD
LONG SHOT of the limousine moving through the streets.

127. INT  DAY  LIMOUSINE
The driver turns and passes through the gates of the Sarah Reed Children's Shelter.

128. EXT  DAY  SHELTER
The limousine pulls up to the parking lot of the shelter.

129. INT  DAY  LIMOUSINE

          CATHERINE
        (giving in to the
        confusion within)
Tom, I'm frightened. Maybe I should leave her here. At least she's safe.

(129 continued)

>FATHER TOM
>Don't be ridiculous, Kay. She needs you now. The police will be watching you both. (trying to convince her) I promise you there's nothing to fear.

>CATHERINE
>For how long, Tom? What happens if they don't find the murderer?

They both pause, looking at each other.

>FATHER TOM
>Alice is waiting.

They leave the limousine.

130. INT  DAY  LIVING ROOM
Alice is sitting in a chair with her coat on. The door is unlocked by a matron. Catherine enters, followed by Father Tom.

>ALICE
>(jumping up eagerly and grabbing her suitcase)
>I'm all ready. (She looks from her mother to the priest; then disappointed) Where's Daddy?

>CATHERINE
>He had to go back.

>ALICE
>(hurt)
>How come?

>CATHERINE
>Let's go home. (taking the suitcase) We'll talk about it later.

>ALICE
>(stubbornly not moving)
>He didn't even say good-bye.

>CATHERINE
>(going to her and putting her arms on her shoulders)
>Please don't feel that way. He kept his promise to you. (looking into her eyes) It's because of him you're coming home. (Catherine's eyes are filled with tears.)

131. INT   DAY   RECTORY

CLOSE UP of a rigidly arranged collection of dolls, some hand-made, some in the costumes of exotic countries. It is clear they have never been the playthings of a doting "child-mother." They seem to be concentrating on someone in the room. The CAMERA PANS to Mrs. Tredoni, who is standing by the bed in her hooded coat, putting her kitchen knife into her shopping bag. Over the bed hangs a large crucifix. On the wall is the familiar picture of the Sacred Heart, an artfully woven dried palm stuck into the frame.

The CAMERA PANS with her as she moves to an oak dresser near the bed. Opening a drawer, she removes from under the cotton underwear her mask and veil. She stuffs them into her shopping bag.

On the dresser, which is dominated by a statue of St. Michael, is a photograph of a child in communion garb standing beside a tall man in an old suit. The little girl's face is noticeable blurred. Next to that is a photograph of Father Tom.

Mrs. Tredoni blesses herself and places her hand on the feet of the statue of St. Michael.

132. INT   DAY   HALL

Mrs. Tredoni comes out of the doorway, and begins to move stalthily past the partially open door of Monsignor's room. Monsignor sits dozing in his wheelchair. He flinches in his sleep, groaning. She stops, waiting for Monsignor to quiet down. She continues down the stairs and heads for the back door.

133. INT   DAY   HALL

Dressed in her hooded coat, Alice is coming out of the door of her apartment.

      CATHERINE (V.O.)
   (nervously)
  Don't leave the apartment. I'll
  be ready in five minutes. I want
  to leave early.

Alice goes down the stairs, stopping at Alphonso's apartment. She cracks the door: Alphonso is sleeping on the sofa. Closing the door carefully, she descends the steps to the basement.

134. EXT   DAY   STREET

Spina is sitting in the car reading the newspaper. Two boys pass on skate-boards. His eyes follow them for a moment. Reaching for a cigarette, he finds the pack empty. He crumbles it and throws it out the window. He

(134 continued)

opens up the glove compartment and searches through it. Frustrated by not finding any cigarettes, he returns to his vigil. After a few moments he again, almost unconsciously, begins to search through his pockets. Yielding to his need, he keys the mike.

> SPINA
> Detective Unit 31 to Headquarters.
>
> HEADQUARTERS
> Go ahead, 31.
>
> SPINA
> I'll be 10-15 for about five minutes.
>
> HEADQUARTERS
> 10-4.

Spina starts the car and pulls away.

135. INT   DAY   FAVA'S CANDY STORE

Through the window Spina is seen driving up. He enters the store, picks up a newspaper, scans the headlines, and takes it to the counter with him. He orders coffee, an English to go, and a pack of Marlboros. Within a short time the waitress puts a cup of coffee in front of him.

> SPINA
> I said to go...(as she reaches for it)--That's okay, I'll drink this one. Put another in.

As Spina drinks the coffee, behind him through the store window, only partially visible through the hanging masks and magazines, Mrs. Tredoni can be seen walking past.

136. INT   DAY   ALPHONSO'S APARTMENT

EXTREME CLOSE UP of an eyeball peeking through a crack in the door. The CAMERA PANS from the eye to a mound which is Alphonso sleeping on the couch. On the floor next to him is an empty bottle of gin. A cat is asleep on his stomach. SOUNDS of someone tiptoeing toward the couch. The cat wakes up. Alice stands watching Alphonso. The cat's eyes are frozen on Alice. As she pulls a jar of cockroaches from her coat pocket, the cat's eyes narrow; seeing the roaches, he jumps off Alphonso's stomach and runs to hide behind a pile of junk.

Alice opens the jar and empties its contents onto the pillow. The roaches scatter in all directions, some heading for Alphonso's bathrobe.

137. EXT   DAY   HALL

As Catherine comes down the stairs, Alice is leaving Alphonso's apartment.

(137 continued)

                    CATHERINE
          What were you doing in there?

                    ALICE
               (thinking fast)
          I was just saying hello to Mr.
          Alphonso.

                    CATHERINE
               (smiling)
          I'm glad you did that.

     They leave the FRAME and go down the stairs.

138. EXT  DAY  FRONT OF SPAGES HOUSE
          In the rear Mrs. Tredoni can be seen entering the
     back yard, intent on going to the basement. The front door
     opens, and Catherine and Alice come out. They leave the
     FRAME. The CAMERA HOLDS on the house.

139. INT  DAY  APARTMENT
          Mrs. Tredoni comes from the basement and makes
     her way up the stairs to the Spages' apartment. Knife drawn,
     she raps sharply on the apartment door. Alphonso is heard
     screaming below. Panicked, she turns, fleeing down the
     stairs. As she approaches Alphonso's apartment, the door
     jerks open. Wild-eyed, Alphonso comes out, frenziedly shaking
     his robe to dislodge the roaches. His voice rises in a scream
     of terror as he comes face to face with the masked Mrs.
     Tredoni.

                    ALPHONSO
               (realizing, grabs her)
          Alice, you little bitch...
               (tearing off her mask)  I'll
          teach you...

          He stops, stunned by the unexpected face of the
     housekeeper. Seizing the opportunity, Mrs. Tredoni lunges at
     him, her knife finding its home in the massive belly.
     Alphonso looks at the blood spurting from the wound and running
     down his stomach. He slides to the floor, his screams of
     terror increasing out of all proportion to the injury. Mrs.
     Tredoni flees, knife in hand, down the steps to the front
     door. She opens the door confronting Spina, who has been
     alerted by the screams. Quickly slamming the door, she
     disappears into the basement.

140. EXT  DAY  APARTMENT
          With his coat wrapped around his fist, Spina
     breaks the glass, reaches in, and turns the knob. He follows
     the screams of Alphonso.

141. INT  DAY  CHURCH
It is the children's mass, and the church is crowded with families. As it is the Sunday following First Holy Communion, there is a section in the front reserved for members of the First Communion class. Catherine and Alice are in the middle of a pew two-thirds of the way back. The priest is kneeling, adoring the Host; rising, he elevates it. The bells ring. Then, uncovering the chalice, he continues with the consecration of the wine.

In the rear of the church Mrs. Tredoni stands with her head bowed. The bells stop ringing. Nervously she looks up. Catching sight of Alice, she is overwhelmed by the need to be near them. She moves up the aisle, oblivious to the fact that it is the most solemn part of the mass, the consecration of the blood. Although there is no room, she squeezes into the pew directly behind them, forcing the kneeling parishioners to move down. She does not take her eyes off the Spageses. Aware of the movement, Alice turns to look. Her eyes meet Mrs. Tredoni's. She turns back guiltily and, as if Mrs. Tredoni had admonished her, pretends to engross herself in prayer.

The priest kneels and adores the Blood of Christ; rising, he elevates the chalice. The bells are rung. Setting the chalice down, he covers it and adores it again. He prays over the chalice.

From a side door to the sacristy Father Tom enters the church. The CAMERA FOLLOWS him as he walks down the side aisle, surreptitiously searching the congregation. From the corner of her eye, Mrs. Tredoni watches Father Tom. Noticing her, he continues on, trying to avoid her gaze. He makes his way to the rear of the church.

142. EXT  DAY  CHURCH
Two patrol cars are parked outside the church. Standing on the sidewalk are Beame, Spina, and several policemen. Father Tom comes from the church and goes to meet them.

      FATHER TOM
     (tersely)
  She's inside.

      SPINA
  Let's go.

      FATHER TOM
    (holding up his hands)
  Wait a minute. She's too close
  to Catherine and Alice. If she
  sees you, who knows what she'll do?
      (MORE)

(142 continued)

> FATHER TOM (continued)
> (pause) It's almost time for communion. (to Beame) Come with me to the sacristy. When she comes up to receive, I know I can get her to go with you.
>
> SPINA
> What happens if she doesn't come up?
>
> FATHER TOM
> Look, I know her. She'll come up. She's never missed.
>
> SPINA
> (looking at Beame)
> Why can't we put a marksman in the balcony?
>
> FATHER TOM
> (sternly)
> Not in my church. (firmly) I can handle her. She wouldn't do anything to me.
>
> BEAME
> (deciding, to Spina)
> I want men covering all the exits. Keep out of sight. Let's go, Father.

They leave the FRAME.

143. INT DAY CHURCH
The priest genuflects before the altar. Rising, he prays in a low voice.

> FATHER PAT
> Panem caelestem accipiam; et nomen Domini invocabo.

Raising his voice alightly, he prays "Domine, non sum dignus" three times. As he receives the Host and begins gathering the fragments in preparation for the Communion of the Blood, the children in the front get out of the pews. The center aisle begins to fill with parishioners. Catherine and Alice rise. Catherine, turning to pass, leans over to excuse herself to a man kneeling next to her. Karen's cross is visible through her open coat. The light catches it. Mrs. Tredoni's eyes are frozen on the image of the cross. Her hand touches her chest where the cross should be. Mesmerized, she rises to follow Catherine and Alice. As she

(143 continued)

starts toward them, she is cut off by a group of kids, some in school jackets, who pile into the aisle from the pew on the other side. Mrs. Tredoni is caught in the movement of the kids.

144. INT   DAY   SACRISTY

      BEAME
   (hidden from the
    parishioners,
    observing the church)
You were right, Father. She's coming up the aisle.

      FATHER TOM
   (turning to Beame)
I want you to promise you'll give me a chance to have her come freely.

      BEAME
Okay, Father. Be careful.

      FATHER TOM
   (confident)
Don't worry.

145. INT   DAY   CHURCH

Father Tom enters the altar and goes to the kneeling altar boy. The altar boy is holding the server, a small brass tray which is placed under the chin of the communicant to prevent the Host from dropping to the floor. He takes the server from the boy, motioning for him to step aside. He kneels down in the boy's place. Father Pat turns to the congregation, ready for prayer. He looks down somewhat puzzled at Father Tom's presence.

      FATHER TOM
   (mouthing to Father Pat)
Later.

      FATHER PAT
Ecce Agnus Dei, ecce qui tollit peccata mundi. Domine, non sum dignus, ut intres sub tectum meum: sed tantum dis verbo, et sanabitur anima mea.

The first group of parishioners are kneeling at the altar waiting. Not far away Catherine and Alice are on line with those waiting in the center aisle. Mrs. Tredoni is visible a little distance behind them. Father Pat moves toward the right end of the altar rail with Father Tom following him. He begins dispensing communion in the usual order from right to left. As each communicant rises, another takes his place at the rail.

146. INT   DAY   SACRISTY
         Beame in the sacristy watches.

147. INT   DAY   CHURCH
         Catherine steps forward to kneel at the altar. The next communicant rises, and Alice takes the place beside her mother. Father Tom watches from the corner of his eye. Mrs. Tredoni pushes her way ahead of those waiting and takes the newly vacated place beside Alice. Finishing the row, Father Pat moves back to the right end of the rail. He continues dispensing communion.

         CLOSE UP Father Tom.

                    FATHER TOM
                 (to Father Pat)
            Hurry, Pat.

         Father Pat, bewildered, speeds up. They make their way towards Catherine; she receives the Host. Father Tom tenses as she bows her head. Wanting to be sure she is safe, he remains in front of her. Father Pat, prevented by Father Tom from moving to the next communicant, looks in confusion at his superior. Catherine finishes her prayer and leaves the altar. As the priests move toward Alice, Mrs. Tredoni closes her eyes in preparation for communion. Father Tom passes Alice and moves to Mrs. Tredoni. Alice, anticipating communion, has her mouth open and her eyes closed. Father Pat hangs back, unsure of what to do.

                    FATHER TOM
                 (very gently)
            Mr. Tredoni, I want you to come
            with me.

         Alice's eyes open; she stares in confusion.

                    MRS. TREDONI
                 (eyes widening)
            I want communion, Father.

                    FATHER TOM
                 (intimately and softly)
            I can't give it to you now, Mrs.
            Tredoni. I promised them you'd
            come with me.

         As Captain Beame steps forward for a better view, Mrs. Tredoni's eyes connect with his. People nearby wait, watching uncomfortably. Mrs. Tredoni looks to Father Tom as if to say, "you betrayed me." Her hands drop to the shopping bag. Father Tom, hoping to persuade her, puts his hand on her shoulder.

(147 continued)

                    MRS. TREDONI
                    (enraged)
          You gave it to that whore!

                    FATHER TOM
                    (simultaneously)
          Please come with...

    From out of her shopping bag, the large kitchen knife flashes, piercing the leaning priest's abdomen, once, twice. A woman screams. Stunned, Father Pat drops the chalice which falls over the railing and rolls toward Mrs. Tredoni, who has risen. Alice, frightened, jumps back, screaming for her mother. Father Tom falls to his knees, supporting himself on the railing. Mrs. Tredoni's knife enters the priest's neck as he falls through the gate of the railing. His last images are of the raised sword of St. Michael, the tortured face of Catherine, and the fallen chalice. Beame grabs the knife from Mrs. Tredoni, whose glazed eyes envelop the body of the fallen priest. She drops to her knees, cradling Father Tom. Rocking, she moans quietly.

    The CAMERA DRAWS BACK as Beame gently tries to separate her from the priest.

    The stunned crowd watches. Catherine clings to Alice. Responding to the screams, Spina and the police work their way through the crowd. As the CAMERA continues PULLING BACK; the tableau of death grows smaller and smaller.

                    FADE OUT


Any resemblance to any persons living or dead is purely coincidental.

# Chapter 6
## Analyzing *Alice*

**The style and tone** is evident right from the opening titles—at the right side of the frame, there is animated imagery of a veiled figure clutching an ornate crucifix. The soundtrack, with its eerie theme by Stephen Lawrence, seems indebted to Ennio Morricone's creepy themes for numerous *giallo* films, including Dario Argento's *The Bird with the Crystal Plumage* (*L'uccello dalle piume di cristallo*, 1970); Lawrence has referred to Morricone as one of his models[22], so the link is entirely probable. For Sole's part, he was thinking more along the lines of Bernard Herrmann when giving guidance to Lawrence, though he was also a fan of *Klute* (1971), which has a similar eerie sing-song wordless vocal worked into its music. *Klute*, of course, achieved a level of exposure and "respectability" in the U.S. which was never really attained by these Italian imports, though it, too, seems to have been created out of the same basic creative DNA as the contemporaneous Italian offerings. Interestingly, the use of vocals in the music seems to anticipate some of Pino Donaggio's later scores for Argento and Brian De Palma. Donaggio had scored a triumph with his first film score for Nicolas Roeg's *Don't Look Now* (1973), itself the key inspiration on Sole's film; his lush piano-based score for that film didn't feature any such vocals, however. The overall effect is greatly aided by the presence of a whispering voice saying the Lord's prayer; the pressured delivery conveys the sense of a mind in torment, though it's difficult to ascertain whether it's being spoken by a man or a woman, or a child or an adult—a key part of the film's artful game of deception.

From there, Sole begins to establish the mood and atmosphere while also setting up some of the character dynamics. The plotting by Sole and Ritvo is

---
22. Interview with Stephen Lawrence on the Arrow Blu-ray of *Alice, Sweet Alice*.

clean and elegant. Father Tom (Rudolph Willrich), a handsome and affable young priest, opens his home to his parishioners. Unlike some of the older, more staid and conservative members of the clergy, he is established as being readily accessible and willing to listen without passing moral judgements. On that level, at least, he comes across as positively progressive. His housekeeper, Mrs. Tredoni (Mildred Clinton), is presented as a fairly typical old school Catholic. She dotes on Tom and tries to keep his house and his life orderly and above reproach; his willingness to let people in and to ignore his own needs in order to help them is clearly a source of stress for her, which proves to be key to the narrative. For the time being, however, she seems relatively benign, if somewhat foreboding.

When Catherine Spages (Linda Miller) shows up with her daughters Alice (Paula Sheppard) and Karen (Brooke Shields) in tow, it's clearly off-putting for Mrs. Tredoni. Their intrusion serves to disrupt her orderly way of keeping things and she's barely able to conceal her annoyance, preferring instead to channel her energies into scrubbing the kitchen floor. Tom has no such reservations and he directs much of his attention towards Karen, who is poised to take her first Holy Communion in just a few days. The favoritism displayed towards Karen is plain to see and it's equally plain that Alice resents it bitterly. Her irritation is understandable, in that she is looking for validation and consideration, but Catherine seems more comfortable dealing with the prim and proper Karen as opposed to Alice, who is poised on the brink of young adulthood.

When Alice goes off on her own, ostensibly to use the bathroom, Sole takes his time to show her snooping around the house, which is a shrine of sorts to Catholic iconography. Rather than depict this iconography in warm and inviting terms, Sole makes the icons look sinister and baleful, as they look down dispassionately on the characters. Sole and film editor Edward Salier maximize the creepy effectiveness of the set decorations by isolating various details in fetishistic close-ups.

The first real "scare" occurs when Mrs. Tredoni is surprised by Alice, who has donned a particularly unsettling clear plastic mask with adult-style lipstick and makeup. Alice clearly enjoys getting under the skins of everybody she meets and Mrs. Tredoni responds by calling her a "nasty child." The fuss causes Catherine to erupt: *"Try to act like a lady!"*

It's interesting that while Catherine tends to view her children as children, in certain contexts she's eager to foster the notion that Alice is no longer a child and needs to behave accordingly. In light of subsequent revelations about Alice and the biological changes she's starting to undergo, this admonishment to act like a lady takes on a deeper resonance. Alice is stuck in the symbolic purgatory of adolescence; she has one foot still in childhood, another in young adulthood, and the need for acceptance, validation, and to feel as if she belongs is greater than ever. Catherine is too distracted to recognize this and Alice's social awkwardness ensures that she's going to have a particularly difficult time of it.

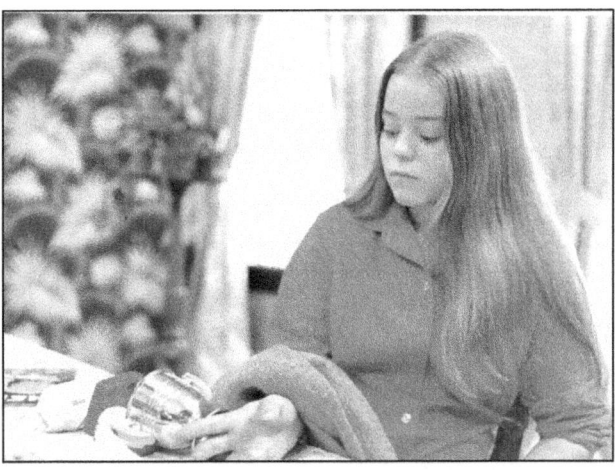

Alice (Paula Sheppard) feels neglected and invalidated throughout the film; she proves to be the ideal red herring.

The use of color is also very striking. Karen is in yellow—or *giallo*, as the case may be. Yellow also carries the connotation of cowardice. Alice is dressed in red—the color associated with sexuality and with violence. It's a great shorthand way of suggesting the dynamic between the two sisters, with Karen as the perpetual victim and Alice as the aggressor.

In these early scenes, Sole does a splendid job of establishing the sense of banal domesticity. The cluttered but orderly world of Father Tom and the small but pristine apartment dwelling of the Spages are loaded with the sort of detail that speak to Sole's background in architecture, but they're precisely the sort of places where bad things never happen. In common with Alfred Hitchcock in *Psycho* (1960, which gets an explicit name check later in the film, when Father Tom walks by a poster for the film) and Roman Polanski in *Rosemary's Baby* (1968), Sole goes to great pains to set his horrors in a demonstrably real environment. Disquieting details abound, especially when the action shifts to certain key locations, but this is as far removed from the fairy tale world of German Expressionism as one can get. Even the Italian *giallo* films are much more overtly artificial by comparison.

And yet, Sole's approach to framing and his use of lenses is anything but naturalistic. The contrast between the bizarre angles and distorted views with the mundane, vaguely run-down settings is key to the film's aesthetic appeal. It's arguably one of the things that appeals to some viewers, while putting off others. Somehow the combination of the urban and the domestic with the skewed stylistic approach makes for a curious marriage, but it's one which is consistently worked throughout the picture. Like it or not, it's most definitely not accidental.

Beneath the air of the placid and the ordinary, violence is never far away. It manifests first on an emotional level, as the Spages' apartment functions as a sort of symbolic pressure cooker. The small space doesn't allow for much in the way of privacy and the relationship between Catherine and her daughters is fraught with tension. Karen is the spoiled child; she's prone to whining when things don't go her way, and she projects an air of virtue and innocence that's absolutely cloying. While she doesn't deserve what fate has in store for her, she's far from a sympathetic character. Alice is admittedly beset with a cruel streak and with a ready-made victim like Karen at her disposal, this leads to plenty of complications. Catherine, whose divorce had made her into a single parent, does the best that she can, but she is ill-equipped to diffuse the situation. She reacts by berating Alice, which only serves to make the child more and more defiant. It also drives a wedge between them, as they're both too stubborn and willful to give an inch where compromise is concerned.

Things come to a head when Alice steals Karen's favorite baby doll. It's typical of Sole's approach that the doll is far from banal: instead, it has a creepy two-faced visage. Turn it one way and it appears to be sleeping; turn it the other and it appears to be smiling. It's a truly bizarre effect, thus making Karen's fixation on it all the more troubling. Of course it's not unusual for siblings to fight; one could even say that it comes with the turf. The Alice/Karen dynamic goes well beyond this, however. Karen sees Alice stealing off to an abandoned warehouse and she follows her there. Sole maximizes the potential for suspense with numerous long takes as Karen makes her way through the maze of dusty, run-down corridors, climaxing with a terrific shock effect when Alice suddenly appears wearing the same mask she had previously used to frighten Mrs. Tredoni. Alice asserts her dominance by promising to destroy the beloved baby doll if Karen tells on her, so the younger sister reluctantly agrees to play along. When the kids return home, Catherine is agitated because Alice disappeared without doing her chores. Alice answers her back, asking why she cares where she gets to: "I'm not Karen!" It's clear that Alice feels unloved and neglected, while pretty little Karen is the apple of everybody's eye. Catherine has no idea how to cope with this and the ensuing shouting match underlines their inability to communicate with one another.

Alice ends up running in to their landlord, Mr. Alphonso (Alphonso DeNoble). The scenes featuring Mr. Alphonso are arguably the most famous in the film. A lot of this is undoubtedly down to the presence of DeNoble himself. Weighing somewhere in the range of 400 to 500 pounds, wearing a wife beater stained with spaghetti sauce and pants clearly stained with urine, and with his eyebrows evidently shaved off, he can't help but make a vivid impression.

The loathsome landlord Mr. Alphonso (Alphonso DeNoble) provides the film with some of its most memorable sequences. Courtesy of Nathaniel Thompson.

Sole first worked with DeNoble in the Fellini-inspired *American Soap*, and DeNoble definitely feels like he would have been at home in the Italian *maestro*'s grotesque fantasy world. He isn't just striking to look at, however. There's also a sick undercurrent of perversity in his interactions with Alice, though it has to be admitted that the interaction is not one-sided. Alice, on the brink of exploring her own nascent sexuality, seems to get a sick charge out of teasing Mr. Alphonso. She's insulting, calling him "fatso" to his face, and making it plainly clear that she's not afraid of him. Alphonso seems to appreciate her feisty demeanor, but he also loathes her acid tongue. The two never miss an opportunity to try and knock the other down a peg or two. She makes fun of his weight and he calls her a "little bitch." Sole's attention to detail in these scenes makes the most of every queasy flourish, from the tinny phonograph music emanating from his old Victrola to the way he dotes on his cats while eating some of the wet food from their can. According to Sole, Alphonso's apartment was the only fabricated location in the film—everything from the tacky wallpaper to the creepy artwork on the walls was selected with an eye towards making it into the ultimate apartment from hell.

Holy Communion provides the film with its central set piece; it's the fulcrum from which the rest of the narrative functions. Sole contrasts the pageantry of the event with grotesque character details. Nowhere is this more evident than in the character of Catherine's sister, Annie (Jane Lowry). She's done up to the nines for the occasion, but the makeup is too heavy and the clothes look cheap. She clearly thinks of herself as being above it all, but these details make it plain that she's no better than anyone else. Crucially, she is also an inveterate gossip and her relationship with Alice is particularly strained. She sits in the pew beside Catherine, with her henpecked and ineffectual husband Jim (Gary Allen) at her side; there's no sense of warmth or love between any of these characters. Annie is a harpy who loves to boss people around. Catherine is trying to hold her head above water. Jim retreats into his own little world, where presumably he isn't constantly being emasculated. The occasion is meant to be a happy and momentous one for any Catholic family, but things soon turn on their ear and everybody will be irrevocably changed as a result.

Sole and Salier make use of cross-cutting in the scene and the contrast between the religious ceremony and the violence erupting behind the scenes can't help but remind one of the famous baptism montage in *The Godfather* (1972). Sole is an admirer of Coppola, so the resemblance is surely intentional. The symbolic violence of Communion—with people eating wafers emblematic of the flesh of Christ and wine which represents His blood—is emphasized by the literal violence of the attack on Karen. We see her struggling with somebody in a yellow rain slicker and an eerie clear plastic mask—the same get-up, in fact, that we've already seen Alice donning earlier in the film. The assailant strangles the child and drags her body across the floor before depositing it inside a chest in one of the empty rooms of the Church; all eyes are on the ceremony unfolding in the main area, and nobody is aware of what is taking place. The killer then deposits a burning candle inside the chest, setting the corpse on fire.

Sole ensures that Alice remains a prime suspect by showing her arriving late; she even finds Kathy's veil on the floor and dons it herself, so that she can go and take Communion. Annie notices Alice at the altar and raises a fuss about it, but Catherine doesn't want to cause a scene and doesn't intervene. Alice's need to feel validated and accepted is one of the key themes in the film. She's rebellious, as most kids of her age tend to be, but she also desperately wants to find some sense of meaning in her life. Alice wants to be doted on by her mother and Father Tom in the same way that they fuss over Karen, but despite her efforts it never goes the way she wants it to. A nun smells the smoke emanating from the back room and discovers Karen's corpse; her shrieks stop the ceremony cold in its tracks, and Alice is denied Communion as a result. It's Annie who goes to see what the commotion is about and one can't help but get the impression that she derives some twisted satisfaction out of being the one to break the news to Catherine; her tears and hysterics feel phony and overwrought for effect, and this is indeed consistent with her reactions throughout the bulk of the picture.

The wake and ensuing funeral are dispensed with economically by Sole. Legendary wrestler Antonino Rocca can be seen callously slinging Karen's coffin into the hearse. It's a touch of black humor that registers whether one is familiar with Rocca or not, though inevitably it carries even more weight if one recognizes him. The funeral also brings Dominick (Niles McMaster), Catherine's former husband and the girls' father, back into the picture. Dominick is established as a kind and caring man, but the complicated social attitudes towards the topic of divorce make him into a kind of a pariah figure. In a typically callous moment, Annie comments, "Well at least he managed to get here before they put her in the ground." In Annie's eyes—and the eyes of so many other parishioners—it's bad enough that he and Catherine got a divorce; the fact that he had the audacity to marry again is tantamount to Original Sin.

Suspicion and veiled accusations begin to manifest as Annie asserts her presence in the household. She tries to come off like she's only there to help, but she does everything in her power to drive the wedge between Catherine and Alice even deeper. She's convinced of Alice's guilt and makes numerous comments to that effect. Alice picks up on it and pushes back against her aunt wherever she can, but she's fighting a losing battle. She's already seen as being

Annie (Jane Lowry) and Jim (Gary Allen) react to the discovery of Karen's body. Courtesy of Nathaniel Thompson.

"weird," and as an outsider that makes it even more difficult for her to establish her innocence. Through it all, Dominick remains convinced of her innocence. Catherine is more ambivalent, though she continues to try and mend the fences so that she can win back Alice's trust.

The wake is rife with touches of grim humor, with visiting relatives taking advantage of the food and booze on display while putting on an air of grief and contrition. Annie continues to dig her claws in more deeply and she volunteers to stay with Catherine while she tries to readjust to a new life without Karen. Alice resents her presence and the resentment is mutual. The tension between the two characters is beautifully conveyed by the actors as well as Sole's expert use of framing; shots of Annie glaring in Alice's direction, unbeknownst to Catherine who has her back to her, make it clear that she intends to do what she can to "expose" Alice. The harder Annie tries to make herself useful, the more obnoxious she becomes.

Catherine sends Alice down to Mr. Alphonso's apartment. One doesn't get the impression that he's fond of ever leaving his disheveled apartment, but he

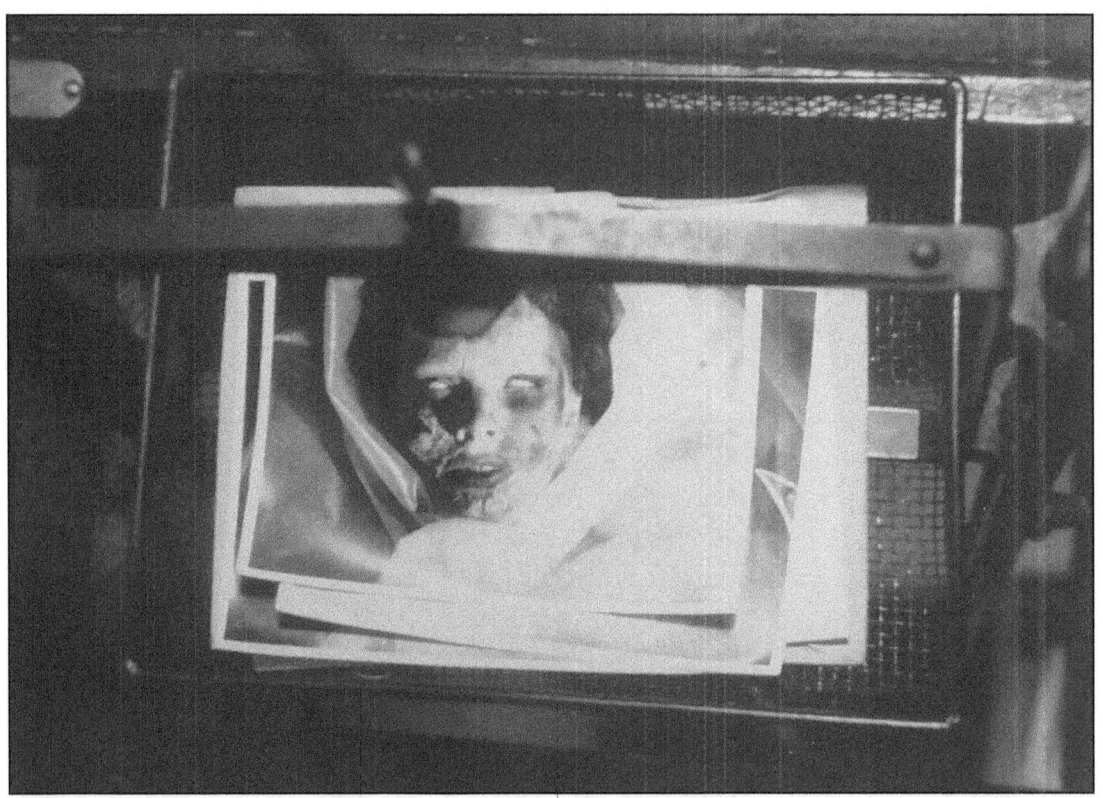

The horrific burn make-up on Karen (Brooke Shields) is glimpsed only briefly via this forensic photograph.

made the token gesture of sending flowers to the funeral, so Catherine wants him to have some leftover cake. Here again, Paula Sheppard as Alice and Alphonso DeNoble as Alphonso are in their elements. Alice makes no attempt to conceal her disgust for Alphonso, and he delights in being perversely inappropriate towards her. His callousness really comes to the foreground when he observes, "God always takes the pretty ones." There's nothing remotely sympathetic about Alphonso, and DeNoble is to be commended to committing to such a loathsome characterization. The fact that these two characters can't stand each other and openly wish each other dead gives their scenes a raw emotional intensity.

The scenes detailing the police investigation are undoubtedly the least successful in the film. It's not that the scenes are poorly done; far from it. Instead, they feel like a concession to the conventional in an otherwise very unconventional narrative. They're necessary on one level, but they seldom rise above the pedestrian. Fortunately, Sole knows better than to dwell on these scenes for too long, and even here he allows himself the occasional stylistic flourish. For example, the opening of the first major scene at the police station is a great example of Sole making use of a practical location for a specific effect. There's a shot of Alice's charred visage, courtesy of a black and white police photograph, and Sole shows us this gruesome image bathed in a hellish red light. The picture is in a tray which is lowered down to one of the offices on another floor by way of a sort of dumbwaiter system. According to Sole, this was a happy accident of sorts and he got the idea for the shot when he saw this system being utilized at the Paterson Police Department, where he was permitted to film these scenes.

Detectives Brennan (Tom Signorelli) and Spina (Michael Hardstark) aren't terribly well-delineated, but on a certain level they don't really need to be. They're there to advance the plot and to help keep the narrative grounded to some extent in reality. Their inner conflicts and personality quirks don't particularly matter in this context and Sole doesn't make much of an attempt to humanize them. They're cold and resolved to do their job as dispassionately as possible, which is perfectly in keeping with protocol, but which doesn't make them terribly engaging as screen presences. They soon come into conflict with Catherine and Dominick, and the latter eventually decides to launch his own investigation.

When Alice goes to see Mr. Alphonso with the rent check, things escalate even further. She taunts the landlord and defiantly teases him. He picks up on this and sets her off by saying he believes Annie to be correct about Alice being a killer. Alice destroys the check and Alphonso lurches towards her like a monster, pinning her against the wall and trying to kiss her. The implications

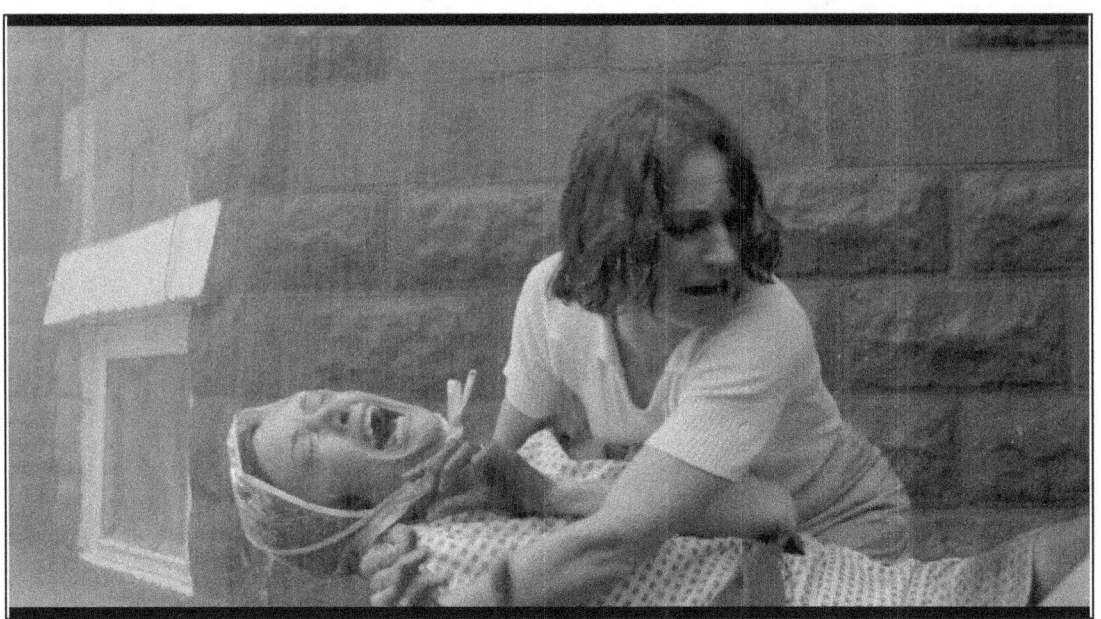

The aftermath of the attempt on Annie's (Jane Lowry) life; Catherine (Linda Miller) screams for help in the pouring rain. Courtesy of Nathaniel Thompson.

of pedophilia are far from subtle and add a skin-crawling dimension to the sequence. Alice frees herself by grabbing one of Alphonso's kittens and sadistically flinging it to the floor. Some viewers have taken exception to this scene, less for its implicit pedophilia (it pays to remember that Sheppard was 18 at the time of filming) than for its animal cruelty. While it's clear that Sheppard roughly grabs a real kitten by its neck, there's nothing to support any contention that any animal cruelty was utilized in creating the scene; she throws the kitten out of frame, where a crew member caught it, and the confrontation ends with Alphonso wailing off camera that she has killed his cat. It's a disturbing scene, no question, but it's less about what Sole shows and more about what he conveys in a very artful fashion. Even so, this didn't stop the British censor from removing several seconds from this sequence; it's only in recent years that the uncut version was finally passed by the British Board of Film Censors.

When Annie heads out on some errands, she's surprised in the stairwell by the same figure in the yellow slicker and the clear plastic mask. Sole plays the scene for maximum physical impact by emphasizing sudden quick cuts in the editing as the assailant stabs Annie in the thigh and then in the foot. While Sole wasn't directly inspired by Dario Argento, one is reminded of the painful murder scenes in *Deep Red* (*Profondo rosso*, 1975), which filmed a year prior to this film. The emphasis on tactile physical things which can elicit a sympathetic response in the viewer is much the same in both films—and indeed, there's an even more similar bit of violent mayhem in store, as well. Annie's hysterical response, as she drags herself into the pouring rain and screams for help, provides the perfect capper; the assailant runs off, but between Annie's histrionic accusations and Alphonso glimpsing the attacker's get-up, already associated with Alice, ensures that both characters are going to get their wish by getting the child into serious trouble.

Alice soon falls under suspicion and when Spina gets hold of her records from school, they discover that she has a history of emotional disturbance. This is sufficient for them to arrange to have Alice put into an institution, where she'll undergo a comprehensive psychological evaluation. Alice regards this as a betrayal and aims her anger towards her mother; her absent father seems to have a better rapport with her and it's in their interactions that the audience sees the softer, more vulnerable side of her personality.

Catherine tries to compel Annie, still recuperating in hospital, into recanting her accusation, but Annie plays the pious victim to perfection and refuses to acknowledge the possibility that it could be anybody other than Alice. Despite her own fraught relationship with her daughter, Catherine recognizes how unfairly Alice is being treated. "People believe what they want to believe," she cries. Of course, she's absolutely correct. Alice is automatically pegged as the likely perpetrator because she has a reputation for being troubled. She fits the bill to perfection and that's quite sufficient where society at large is concerned. Probably the most telling bit of dialogue occurs when Catherine accuses Annie of hating Alice because Catherine was pregnant with Alice before she got married. Annie denies it, of course, but given her holier-than-thou attitude towards Dominick and her obvious antipathy for Alice, it's clearly accurate. Sole's criticism of Catholicism—at least in the hands of the wrong people—is evident throughout the film. In exchanges such as this, it makes it clear that, from his perspective, the emotional and physical violence which permeate the film arise out of a fundamentally twisted and corrupt form of dogma. Religion, in its worst form, is therefore at the heart of the film's dialogue about hypocrisy, intolerance, and violence. The suppression of natural urges regarding sexuality can therefore lead to explosive consequences.

The scene of Alice being brought into the police station for a lie detector test is one of the film's highlights. Sole emphasizes her confusion and disorientation as he quickly cuts from point of view shots to objective shots, utilizing rapid dolly movements as she's led through the cold, foreboding police station. The ensuing test is played for a mixture of suspense and grim humor as she denies involvement in the murder of Karen and the attack on Annie; the results seem to confirm her innocence, but the water is muddied by her claim that Karen attacked Annie. It's interesting that both children had matching rain slickers, and both were seen wearing similar plastic masks at one point or other, thus adding to the air of paranoia and the deceptive nature of appearances. Alphonso and Annie are convinced it was Alice because of this get-up, while Alice is equally sure that Karen has come back from the dead. Taking things at face value and not questioning the veracity of what they see ensures that all three characters are led down the wrong path.

Alice's burgeoning womanhood is also brought into play here. The man administering the lie detector test smugly tells Spina, "Did you notice her tits? When I went to put the tube around her, she looked up at me like she wanted me to feel her up." The casual sexism and misogyny of their exchange speaks volumes about their characters, as well as the unfair way Alice is being judged by people in authority. As a twelve-year-old transitioning into young adulthood, Alice is already undergoing significant emotional and psychological changes; the male authority figures use this as justification to suggest that she is sufficiently unbalanced to be capable of acts of extreme violence. Alice gets the last laugh by pushing the lie detector machine off the table and smashing it to bits, thus providing a satisfying comic coda to the sequence.

Dominick's role as an amateur sleuth is another area that connects the film into the *giallo* genre, but in fairness this is also typical of Hitchcock's work, as well. It was Hitchcock who famously said that the characters in his films didn't go to the police because the police are boring. Spina and Brennan definitely validate this thesis. Dominick, conflicted over his renewed feelings for Catherine and grieving the loss of his daughter, adopts the role of hero in a film that is totally lacking in heroic types. It's typical of Sole's subversion of expectations, however, that he will not prove to be capable of overcoming the insanity that has thrown his world into disarray.

Having failed her lie detector test, Alice is shuttled off to a clinic where she undergoes a comprehensive psychological evaluation. She resents being displaced and removed from her home, but Catherine and Dominick explain that they are powerless to do anything about it. The psychiatrist on staff, Dr. Whitman (Louisa Horton), is depicted as competent but unduly set in her ways. She doesn't seem to fully grasp the complexity of their familial situation and her diagnosis suffers accordingly. Based on the results of her tests, she feels that Alice is better off in their facility and advocates to keep her there. The unraveling of the family unit is more-or-less unstoppable and Dominick's determination to uncover the truth seems to be the only potential source of salvation.

Dominick (Niles McMaster) and Catherine (Linda Miller) meet with the psychiatrist Dr. Whitman (Louisa Horton). Courtesy of Nathaniel Thompson.

The most interesting revelation made by Dr. Whitman is that Alice has begun menstruating. Catherine is shocked, because in her mind, Alice is perpetually a child. She's not prepared for her transition into young adulthood. It's not enough that Alice is already dealing with the difficulties inherent in a dysfunctional family environment, she's also coping with the realization that her body and her own sense of self are undergoing changes. This is a challenging period of time for all young people and without the understanding and support of a loving family, she has a particularly difficult time of it. It's not that Catherine doesn't love her or that she's a bad mother; as in so many areas, she's simply overwhelmed and ill-equipped to deal with the reality of the situation. She feels hurt that Alice hasn't shared this news with her, but even here she misses the point: Alice didn't share it with her because she didn't feel her mother would be interested, focused as she always is on Karen's every want and need. In spoiling Karen and ignoring Alice, Catherine has helped to create an extremely volatile family dynamic.

Sole's love of *Don't Look Now* is evident throughout, but it is particularly evident in the relationship between Dominick and Catherine. In Roeg's film, John (Donald Sutherland) and Laura (Julie Christie) undergo marital crisis following the death of their daughter; shortly before tragedy strikes again, they manage to rekindle their passion and unite as a more deeply committed couple. Much the same is destined to happen here, as well.

Deleted scene featuring Dominick (Niles McMaster) and Catherine (Linda Miller) coming to grips with their feelings.

Their temporary idyll is interrupted by a series of phone calls: the first two are from the killer, who breathes heavily into the receiver without saying a word. This is a familiar trope in thrillers in general, but it certainly also evokes the *gialli* of the period, notably the "Telephone" segment of Bava's *Black Sabbath* (*I tre volti della paura*, 1963) and Argento's *The Bird with the Crystal Plumage*. It also calls to mind the obscene phone calls of Bob Clark's proto-slasher *Black Christmas* (1974). The third call is the most jarring, in that it comes from Dominick's unseen "new" wife. Dominick came back to Paterson having settled into a comfortable new life, but the stress of Karen's murder and his attempts to shield Alice from being blamed for it has helped to bring him and Catherine back together. They yield to temptation by kissing, but the phone call disrupts the possibility of anything else happening. It brings Dominick back to earth and reminds Catherine of how impractical a reconciliation is under the circumstances. It's a lovely, tender little scene in a movie that isn't exactly overflowing with such moments. It helps to vary the emotional tone of the piece, for at least a brief interlude, but it is too late for it to affect a permanent change.

Another phone call sends Dominick on a fateful journey. It supposedly comes from Annie's daughter, who is confessing to having attacked her mother, but Sole tips the audience that this information is not to be trusted. Dominick, desperate to clear Alice and restore some stability to the shattered family unit, rushes off to meet her in an abandoned warehouse—the same one we already saw Alice threatening Karen in earlier in the picture. By this stage, it's clear enough that Alice cannot be to blame. She's still locked away in the institution, undergoing psychological evaluation, and Dominick is convinced that he's been successful in his mission.

Throughout the film, Sole and editor Edward Salier utilize a variety of clever techniques to ratchet the tension. For example, they will often transition from loud, almost operatic scenes of violence or heightened emotion to comparatively quiet moments; it's a technique that William Friedkin used to nerve-shredding effect in *The Exorcist* (1973). Sole also does a terrific job of lulling the viewer

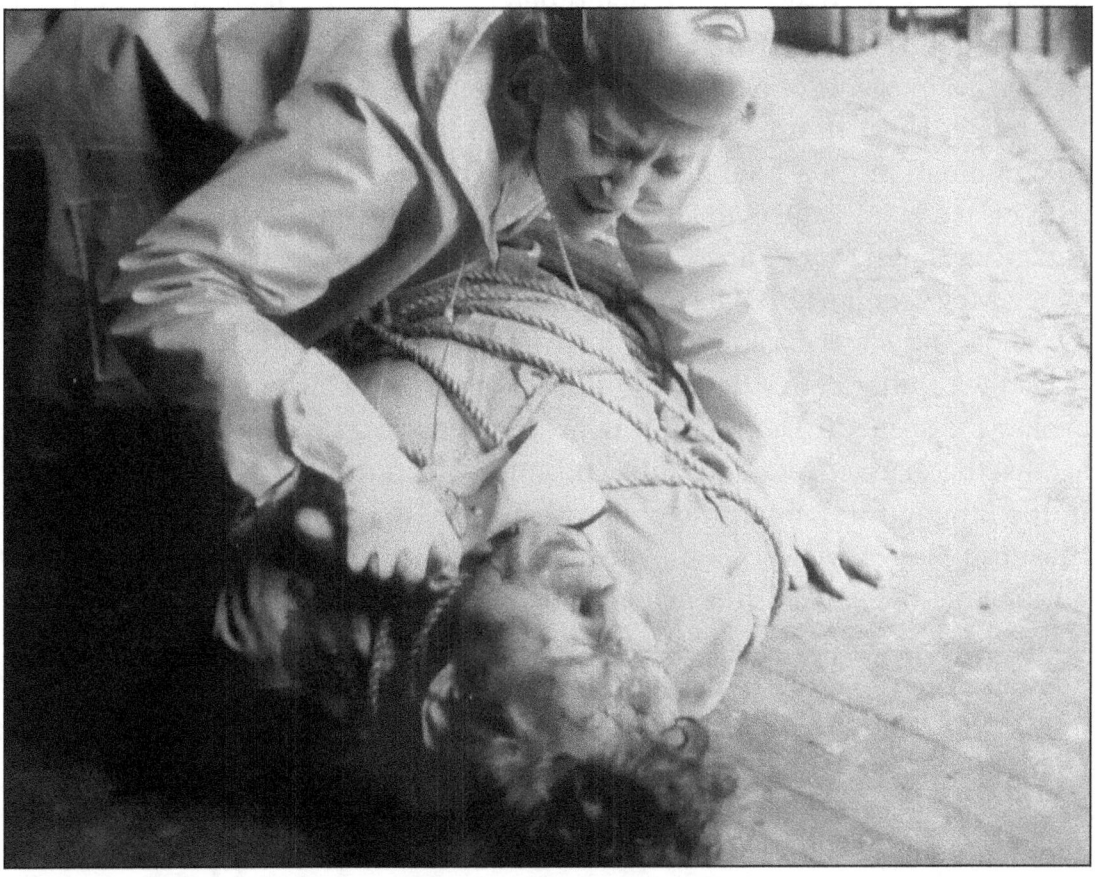

Dominick (Niles McMaster) discovers that Mrs. Tredoni (Mildred Clinton) is the killer, but he doesn't live to tell anyone about it.

into a state of protracted unease by building suspense through lengthy build-ups followed by sudden bursts of violence. Nowhere is this more evident than in Dominick's journey to the warehouse. The sunny, bucolic exteriors create an atmosphere in which nothing can possibly go awry; once Dominick enters the crumbling, shadowy building, the general feel of the scene begins to change, darkening on both a literal and a symbolic level. He has been established as a sincere and decent person and his attempt to clear Alice is truly selfless; he's not doing it for the sake of the family name or to prove something to the former relatives who now despise him. He simply loves his daughter and he believes in her. This makes what happens all the more heartbreaking. After being attacked and stabbed in the arm in the stairwell, Dominick finds the yellow raincoat-clad assailant in one of the lofts and tries to assure the figure that everything is OK. Far from being OK, the assailant suddenly lunges with a brick and smashes Dominick in the head. As the killer binds Dominick with a rope and begins to drag him towards his certain doom, the truth comes out. The killer is unmasked, literally and figuratively, as Mrs. Tredoni. Dominick pleads for his life, but it is too no avail. Crazed and determined to finish what she's started, Mrs. Tredoni lets loose with a diatribe about punishing sinners; Dominick and Catherine, by virtue of being divorced, are rendered into monsters in her eyes. Her religious beliefs are so extreme and conservative that she regards them as an abomination. In a final heroic gesture, Dominick gets hold of her crucifix with his teeth and refuses to let it go—in fact, it is the same crucifix Father Tom had given Karen for her first Holy Communion, so it is a particularly vital clue. When Mrs. Tredoni is unable to get Dominick to let go of the cross, she removes her shoe and starts bashing him in the teeth. It's a genuinely painful scene, played with utter conviction by both McMaster and Clinton, and it definitely evokes the scene in *Deep Red* in which one character has his teeth shattered against the sharp edges of a mantle and a desk. It's one of the most brutal scenes in the film and it's one of the scenes that upset the more conservative critics the most. Many reviewers complained of the excessive violence and bloodshed, but as Sole recognized, the playing field had changed by the mid-70s, and it was necessary to stay ahead of the competition by going for broke where possible. The violence is not gratuitous, however. Indeed, with all the emphasis on Catholicism, the murder scenes take on an almost ritualistic significance. In trying to protect his daughter and shore up a hopelessly dysfunctional family unit, Dominick puts himself in danger and pays the ultimate price. Enraged after failing to get the crucifix out of his mouth, Mrs. Tredoni pushes him out the loft window and he falls to his death, hitting the ground with a sickening thud. It's a simple but convincing effect, perfectly captured by Sole and his

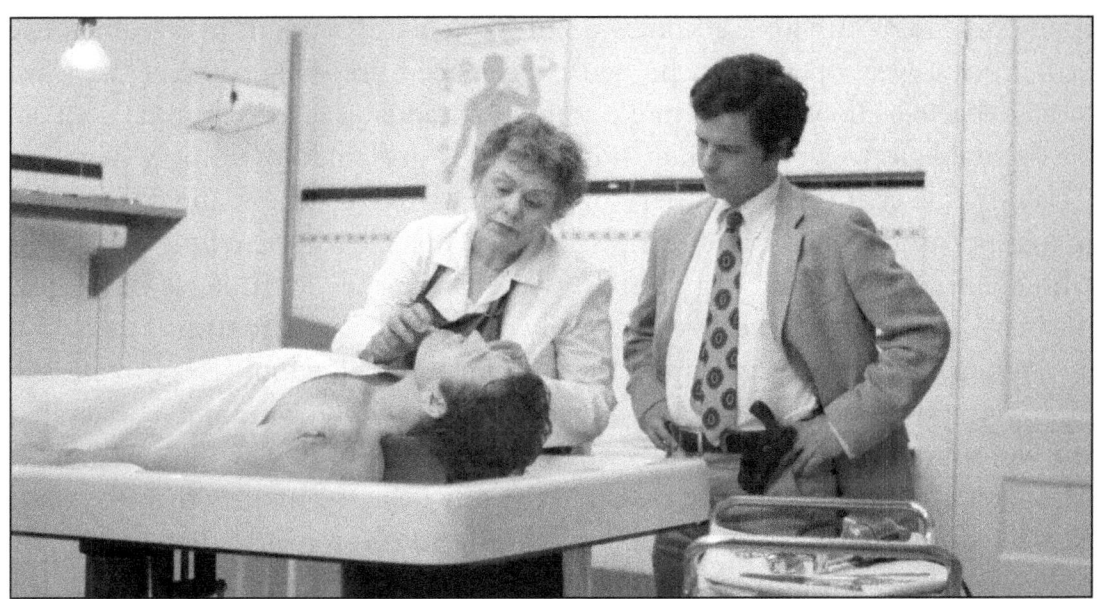

The pathologist (Lillian Roth) and Detective Spina (Michael Hardstark) examine Dominick's corpse. Courtesy of Nathaniel Thompson.

cameraman (whichever cameraman it was by this stage in the filming; by Sole's own admission, he burned through quite a few), as the audience sees a dummy fall from the window, the sight caught in the reflection of a piece of broken mirror, with the climax performed by McMaster himself as he wrenches back into frame as if he's hitting the ground at full impact.

The police soon find Dominick's body and the police pathologist (Lillian Roth) is able to provide a time of death which completely exonerates Alice of any possible role in the murder. Roth's appearance—for which she got a special credit as "Miss" Lillian Roth—marked her first time on cinema screens in many years; the role frankly doesn't give her much to do, but she still performs with the gravitas and dignity of an experience professional.

Mrs. Tredoni, meanwhile, goes to confession. Fittingly, she turns to Father Tom. Despite the secrecy of the confessional, he recognizes her voice and assures her that the minor sins she confesses (including anger towards an enfeebled employer and forgetting to say her morning prayers) are nothing for her to feel so troubled about. Mrs. Tredoni is insane, of course, but she's also a hypocrite. She hides behind the sanctity of her faith, using it as justification to commit horrible acts of violence, but she accepts no real accountability for these actions. She has the opportunity to confess and atone, but in her mind her real transgressions aren't the murders of Karen and Dominick or the attempted murder of Annie; on that level, she feels as if she's doing God's work. Here again, Sole's issues with Catholicism and the sort of fervent, overzealous use of faith as a weapon—which he had experienced first-hand during the *Deep Sleep* debacle—allows him to make some pointed jabs at the Church. Even so, it's debatable as to whether the Church itself is presented as entirely negative. Certainly the character of Father Tom comes across as decent and progressive in his approach. Instead, it's the old school zealots like Mrs. Tredoni—the types who spend every Sunday in church, while getting up to all sorts of terrible business the rest of the week—who really come in for his criticism.

When Catherine shows up at Father Tom's, Mrs. Tredoni feels threatened. She continues to resent Catherine's presence in Father Tom's life and worries that she will somehow take him away from her. In a delightfully awkward exchange, Mrs. Tredoni unveils her motivation to the unwitting woman. It turns out that Mrs. Tredoni once had a daughter and that she, like Karen, also died on the day of her first Holy Communion. In her twisted, fanatical mind, the death of her daughter served as a lesson from God. "He waited until then to teach me that children pay for the sins of their parents." Catherine is too trusting and naïve to understand what she's saying, but the rationale is clear enough: Karen is made to pay for the dissolution of Catherine and Dominick's marriage, and they, too, will pay for going against God's will. Mrs. Tredoni is the classic murder "type" in this sort of thriller. As an apparently mild—if spiky—old lady, she seems to be immediately above suspicion. This enables her to move about undetected, and the plodding police are slow to pick up on her erratic behavior, as well. It never even occurs to Catherine to regard her as a possible suspect; her life is falling apart, with the deaths of her daughter and her estranged husband, and not even a symbolic confession from the killer is enough to shock her into a state of awareness.

From there, the pace tightens considerably as Sole moves towards the film's operatic climax. Mrs. Tredoni decides to try and remove Catherine from the equation, but her plan is foiled by the sudden return of Alice. It's perhaps symptomatic of Alice's state of mind that her first action upon being returned to her home is to play a cruel prank on Mr. Alphonso. She slips into the landlord's apartment while he's snoring on the couch and deposits a jar of cockroaches on his stomach; the jar tips over and Alphonso awakens, shrieking as the bugs crawl all over him. Mrs. Tredoni is frightened by the commotion and tries to escape, but Alphonso catches her in the hall and, thinking it to be Alice, tries to stop her; he pays for his mistake by being knifed to death. The murder of Alphonso is painfully awkward, and the final flourish of having him knock over his fishbowl, with the blood from his arm dripping into the clear water, is positively inspired. Alice has gotten her revenge on the man who helped to put her into the institution, but of course that wasn't at all what she had in mind.

Mrs. Tredoni flees back to the church, where Father Tom is about to perform Communion. By this point, the police are on to her and they enlist Tom to help bring her in. Tom believes that he can reason with Mrs. Tredoni, so he rejects Detective Spina's offer to put a sharp shooter inside the church. Father Tom isn't an arrogant man but, like Catherine, he is much too trusting. He believes that, with his history with Mrs. Tredoni, he understands her and what makes her tick. Unfortunately for him, he underestimates just how profoundly disturbed she really is.

Mrs. Tredoni (Mildred Clinton) is not to be trifled with—or underestimated.

Alice once again arrives late, looking to partake in Communion. It's a delicious irony of sorts that she is once more passed over when Tom speeds things along in order to get to Mrs. Tredoni. Through it all, Alice has remained the ultimate red herring—her psychological problems and inability to fit in make her the perfect "misfit," but despite her capacity for cruelty, she really just wants to be validated. As a Catholic, participating in Communion has a special resonance for her; but for the second time in the narrative, she is denied this little bit of solace.

Mrs. Tredoni is also denied Communion, but her reaction goes beyond the disappointment of Alice. She explodes in a rage, saying that Tom gave it to "that whore," while gesturing towards Catherine. Determined to keep Tom for herself, Mrs. Tredoni stabs him in the throat with her butcher knife. The stabbing is brutal and bloody, and the congregation explodes into hysterics as the police swarm in to surround Mrs. Tredoni. She's too far gone to care about what happens to her; instead, she cradles Father Tom in her arms, suggesting a sick parody of the *Pietá*. Father Tom's inability to correctly "read" Mrs. Tredoni puts him in the same category as Dominick, and the two would-be heroes end up brutally murdered, leaving the plodding policemen to come in and clean up the mess.

The final, ironic image is of Alice as she staggers towards the camera, apparently in a daze over what she's just witnessed. She's clutching Mrs. Tredoni's bag—and she withdraws the bloody butcher knife. The theme of

Mexican lobby card; the title translates roughly as "The Mask of Crime"— a bit bland as titles go.

violence and sin as a sort of familial disease which is passed on from generation to generation gets its final fitting realization as Sole focuses in on Alice's blank, passive expression. We don't know what will become of her or how this will affect her, but Sole makes it plain enough: Alice is not going to come through this unscathed. The cyclical nature of violence is destined to continue, with Alice as its latest psychologically-scarred casualty.

Whether one calls the film *Communion* or *Alice, Sweet Alice* or *Holy Terror*, there's no doubt it remains one of the key horror-thrillers of its vintage. Sole's comparative lack of directing experience never betrays itself. While some critics would lambast his use of symbolism, these same critics would likely have been overjoyed if the same exact symbolism had been served up by one of their canon of established arthouse *auteurs*.

Quite simply, Sole's remarkable achievement fell victim to good old-fashioned snobbery in most sectors. Without the benefit of a major "name" in the cast or a back catalogue of "respectable" work for Sole to point to, the film seemed to arrive out of thin air; sooner than embrace it for what it managed to achieve on such meager resources, many of the mainstream critics turned up their noses and dismissed it as yet another disposable "B" movie. Careful and attentive viewing reveals a film of remarkable intelligence and surprising assuredness. Only in some of the bland investigatory scenes does that pace slacken; elsewhere, Sole manages to keep things remarkably gripping throughout. Its shock sequences have lost none of their power, its observations about repression and religious hypocrisy remain as timely as ever, and the performances, ranging from the pleasantly understated to the borderline baroque, perfectly serve the material. If there is a tragedy in all of this, it's that Alfred Sole and Rosemary Ritvo were deprived of the opportunity to deliver on its promise; but at the very least they were able to capture lightning in a bottle at least once—and that's more than can be said of many filmmakers.

# Chapter 7
## What the Critics Said

**Like so many films** now regarded as classics, *Alice, Sweet Alice* didn't generate widespread acclaim when it started to stagger into theaters in November of 1976. At best, the most "sympathetic" reviewers praised aspects while damning the film for being a "mere" genre effort. At worst, the least sympathetic critics took offense to its then-shocking violence and condemned it as sheer brain dead sensationalism. In order to get a better idea of how the film was received, we've rounded up as many then-contemporary critiques as we could lay our hands on.

These reviews have been faithfully transcribed, save for edits where deemed appropriate, so all spelling errors are reproduced as originally published.

> *Variety*'s "Coli," caught the film at the September 8, 1977 screening in London; the review in the September 21 edition was very enthusiastic:
>
> By any standards, Communion is quintessential American filmmaking: entertaining, intelligent, and derivative. Alfred Sole's third feature (the first entitled *Deep Sleep* ran afoul of the British censor and the second, *American Soap*, awaits release[23]) is an inspired homage to Hitchcock that should gain him the attention he deserves.
>
> The film was independently produced by Richard K. Rosenberg, shot on location in Paterson, New Jersey, using a talented cast drawn from the stage and television. With the right marketing it should be solid. […]

---

23. This appears to have been the only mainstream reference to *American Soap*, which was never released in any form.

As the pic borrows selected elements from the demonology genre—Catholic iconography and an evil incarnate child—at the start it seems as if Sole intends to resurrect the *Exorcist* formula. But the film soon acknowledges its Hitchcockian inspiration and sets about shocking and teasing the audience in a manner worthy of the master.

In fact, *Communion* almost seems like a project slyly constructed to endorse prevalent French theories about "Catholic guilt" being Hitchcock's most persistent thematic concern.

Be that or not, it's certainly an impressive feature on a multitude of levels. Rosemary Ritvo's and Sole's script brilliantly psychoanalyzes a family's inter-relationships—the jealousy between sisters, the bond between mother and child, etc.—through the immediacy of a tight, suspenseful search for a butcher-knife assassin. And in the process deliver some detailed criticisms of absolute beliefs whether they be religiously, socially, or familiarly rooted.

The gory setpieces (the initial killing, the father's protracted death in an abandoned warehouse, and the stabbing of the family's grotesquely obese landlord, Mr. Alphonso) are all frighteningly conveyed and realized.

Sole was born and raised in Paterson and it's evident that he used his native familiarity when selecting locations or detailing specific characters, like the rectory housekeeper, Mrs. Tradoni, well played by Mildred Clinton.

But what's even more obvious is his innate sense of cinema and direction. The way in which his camera tracks rather than zooms, his evocative composition, and unexpected cutting all contribute to the film's disturbing ambience and progression. Only in the portrayal of Mr. Alphonso does his touch (and script) falter. [...]

In producer Richard K. Rosenberg Sole has found an admirable partner. It must be to his credit that *Communion*, as a completely independent production, has no rough edges.

Barbara Klein's write-up in *The News*, dated November 15, 1977, was generally positive and may well have had Sole and company cautiously optimistic about their chances:

*Communion*, which premiered here Saturday, is a suspenseful, slightly long thriller. It includes several knifings and blood—thus, an R rating. But, if horror is your bag, *Communion* is a movie you'll want to see.

The story is about murder, murder and more murder. [...] The filming of these scarey [sic] events proves to be director Alfred Sole's finest work. I skimmed through the script of *Communion* when it first went into production, so I knew who was good, bad and ugly and what they were up to. Still, the flawless set-up of the film's most moving scenes sent me slightly out of my seat.

Stephen Lawrence's music is very good. The special effects are excellent.

A particularly impressive performance is given by Paula Sheppard, making her acting debut in *Communion*. She's actually a college student. She plays a 12-year old.

Mildred Clinton, who appeared in the film *Serpico* and does a lot of television work, is perfect in the part of Mrs. Trudoni, a rectory housekeeper.

*Communion* could be improved with editing. Some of the dialogue is dull. A long, languid love scene is unnecessary. Indulgence in "arty" photography slows down the 110 minute film.

The time setting of the story—1961—puzzled me. Why not today?

Also, a clarification of the close relationship between Father Tom, played by Rudolph Willrich, and Katherine Spages, played by Linda Miller, would be appropriate early in the film. He could be her brother, a former neighbor, or family friend. No explanation is offered.

With a relatively small budget, Alfred Sole has fashioned a good mystery movie from a screenplay written by him and another Patersonian, Rosemary Ritvo. It's a film that begins simply and builds to an intriguing climax.

*Communion* probably won't be widely distributed until next year. Thriller fans have something to look forward to.

Bill Brownstein, writing in the November 19, 1977, issue of the *Montreal Gazette* was mightily impressed:

Many have tried, but few have been successful in achieving abject horror recently.

> Someone like Steven Spielberg seizes upon the terror of sharks lurking in seemingly placid bodies of water in *Jaws*—and countless other directors try the same formula until it is watered down to

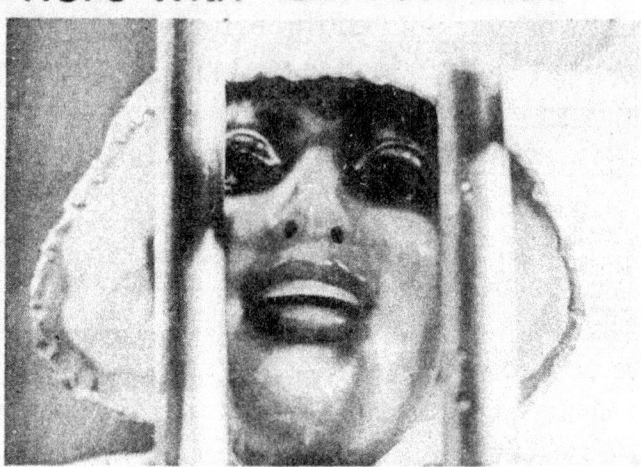

The November 19, 1977 edition of the *Montreal Gazette*, featuring an article about Alfred Sole.

the extent that it raises nary a sigh from even the most squeamish. Similarly, the supernatural and demonic element worked well in *The Exorcist*, but ensuing copies succeeded more as sedatives than anything else.

But Alfred Sole's *Alice, Sweet Alice* comes as a surprise—a gory and effective one at that. Without relying on snacking sharks or monster squids or devilish and invisible demons, Sole succeeds in terrifying you.

It would be grossly unfair to delve into the plot other than to mention that it deals with a New Jersey Italian Catholic family whose youngest daughter is murdered on her first communion. This triggers off a series of bizarre and bloody events.

Sole's innovative use of a wide angle lens throughout—which gives an eerie and slightly distorted effect when it is close up—and an excellent job of editing combine to elicit the maximum in suspense. Like Hitchcock's *Psycho* and unlike many other films, pain inflicted upon the victims is also felt by the audience.

The actors, most of whom are unknown, add another dimension of fear because you don't associate them with previous screen images—hence, they're totally unpredictable.

*Alice, Sweet Alice* does have its rough edges. The story line has gaps, and inconsistencies do crop up. Also given the $400,000 budget, there are occasional problems with the sound and color reproduction. None of this, however, detracts very much, and the film is more likely than not to leave you numb.

A word of caution to the faint of heart. Enough blood is spilled in *Alice, Sweet Alice* to keep a Red Cross blood bank going for a year.

Bill von Mauer's 19 November, 1977, write up in *The Miami News* was far more condescending—and he even tried to tip the audience off to the murderer's identity, in addition to some other spoilers; talk about a spoiled sport!

Alice, you have to admit, is a little strange, even schizoid, says Lillian Roth who plays a child psychologist in the movie *Alice, Sweet Alice*, but is she the one who is going around carving everybody up with a butcher knife?

Was it Alice, only 14, who killed her younger sister Karen on confirmation day and dragged her body into a chest during the ceremony and threw a lighted candle after it, but not before she snatched the cross from around the dead girl's neck. [...]

And then when Alice's daddy is carved up and tossed off the top of an abandoned warehouse, it looks bad again for Alice, particularly in the eyes of her Aunt Annie, who suspects her of just about everything.

Then when the 300-pound building superintendent of the apartment house where Alice lives gets it in the stomach with another knife you get to pondering about Alice once more and wondering if she's being naughty again. [...]

The most interesting thing about this movie is the chance to get a first look at Brooke Shields (Karen), the 12-year old beauty who plays a controversial nude scene in the upcoming movie *Pretty Baby*. The rest of the movie is murder. But keep your eye on Father Tom's housekeeper.

William Whitaker, in his November 20, 1977 write up in *Abilene Reporter News*, adopted the familiar attitude of "it's pretty good—for this sort of a thing," but at least he was a lot more enthusiastic than some:

Beastly brats, avenging angels of death and lots of blood are in the offering in Alfred Sole's production of *Alice, Sweet Alice*—and actually, it's not a bad little flick.

The blood and gore get to be too much after a while, but the script has enough imagination and the direction enough insight to make it passable fare as far as these kinds of films go.

Sole, who had a hand in the writing of the script in addition to serving as director here, shows a lot of promise for the future should someone eventually invest some time and money in him. Besides just telling a horror story, *Alice, Sweet Alice* is loaded with all sorts of subtle hints—never insisted upon, but always suggested. [...]

Sole leaves subtle, sometime symbolic hints all over the place as he goes along the way. As the mother of the daughter is getting off the bus, the camera concentrates on the lettering on the bus steps: *watch your step*.

Also interesting is the irony how communion—which the nasty young girl continually seeks—always eludes her, right until the blood-drenched ending. This becomes especially significant when you know the circumstances surrounding Alice and the rest of the characters.

And then, there's the shuddery scene where the murder, talking to an intended victim, slices up a fish—a powerful symbol of Christianity—as she hints of vengeance for the evil the victim has allegedly committed.

It must be admitted, however, that the film is not completely successful, but it's not bad for the genre. Many of the imaginative camera angles turn out to be too mechanical to be effective, and the dialogue—particularly in the beginning of the film when things need to be set up—could use some work.

The cast is largely an unknown one, though most are competent. The real credit for the picture's good points, however, must go to Sole.

Much the same attitude is evident in Daniel Ruth's critique in the November 21, 1977 edition of the *Tampa Tribune*; it's a commentary on the film's delayed release that Sole and Ritvo are accused of swiping elements from Brian De Palma's *Carrie* (1976) and Robert Wise's *Audrey Rose* (1977), both of which premiered well after production wrapped in 1975:

It is hard to tell whether *Alice, Sweet Alice* is a thriller murder mystery or a subtle promotional campaign for blood donations. The stuff is flowing in almost every scene.

It is also quite clear that the Catholic Church seems to be going through a bad time in the movies these days.

Most recently we had *Nasty Habits*, a terrible satire on Watergate that takes place in a convent. *The Kentucky Fried Movie* also takes its swipes at the church and now *Alice, Sweet Alice* revolves about rectory intrigue as its numerous characters meet their deaths at the point of huge kitchen knives.

Actually, the film is not all that bad. Screenwriters Rosemary Ritvo and Alfred Sole have given us a tight, well-paced melodrama that keeps its audience guessing as to who the murderer is until the last possible moment, leading us down several trails until the film's tense climax.

Sole also directed the film and has done a credible job, although he employs the usual gimmicks to excite his audience.

To be sure, *Alice, Sweet Alice* is far from an original piece of work. Elements of *Psycho*, *Carrie*, *Audrey Rose* and a number of other films too numerous to mention are represented here. But at least Ritvo and Sole had the good sense to steal some of those films' better aspects.

Consequently, we have a film that passes for pretty good thriller fare. […]

The film is so full of symbolism that it would take St. Jerome to figure it all out. Crosses, shadows of crosses, statues, shadows of statues and almost as much holy water as blood are used either to set up scenes or end them. […]

The film is set in the early 1960s when the church took a staunch view of sex and divorce, so in this respect *Alice, Sweet Alice* is somewhat dated.

Since Alfred Hitchcock and Brian De Palma have not made anything for us this year, I suppose we'll have to settle for the second team in Sole. And as a substitute player, he'll do until the real masters decide to produce another film.

Even worse was Bill Cosford's critique, in the November 23, 1977 edition of the *Miami Herald*:

Played out against the carefully dreary backgrounds of Paterson, N.J.—a place quite dreary enough on its own hook, actually—*Alice, Sweet Alice* has all the elements; the film ought to be a terror.

Instead, it belongs in the jar with the roaches. And the fault can't really be laid to the string of stock performances by some earnest actors (among whom Alphonso DeNoble stands out, portraying the wretched landlord as one of the most repulsive creatures in modern screen history). Nor is it so much the screenplay, admittedly long and shallow but salvageable nonetheless. No, director Alfred Sole is the real villain.

Directing his grisly little tale as if it were a master's degree project for a film school, Cole [sic] stages his action as self-consciously as possible, then films it all from camera angles progressively more bizarre, until one is aware—at the height of the action, no less—of nothing so much as the filmmaker's artless presence.

Eventually, so many otherwise harmless objects are invested with the Sole pregnant pause—a traffic light switches ominously from green, through yellow to red, while the camera lingers and nothing, *nothing* happens—that the possibilities for terror are lost. Where *Alice, Sweet Alice* tries for Hitchcock, it finds Woody Allen.

And where Allen is plainly not enough for thrillers, ersatz Peckinpah is made to do. Sole's only real shock effects are those recorded during a particularly nasty beating. Sadly, having a man having his mouth bashed in is not so much frightening as repulsive.

What's lost? The richly filmed atmospherics of the New Jersey city; a plot with enough twists that it might have done for an hour-long TV melodrama; a score that is as scary as it is derivative of *Psycho*'s. And, lest you've missed the ads, the "introduction" of Brooke Shields, the 12-year old actress soon to step out as a pubescent prostitute in the upcoming *Pretty Baby*. Alas, Shields is introduced and killed off in quick order. Small loss for us, substantial gain, no doubt, to the nascent Shields career.

Somewhere in *Alice* there was a horror film screaming to get out. But too much Sole and not enough soul makes this one a dull evening.]

Reviewing for the June 1, 1978 edition of the *Chicago Sun-Times*, Roger Ebert came to the film's defense—just as he would with *Halloween* the following year. Ironically, he would become a vociferous presence railing against the "slasher" fare that followed:

*Alice, Sweet Alice* is a sleeper; an odd, strange, macabre thriller that works on its own terms, no matter if Brooke Shields is in it. It's a 1976 production, *Communion*, that apparently went directly onto the shelf. But then Brooke Shields made the excellent *Pretty Baby*, and *Communion* was retitled and rereleased. […]

The movie walks a tightrope between thrills and comedy. Some of the scenes are obviously in homage to Hitchcock, and others seem determined to make *National Lampoon* look like *National Geographic*. The scary scenes do work, though: the director, Alfred Sole, has a nice touch for creepy moments. […]

Movies like *Alice, Sweet Alice* come along about once a year, and are in totally bad taste, and are routinely attacked by movie critics. But sometimes they achieve a weird sort of effectiveness.

It's well made, it's never boring, it constructs its bizarre world and then stays resolutely within it—and it's depraved and decadent. Some of you will want to be warned of that, and others will just want to be notified.

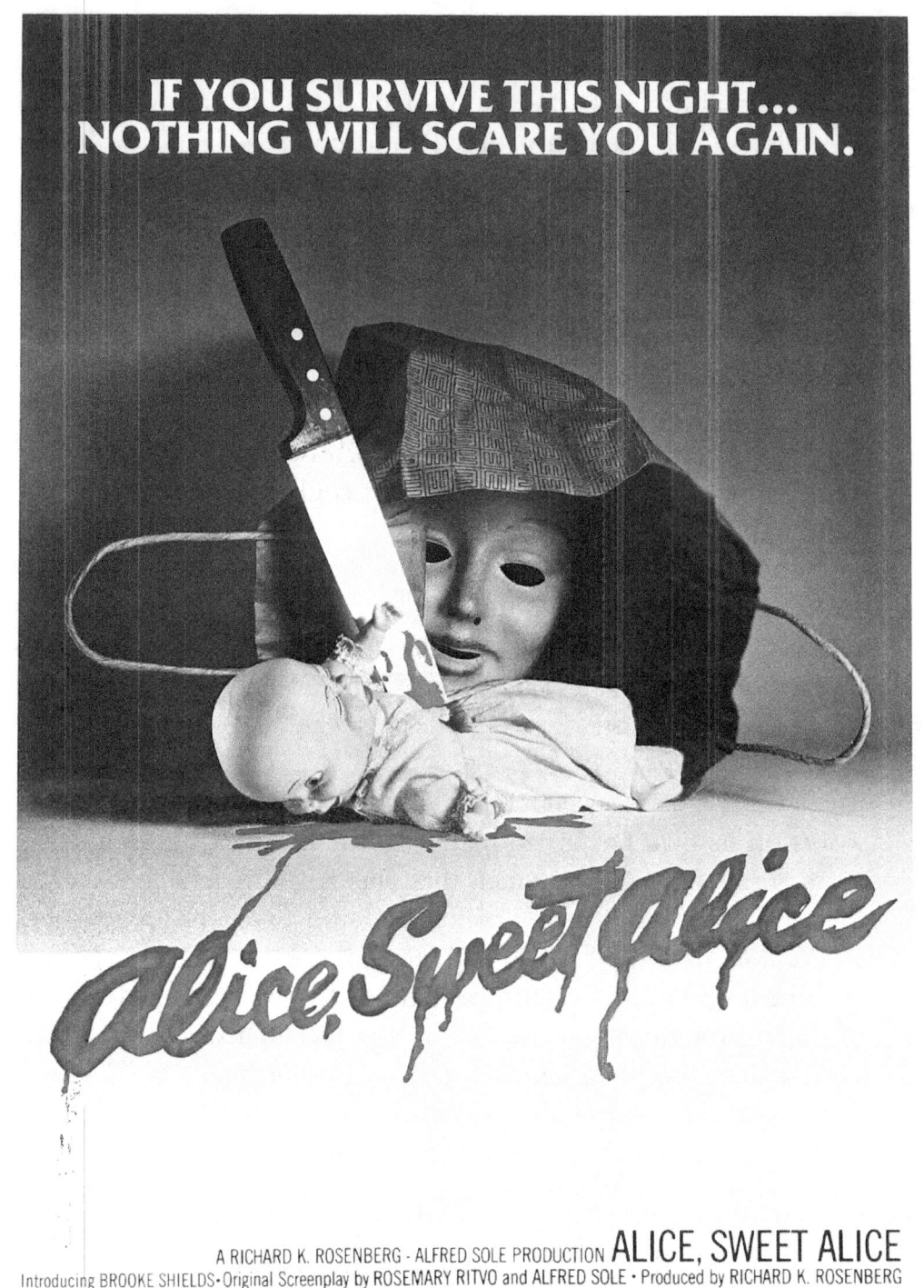

Sole may have objected to the change in title, but Allied Artists still put together an eye-catching ad campaign.

In the June 8, 1978 edition of the *Minneapolis Star*, Don Morrison offered an exceedingly ignorant take; his elitist attitude is made clear from his opening admission:

> This will be a necessarily incomplete report on *Alice, Sweet Alice*, inasmuch as I walked out on it after less than 20 minutes.
>
> It is chiefly in the spirit of alert consumerism that I mention the movie at all. It provides a chillingly persuasive illustration of Morrison's First Law, which is "Movies you don't walk in on you don't have to walk out on." Whereas I get paid to take such chances in the cinematic lottery, you are better advised to invest your money in ukulele lessons than in *Sweet Alice*.
>
> There's little I can tell you about the movie's origins, credentials, provenance or even date of issue. You have never heard of any members of the cast (with one glaring exception) or of Alfred Sole, who co-wrote the screenplay with Rosemary Ritvo. This hardly matters since, by now, they doubtless have given up all ambition to engage in amateur theatricals, changed their names and possibly moved to small towns in Idaho. [...]
>
> The glaring exception to prevailing anonymity is, of course, Brooke Shields, who is given top billing on the theater marquees and in ads for *Sweet Alice*. [...]
>
> Young Mistress Brooke is an undeniably beautiful child, although her career since infancy as a photographer's model appears to have afforded her little opportunity to be a child. She gives me the impression of self-consciously carrying her beauty around like a rare *objet d'art*—which is not only sad but something of a handicap to a dramatic performance. [...]
>
> The really convincing indication that *Sweet Alice* was not Brooke Shields' major film debut lies in the fact that she gets killed in the first reel—moments before I walked out.

Patrick Taggart, writing in the September 9, 1978 edition of the *Austin American-Statesman*, was similarly unimpressed:

> In the first place, it takes a lot of temerity to claim that Brooke Shields "stars" in the cheap horror film *Alice, Sweet Alice*. Ten minutes does not a starring role make, though producer Richard Rosenberg obviously needs to summon all the box office appeal he can muster.

> *Alice* is yet more effluent being poured into an already fouled stream of late summer movies. Inept in almost every regard, the film will put you to sleep faster than it will kill you.
>
> The acting has been left to various nobodies, has-beens and never-weres. But their efforts virtually tower over that of the director, editor, cinematographer, composer—you name it. [...]
>
> The only joke here is the film, and folks, it's on us.

The brickbats continued when Linda Gross reviewed the film in the May 12, 1978 edition of the *Los Angeles Times*:

> *Alice, Sweet Alice*, originally called *Communion*, is a foul movie about a series of murders assumed to be committed by a psychotic 12-year old. The film, which features child actress Brooke Shields as an early victim, was made before *Pretty Baby* but is now being released presumably to cash in on her current notoriety.
>
> Alice, which offers 105 minutes of atrociousness and bloody homicides perpetrated on children by other children and infirm adults, is an obscenity. The violence is punctuated with sneering depictions of the Catholic Church and portrayals of women as unhinged, overbearing, repressed or victimized.
>
> Claustrophobically set in Paterson, N.J. in 1961 in a lower-middle-class Catholic milieu, the film is directed in Grand Guignol style by Alfred Sole, whose flair for mood, tension and character doesn't redeem his excesses in sadistic gore.
>
> The warped screenplay by Sole and Rosemary Ritvo lacks taste and dignity—making fun of those who are fat, feeble or religious, hurling out random sexist insults as well as leering remarks. [...]
>
> The performances, especially those of the two leading children, are credible. Shields shows a mixture of vulnerability and smugness and Sheppard is excellent as her very disturbed older sister. Linda Miller plays the troubled mother with high-strung conviction. Stephen Lawrence composed the edgy score.
>
> Rated R for nauseating violence, *Alice, Sweet Alice*, produced by Richard K. Rosenberg, is one film children should not be permitted to see and one which discerning adults should stay away from as well.

Fan art for the film designed by Silver Ferox Design.

In the June 14, 1978 edition of the *Pittsburgh Post-Gazette*, James Irwin seemed to like aspects of it—but felt that it epitomized a trend towards blaming young women for the ills of the world:

> Why are filmmakers blaming adolescent girls for the violence in the world? From *The Exorcist* to *Carrie* we are expected to believe that a first menstruation or emotional stress from a parental divorce is enough to turn nice schoolgirls into raving murderers and lunatics. […]
>
> The latest is *Alice, Sweet Alice* at the Fulton and 14 area theaters. Though when it is good it is best of the genre so far this year and at least has plot logic, it still has plenty of nonsense in it and demands we expect evil intentions from someone too innocent to be capable of it.
>
> That qualification "when it is good" is important, for it isn't very good often. And when it is it steals everything from Nick Roeg's exquisitely frightening *Don't Look Now*. But it thankfully doesn't give the villain psychokinesis or make her possessed by devils. […]
>
> Director Alfred Sole isn't bad at copying old Alfred Hitchcock sequences to build suspense and create a good deal of tension. But he is terrible at dialogue scenes and one can almost hear the film come to a screeching halt when such a scene comes on. Writers Sole and Rosemary Ritvo effectively rehashed well-trodden ground.
>
> There is too much concentration on knives sliding into bodies and blood pouring over everything, but this is where the cheap thrills come from in today's suspense film.

Frank Daley gave the film a brief write-up in the June 27, 1978 edition of the *Ottawa Journal*; his take was a good deal more enthusiastic:

> *Alice, Sweet Alice* is a modestly made little thriller that heralds the return of the Mayfair Theatre to mainstream programming after a flirtation with soft pornography. The film was made a couple of years ago and has been released clearly because one of the featured players is Brooke Shields, the slender actress-star of *Pretty Baby*. But it could have been released before because although it is not a pretty movie, it demonstrates the talent of its director and co-writer Alfred Sole. […]

> Soles [sic] and company use repressive, religious twists and turns that see jealousy, sexual repression, religious fanaticism and revenge in the form of violent and gory murder.
>
> The actors have been well rehearsed and are believable, the music and sound effects are far better than average, the direction, while faltering in the center and towards the end occasionally, is of a high level.
>
> *Alice, Sweet Alice* is a thriller with style and punch. Even if you can see the holes in the production the holes in the bodies will scare you.

Michael Blowen, in the July 15, 1978, edition of the *Boston Globe* was not particularly sympathetic:

> *Alice, Sweet Alice* begins as a slick, glossy thriller that gradually degenerates into a bloody mess. [...]
>
> Director Alfred Sole employs craftsmanlike camerawork and swift editing in an attempt to gloss over the inconsistent script, but the film's complete lack of originality cannot be hidden. It is totally derivative.
>
> *Alice, Sweet Alice* does contain some interesting material for trivia buffs. Brooke Shields, Louis Malle's *Pretty Baby*, has a minor role as Alice's sister and Lillian Roth, whose life was the subject of the 1955 melodrama *I'll Cry Tomorrow*, with Susan Hayward, plays the only practical character in the film—a pathologist for the police department.
>
> There is a difference between the intelligent manipulation of a typical Hitchcock thriller and the gross vulgarity of an exploitation picture like *Alice, Sweet Alice*. The former builds the suspense through selective characterizations, appropriate music and bits of humor while the latter simply fills the space between murders with meaningless dialogue, obscure religious imagery and pedantic speculation by police investigators.

Dick Shippy's write-up in the September 13, 1978 edition of the *Akron Beacon Journal* was similarly negative:

> The movie is an attempt by Richard Rosenberg and Alfred Sole to peddle cheap horror in the guise of a murder mystery. Or maybe a cheap mystery in the guise of a horror show. Whichever, the operative condition is cheap—and shoddy.

> The shoddiness extends even to the billing, and Brooke Shields is victimized here. Distributors of *Sweet Alice* would have you believe Brooke has a starring role, hoping to capitalize on publicity (or perhaps notoriety) young Ms. Shields has received as the child prostitute of Louis Malle's *Pretty Baby*. […]
> Someone wearing a fright mask (which director Sole, the all-purpose shock merchant, keeps thrusting at us like a totem) has been perpetrating these horrors—and the supposition is it's Alice.
> You can't say beware of the obvious. There's no tripping over that which you can walk around. The side-stepping is made mandatory by the clumsily manipulative narrative of *Sweet Alice*.
> The movie stretches for fearful suspense but it reaches fearful apathy.

Joe Leydon, in the October 26, 1978 edition of the *Shreveport Times* felt that the bad outweighed the good:

> There are so many imaginative touches in *Alice, Sweet Alice* that one wishes it were not such an awful movie.
> With just a little more effort, this low-budget shocker could have at least been mediocre. […]
> The film, alas, is glaringly ineffective. Sole is an absolute amateur when it comes to building suspense, depending more on screeching violin music and grisly violence than steadily rising tension. The film has been set for some strange reason in the early 1960s, and that is a mistake—the budget is just not sufficient to maintain the period flavor, and one is frequently distracted by anachronisms. (The pay telephones are obvious products of the 1970s.)
> All of this could have been forgiven if the acting merely approached the level of adequacy. But the players—ranging from the briefly seen Brooke Shields (as the victim) to Linda Miller (as the girl's mother)—are just terrible. Those people who do not overplay are absolute ciphers. One seldom finds fine acting in films like this, but one hopes to at least encounter competence. The actors in this film cannot even provide that.
> It's a pity, because *Alice, Sweet Alice* is offbeat enough to rise slightly above the usual run of cheapie thrillers. Very slightly, mind you, but enough to make one wish it could have been better.

Incredibly misleading ad campaign, playing up the presence of Brooke Shields—represented with a sultry picture of her from several years after the picture was made. Note the "Introducing" label slapped carelessly atop her name, a concession to the fact that the ads made it appear as if it was a new film.

Rita Rose spent much of her March 10, 1981 write-up for the *Indianapolis Star* attacking the film's misleading promotional campaign, with its emphasis on Brooke Shields as the star; her take on the film was surprisingly sympathetic, however:

> As for the plot, *Holy Terror/Alice/Communion* holds its own in the genre of suspense-horror films. There are plenty of stabbings to fill your Gore Quotient, and oddball characters add the proper touch of insanity.
>
> Especially good is Paula Sheppard as Alice—a 21-year old actress in the role of a round-faced 12-year old—and Mildred Clinton as the nervous housekeeper for a handsome priest. And for what it's worth, Brooke Shields made a great cadaver.

Archer Winsten, reviewing it in the April 3, 1981 edition of the *New York Post,* gave the movie a back-handed seal of approval while taking plenty of digs at the people of Paterson:

> You might think that people living in Paterson, N.J. have been punished enough, but *Holy Terror* works them through a murder mystery in Catholic surroundings and family battles of the direst sort. […]
>
> Considering the fact that the picture has had a checkered career under three names in several countries, *not* including New York City, it's not bad at all. First they called it *Communion* for distribution in Europe, then *Alice, Sweet Alice* for parts of America. Now *Holy Terror* is upon us and you do have to say that it's as big a chiller as the next goosepimpler.
>
> Producer Richard K. Rosenberg, a lawyer born in Paterson, seized the opportunity to set those several murders on his native heath, and director Alfred Sole, a newcomer, was assisted in writing the script by Rosemary Ritvo who lives right in Paterson herself. You might call this picture a cottage industry that proves that people can make something out of what they know best. This is not to say that the actual crime statistics of Paterson are sensational.

In the April 3, 1981 edition of *The New York Times*, the sometimes-prickly Vincent Canby seemed more impressed than usual:

*Holy Terror*, the 1977 horror film that opens today at the Astor Plaza and other theaters, will go into the record books as the movie in which Brooke Shields made her screen debut, though the film itself is a creditable example of its genre and Miss Shields is in the picture for an extremely short time.

*Holy Terror*, which was once titled *Alice, Sweet Alice*, was shot entirely in Paterson, N.J., under the direction of Alfred Sole from a screenplay by him and Rosemary Ritvo. The "holy terror" is a series of quite gruesome murders, the first of which takes place in a Roman Catholic church just as a little girl is about to make her first communion. The principal suspect is the victim's jealous, slightly older sister, Alice, played with coolly remarkable authority by Paula Sheppard. [...]

The actors, none well known except for the late Lillian Roth, who makes a quick on-and-off appearance as a pathologist performing an autopsy, are all good professionals. Mr. Sole, whose first feature this is, knows how to direct actors, how to manipulate suspense and when to shift gears: the identity of the killer is revealed at just that point when the audience is about to make the identification, after which the film becomes less of a horror film than an exercise in suspense. He also has a good feeling for the lower middle-class locale and the realities of the lives of the people who live in it.

Miss Shields, who made this film before Louis Malle's *Pretty Baby*, released in 1978, looks to be a mere tot, a beautiful one but not exactly the sort of child who would one day become famous as the body contained in a pair of nicely snug jeans.

Tom McElfresh, writing in the April 6, 1981 edition of the *Cincinnati Enquirer*, pretty much hated it:

It is, to be fair, possible the present actors—given words to speak and some guidance in speaking them—might have made a passable movie; they'll go nameless and blameless here.

Alfred Sole, director of this mess, will not.

His is the hand which made the story a cheap, cheating mishmash full of sexual innuendo and rage at the Catholic Church. His is the hand which permitted actors fits of screaming, slamming emotion—whether it worked within character and plot structure or not. His is the hand which created the single most offensive murder ever acted on film—the bread knife jabbed into the priest's neck as he passes Communion wafers. His is the hand which left the resolution hanging so the plot could be set for a sequel.

His, further, is the eye which shot after shot called attention to the photography, the camera angles, the sets, the locations—needless, confusing detail in the people and places. [...]

*Holy Terror* is wholly, totally terrible.

In his April 6, 1981 write-up for the *New York Daily News*, Ernest Leogrande awarded the film two-and-a-half stars:

*Holy Terror* is being promoted as Brooke Shields' first movie. [...]

The movie has qualities that take it out of the usual run of sanguinary homicidal horror movies, an attention given to dialogue, to authenticity of setting and to revelatory and atmospheric touches. For one thing the depiction of the strained relationship between the divorced couple, who still care for each other, is presented in a believable way. For another there is a hospital bedside scene in which the patient actually looks like a hospital patient, no small potatoes in the world of cinema.

For its debit side the movie spreads around some ridiculous improbabilities and red herrings, such as the fact that yellow rain slickers keep showing up, even in fair weather, and unnecessarily emphasizes the obesity of a strange landlord who seems to have been cast just for his physical appearance.

And in the May 11, 1981 edition of *People* magazine, their unnamed reviewer really tore it apart:

Wholly terrible is more like it. This 1977 stiff (titled *Alice, Sweet Alice* in its deservedly brief first life) is a shameless attempt to cash in on two current fads—horror films and Brooke Shields. [...] For anyone who makes it to the end, neophyte director Alfred Sole offers a twist. It hardly compensates for the time wasted, literally in the dark. In one shatteringly distasteful scene, Sheppard goes downstairs to pay her family's rent to the nauseatingly fat, bald, goateed, lecherous landlord, who snacks on cat food. When he threatens to blackmail the apparently wicked girl, she rips up the check; he then luridly threatens her and she responds by strangling his beloved kitten. It's that kind of loser: desperate, emptily sensational.

# Chapter 8
## Interview with Alfred Sole

***The following interview*** *was conducted on the evening of August 14, 2019. A follow-up session to clear up some additional questions followed on the afternoon of October 21, 2020. Mr. Sole has my gratitude for taking the time to talk to me about his life and career, and Dante Tomaselli has my sincere thanks for arranging this interview.*

**Troy HowarTH:** *Would you describe yourself as an architect, as a filmmaker, or both?*

**Alfred Sole:** I think I would describe myself as a filmmaker. I started off in architecture, then eventually got into films. Who knows, maybe I should have stayed in architecture, but I wound up directing obviously, and also becoming a production designer. But my heart is in directing, absolutely.

**TH:** *Can you tell me a bit about your childhood?*

**AS:** *(laughs)* Well, what all would you like to know?

**TH:** *Well, how about your background in terms of being exposed to the arts?*

**AS:** Working class Italian family. I grew up in New Jersey. I guess I was always just a visual person, and my father used to love the movies. I used to go to the movies with him a lot. My mother, also, but he really loved the movies. I used to sit in movie theaters and have all these fantasies about what the world is really like, and the movie world, and the magic of making movies. And then

253

if you're fortunate to get into it yourself, you realize that the experience you had imagining what it must be like is not like the reality of making movies. It's completely different—but good. I remember certain films that just blew me away. For some reason, I don't know why, I got into camera moves. I remember seeing *Diabolique* (*Les diaboliques*, 1955); I don't know if you remember that movie?

**TH:** *Oh yes.*

**AS:** I figured you probably knew it. That movie absolutely blew me away. That was the beginning. Then it was Hitchcock, Bergman. But it was always about the sense of the camera moves and the style of filmmaking. I'm so attracted to that. It just felt so magical to me.

**TH:** *What was it like studying architecture in Italy?*

**AS:** Well, I had seen this movie called *Rome Adventure* (1962)[24]. I was sitting in the theater and I thought, "I've gotta go there." I worked a lot when I was a kid, so I had some money saved. My parents were freaking out. So my grandmother helped me, and I got on a boat, and before you knew it, I was in Italy. I went there to go to school. I wanted to be a painter originally. I was in love with Salvador Dalí. I had a roommate, and we were studying in Florence. And once I was in school, I realized I wasn't very good; I wasn't a good painter. But we were right near the University of Florence, and I decided to switch over to taking classes in architecture. That experience of living in Italy and traveling in Italy really framed my idea of what things should be. It was a terrific experience. I was incredibly fortunate.

**TH:** *Do you see any parallels between architecture and making films?*

**AS:** Oh yes, of course. Especially in the design of a set; of course. But also there are a lot of parallels in terms of the visual. Somebody has to go from A to B to C in order to make a movie, and they have to hit their marks. The framing is very architectural. It's all visual; it's all part of the package.

**TH:** *I believe you made some short features before making your first long feature?*

**AS:** Yeah, but they were just amateur things. I shot them myself on 16mm.

---

24. Directed by Delmer Daves and starring Suzanne Pleshette and Troy Donahue.

**TH:** *Did they ever get shown anywhere?*

**AS:** I think I entered one in a film festival, but I'm not sure. It's been so long. There was one called *I'll Be Your Bride*, I remember. But I can't even find the prints. I know I have them, but I don't know where they are. I'm a self-taught filmmaker. I just learned from reading books and watching movies.

**TH:** *Flashing forward a bit, how did you enjoy the experience of making your first film* Deep Sleep, *and how difficult was it to get the money to make it?*

**AS:** It was kind of a strange experience. I was living in New Jersey and I couldn't figure out how to get into the film business. One day I discovered a magazine called *American Cinematographer*. I had a subscription to that. I always used to look forward to the next issue. I just loved the stories of making films in Hollywood and the stories of the actors and the directors. It was like a Bible to me; I loved that magazine. And they used to sell things in the magazine, and I even sent away for a director's viewfinder. I just knew that I always saw pictures of directors with a viewfinder around their neck, so I got my first director's viewfinder *(laughs)* way, way, *way* before I ever got to make a film! I had read that Francis Coppola had made some X-rated films to get started and so I thought, "Well, maybe that's the route to go." There was no formal training. Film schools were pretty much non-existent then. I had a friend who went to college, but that was more for directing television and stuff like that. So I got some friends together and I raised $25,000—and that was my budget for *Deep Sleep*. What an experience. I learned about these two brothers called the Mill brothers, and they were making softcore porn in New York, so I called them up, and I ended up hanging around, working as a sort of P.A., trying to help them out. And I learned quite a bit, just hanging around and watching them. It was kind of difficult. I didn't know how to talk to the actors. It was kind of weird… I don't know—I was on this train and it was moving forward. For some odd reason, I knew… you know how some people look at a car and they can tell how the car was made and how it works?

**TH:** *Yeah.*

**AS:** I had no formal training, but I just knew; I understood the mechanics of it. You know: the camera goes here, and you need this to get this, and you need that to get that. And so I made this porno; it was a really weird experience. Funny—there were a lot of funny moments. I didn't know how to talk to the actors (*laughs*)… you know, put it here, put it here, do this! You know? (*laughs*) All I knew was, in my heart of hearts, I was *making a movie*. I had cameras. I had lights. And I was making this movie that was going to be amazing; it would have music, it would have make-up, it would have a story. You know, I watched a lot of other pornos to see what they were like and it was all fucking, you know… so I was going to make the artiest porno ever. And it wasn't so hardcore at the time. When we finally got a distributor, this really crazy woman, Chelly Wilson—she was a Greek woman, and she owned half of the porno theaters in Manhattan, believe it or not. And she saw the movie and she liked it, and there was a scene where a dog was humping somebody's leg. That happened by accident and I filmed it. She *loved* that. She made all these notes and she had me go back and add all these hardcore close-ups so that she could release the film. And she did.

**TH:** *How shocked were you by the obscenity charges brought against you because of* Deep Sleep?

**AS:** You know what, I wasn't really shocked until I had to go on trial in Oklahoma. Then I was really afraid. Because originally, when I was charged in Paterson, it was "carnal indecency." It was all these crazy charges from the 1800s. That was this Prosecutor named John T. Niccollai. He was trying to make a name for himself, and because the Catholic Church complained, he came after us. I thought, "Well, you tell me what carnal indecency is." That was around the time that porno was playing in the suburbs. It was sort of the golden period of porn, and people would go to see it, and it was OK. But I got really scared when I was on trial in Oklahoma City. That was pretty scary.

**TH:** *Why Oklahoma City?*

**AS:** It was playing in Wayne, New Jersey. At that time, it was actually out-grossing *The Poseidon Adventure*, believe it or not. It was a time when porn was hitting suburbia and playing in theaters. What happened was, I got a call from the theater that somebody stole the print. They needed to track down the distributor because they needed another print. I never thought much about it, I just thought maybe it was just somebody fucking around. About a month or two later I got a call from some guy with UPI saying, "Did you know you were indicted in Oklahoma City?" Apparently what happened was—the law was, any state that the pornographic material flies over, you can be indicted in any state. So they wound up indicting me in Oklahoma City. Apparently the film was put on at a regular theater—it was on for like three minutes and all the FBI agents just happened to be there. Then they closed the theater down and they indicted me. And that was all down to Niccollai. He set that up.

**TH:** *Is it true they confiscated all the profits?*

**AS:** They confiscated all the profits. They confiscated the prints. We had started a trial in Oklahoma. I was down there. I remember being scared out of my mind. In Oklahoma City, we stayed at a place called the Skirvin Hotel. Many years later, I was watching a movie in the theater—a period film, and they apparently shot part of it in the Skirvin Hotel. I started feeling nauseous and then I realized, they shot it in that same hotel. It literally made me feel sick.

**TH:** *Is it true you got death threats?*

**AS:** Yes. Somebody even burned a cross on the front lawn. It's true.

**TH:** *It doesn't sound like it's a film you're particularly proud of…*

**AS:** No, it was… when I saw it again, it was amazing, it was so hardcore. (*laughter*) You know, you get older—I mean, I've seen it all, but when you get older, for some reason, you're like, "*Oh Jesus, did I do that?!*" (*laughter*) What also happened was, I was designing a TV series called *MacGyver*. The producer and I were in a van scouting locations—there were about 10 people in the van, the director, the A.D.s, and everybody. And the producer went on-line and found the movie. He was on his phone and he passed it around and everybody was watching the hardcore scenes. And from that moment on, they all looked at me differently.

**TH:** *Is it true you had a lot of difficulties with the actors in terms of performance anxiety?*

**AS:** Yeah. I used a clear Plexiglas platform so we could film under it and in one scene you can see the colors of the one guy's pubic hair changing. My insurance broker came to see me and that crazy son of a bitch did the final sex scene. He's blonde, so the color of the pubes changed.

**TH:** *So he was a sort of stunt double?*

**AS:** Yeah, it was crazy. Harry Reems couldn't get it up. It was pretty bizarre.

**TH:** *Is it true that you were ex-communicated because of* Deep Sleep?

**AS:** (*laughs*) Yes, I was! I got word. I was at mass, and I got the word. Because the Bishop's house was in the film. I didn't know it was the Bishop's house! (*laughs*) I needed a scene where they were coming out of a mansion, so they ran by the front door and they walked away. The mansion was in the background, so when the Bishop found out, he kind of freaked out. That was the beginning of all my troubles.

**TH:** *So once the dust settled, you were put on probation and not allowed to make any more movies for two years?*

**AS:** That's right. It was a crazy period. I mean, I had my architecture work to fall back on. But they wouldn't let me make any movies for two years.

**TH:** *Then once the probation was finished, you made a film that so far as I know, nobody has ever seen—*American Soap.

**AS:** I wish I had a print.

**TH:** *What can you tell me about* American Soap?

**AS:** It was right before *Communion* and it was really low budget. We had, like, 30 to 40 thousand. Rosemary (Ritvo) and I wrote this script called *American Soap*. It was about a middle-aged woman who falls in love with her neighbor's son. She has a terrible domestic life. Her husband is not nice to her. (*chuckles*) I'm trying to think of the plot right now. But anyway, it was supposed to be very sensual and erotic. She has all these dream sequences, and Alphonso (DeNoble) was in all the dream sequences. It was really…. When I looked at it, it was terrible. (*laughs*) There were some very good moments. The erotic moments between the actress and the young guy who plays the kid… she was in her 40s[25] and he was in his early 20s. It was just this kind of crazy, Fellini-like movie where she was having all these kinds of fantasies. She kills her husband in her fantasy. She was having sex with everybody in her fantasies, while in reality she was in love with this young guy.

---

25. Williams was actually pushing 60 when she appeared in *American Soap*.

**TH:** *I take it Fellini is one of your favorites?*

**AS:** Of course, of course. Given my age and that time period, he was somebody I was crazy about.

**TH:** *Do you remember the names of the actors?*

**AS:** I remember the actress was Kay Williams. And that's the only one that I remember. What happened was, we only had one or two prints made. We couldn't afford to make more. I took one print to California with me and I stayed at a friend's house. I remember he cleaned his basement. I had a print of *Communion* and a print of *American Soap*—and he threw it out.

**TH:** *The one article I read mentioned that United Artists was interested in* American Soap, *then it disappeared.*

**AS:** That's what happened. I was going through a crazy period. I was leaving my wife. I had moved. We only had one or two prints and we didn't know anybody—to be honest, it had its moments, but it wasn't a very good movie.

**TH:** *Now you mentioned it was erotic, but given what happened with* Deep Sleep, *I'm guessing it wasn't a porno movie?*

**AS:** No, no. Definitely not. It was more suggestive. There was no nudity whatsoever. I'd love to know if it still exists somewhere.

**TH:** *It's definitely obscure. None of your filmographies out there that I've seen even list it.*

**AS:** We made it for so little money. It was like 40 grand. We shot it in 16mm. The guy who put up the money for it was a guy by the name of Irwin Greenberg. He was from New Jersey.

**TH:** *Was he a producer or just a businessman looking to make a movie?*

**AS:** He was a businessman. He was actually a client. I was designing his home for him and I convinced him to raise some money to help me make this movie. I'm not sure if he's even still alive after so many years.

**TH:** *Obviously Catholicism is a major presence in* Communion—*did the problems you experienced over* Deep Sleep *impact your presentation of Catholicism in the film?*

**AS:** Well, I was dealing with those problems during the making of *Communion*. So there was a bit of that going on; in the back of my head, I knew I was in trouble for making that movie. I was trying to deal with that and also make a movie. I had all my friends, some of whom were school teachers, in *Deep Sleep*. They were all helping out, and then there was this backlash—they were investigating the teachers who were in a porno. My friend who had a funeral home and let us use it, he was in trouble because porno was being made in his funeral home. I had all that going on when I was making *Communion*. When I was making *Communion*, I was really on cloud nine. I mean, it was difficult. It was very difficult.

**TH:** *What can you tell me about your* Communion *co-writer, Rosemary Ritvo?*

**AS:** Great, great; wonderful person. It was funny, she was my neighbor and she was Catholic. One day we started talking and I was telling her about this idea for a movie. She taught poetry and she was a writer and so we started talking, and before you knew it, we were writing the screenplay together. It was a really wonderful experience.

**TH:** *How many drafts did* Communion *go through prior to its going before the cameras?*

**AS:** I would say just maybe two or three drafts. We talked every day. We wrote about two or three hours every day. We were doing about 10 pages a day. If I'm remembering correctly, I'd say there were only about two or three drafts.

**TH:** *How did you go about raising the funding for the movie?*

**AS:** A friend of mine named Richard Rosenberg was a lawyer. I was approaching everybody I knew and telling them that it could be a good investment, that they could make a lot of money, blah blah blah. You know, like a lot of filmmakers, you become a huckster, selling the movie. It was easy raising money for the porno. The guys who invested were all at a card game, and they agreed to put up some money. When we made the movie, they were all joking and laughing; they got to come on the set and see scenes being made. They all got their money's worth. I think it was 10 guys. For 10 guys, 25 grand is nothing. And they were all professionals: one was a banker, one was a doctor, one was a lawyer, one was an accountant. The accountant was my next door neighbor. Actually, he was the one who got Richard Rosenberg involved. And so, we made the movie.

**TH:** *Were there any scenes or ideas you wanted to incorporate that had to be dropped due to budgetary constraints?*

**AS:** There were lots of places where I had to cut corners. We were always running out of money. There were lots of friends and family involved. My mother fed everybody on a daily basis. I always kind of had this vision of making movies into a big family affair. You know, you go to your friends for help. The hard thing was, the filmmakers who came from New York City, they came, they took the money… not *all* of them, but they had this attitude of, "We'll make this movie, but we're just gonna take the money and run." You know, you stand there talking to them about your vision, and you could see their eyes just glass over; you could tell they weren't really interested. But I got lucky. I got Brooke Shields, and I got lucky in the casting, which was really helpful. It was hard work. I got hepatitis when I was making the movie. But it got made, and I got a movie. That's all I wanted, was a movie.

**TH:** *You've indicated that the filming was very stop-and-start by nature…*

**AS:** Yes, we ran out of money. Linda Miller cut her wrist. We had to stop for that. There were lots of little dramas going on. We kept losing cameramen. We did do a lot of stopping and starting. There were times when I thought this movie would never, ever get made. But, we made it.

**TH:** *Do you remember approximately how long the production lasted… was it a matter of months, or weeks?*

**AS:** To be honest with you…I can't recall for sure. It wasn't *that* long. I know the editing went on for a nice length of time, because we were piecing—you know, we didn't have coverage. I had this great editor, Eddie Salier, and we were piecing this movie together. We took things from other scenes and put them in, putting in close-ups from other scenes, and so on. We didn't have a lot of coverage, but I did know from watching other low budget films that if you don't have the coverage you need to tell your story, it's going to get boring really quick.

**TH:** *I don't imagine there were a lot of crew members available in Paterson; did you get the majority of your crew from New York?*

**AS:** A lot of them were from New York, and I also had friends who just helped out. You know, doing things like typing up the schedules. I had five neighbors on my block who were really good friends—you know, that original card game that came together to fund the porno—and everybody helped out. Everybody was very supportive; it was great.

**TH:** *Did you personally select that very creepy translucent mask that's used in the film?*

**AS:** I did. I was in Paterson. It was in the corner of a toy store. I found the doll and the mask. When I was writing the film, I was going around, collecting things, religious things…so I had all that early on.

**TH:** *You've indicated that you went through a number of different cinematographers; any idea how many there were in total?*

**AS:** At least three or four, I would say.

**TH:** *Chuck Hall and John Friberg are the credited cameramen on the film. You've said before that the cameramen who worked on the film were not supportive; can you go into that a bit?*

**AS:** I wanted to work late, I never really wanted to stop filming. I just wanted to keep on going, keep on going. Friberg was a cameraman out of New York. He had this attitude like, "You don't know what you're doing, kid." I remember saying to him once, "Why are you here? Why did you take the money? You can't get a job in New York, so you're busting *my* balls?" He would always argue over my camera angles. Everything I did was not the right way to do it. You just know, you want your camera here. I knew I wanted my camera there. Of all the people, he was the hardest to deal with. I don't know if he's even around today or not.

**TH:** *I'm not sure. What made you decide to set the film in 1961?*

**AS:** (*laughs*) I actually don't even remember now. I remember my grandmother used to live next to a priest's house. Mrs. Tredoni was actually a woman who ran the priests' lives. She controlled the comings and goings at the house. She fed the priest. And she was in charge. She was the boss. If you wanted to get to anyone, you had to go through her. That was the character of Mrs. Tredoni. Oh yes, I *do* remember: that was the time when divorce was such a big issue. In that time period, women—Catholic women—never got a divorce. It was like the worst thing in the world for a woman to get a divorce during that time period. And that's the reason why I chose that period.

**TH:** *Did the period setting pose many difficulties? It looks like you had access to a lot of period cars and so on…*

**AS:** No. I had great collaborators. My costume designer was really good. She was terrific. And I had people… Cops. My brother-in-law was a cop, and he got cars for me from the police station. We shot in the actual police station in Paterson. We shot in the Board of Health in Paterson. I got all the locations for free. People were all very helpful, because my brother-in-law was a cop. The only problem we had was the church. We couldn't get a church that would let us shoot in it.

**TH:** *Were there any actual sets constructed for the film, or was everything a practical location?*

**AS:** Everything was a practical location, except for Alphonso's…the place where they lived. That was an empty building that was going to be torn down. Everything was a location. I dressed everything. While I was writing, I was shopping for lamps, I was shopping for different set dressing pieces. It was like a mental thing to say that I am making this movie. You know, every time I bought something, I told myself 'well, I *am* going to make this movie.' I kept looking for Catholic things. So that kind of kept me going.

**TH:** *The influence of Alfred Hitchcock and of* Don't Look Now *(1973) are quite obvious…*

**AS:** *Don't Look Now* was a *major* influence.

**TH:** *The film also seems to be an outgrowth of the Italian* giallo *films of the period, though I believe you weren't actually conscious of them at that time?*

**AS:** That's right. I wasn't aware of them then. I saw some of them later.

**TH:** *But* Don't Look Now *was your major touchstone?*

**AS:** Yes, the girl in the slicker. The stabbing. That was definitely a major, major inspiration.

**TH:** *You've indicated you became very ill for part of the shoot; did that slow down production at all, or did you have to soldier on regardless?*

**AS:** I had a doctor friend… I gotta tell you, I have lots of friends (*laughs*)… I was helping design his office, and he came in and gave me a Vitamin B12 shot. He came down to check on me every day, to make sure… I think I maybe stopped for one or two days because I was barfing my brains out. But, he was there… and the more I talk, the more I realize I had a lot of supportive friends. That is really nice. And my neighbor helped me make the knife; he lived right across the street from me. So I told him I wanted a knife that would collapse, and he helped me make the knife.

**TH:** *It's obvious you wanted scenes of horror that were based on things that people could relate to; we've all stubbed a toe on the edge of the furniture…*

**AS:** Right. That's where I got the idea of stabbing her in the foot. I was in New York watching this Mafia movie and people were being shot left and right, and the audience didn't respond. Then one guy spit in somebody's face and they all gasped. I thought, OK, people respond to things they can relate to. They don't know what it's like to be shot or stabbed, but everybody's bumped their foot, so that's how that came about.

**TH:** *I wanted to talk a bit about some of the actors… what are your memories of Mildred Clinton?*

**AS:** She's great. She was very helpful. She was hard working. It was nice working with her, because she was always so professional. Not having a lot of experience working with actors, I would listen to her. She told a lot of great stories. She was very helpful. She had great ideas and would tell me about what she wanted to do. She was terrific.

**TH:** *Now somebody who didn't have any real experience with acting was Alphonso DeNoble…*

**AS:** Right. Alphonso. (*laughs*) I'm sure you know the story about how I met Alphonso.

**TH:** *I've heard it, but I'd love to hear it again!*

**AS:** Well, I was in a graveyard visiting my father's grave, and there was Alphonso dressed up as a priest. I was watching him. He caught my eye. What he did was, he would go to graveyards—the two Italian graveyards… there are too many graveyards in Paterson. And when people were standing by their loved ones, praying, he would walk over and people would say, "Oh, Father, say a prayer for my dead husband, wife, daughter…" He would do it, and they would give him some money. (*laughs*) So that was his gig. I thought that was about the cleverest thing ever.

**TH:** *Yep.*

**AS:** Then I found out he was a bouncer at a gay bar. He was a real character. He was terrific.

**TH:** *Did he find it difficult getting into an acting role, or did it come natural?*

**AS:** No, it came naturally. He was a bit of a ham. He loved it. He was so happy to be doing that character. He just loved it, and he and Paula got along pretty well.

**TH:** *You can almost smell the stench of his apartment; was it unpleasant to film in?*

**AS:** No. I found that wallpaper and we wallpapered the walls, then we got the cockroaches from some lab. They were all gigantic. I had fun putting the pee stains on his pants. It was a lot of laughs. And I found a ton of old furniture… I was always buying stuff. I was storing it, keeping it ready for this moment.

**TH:** *It seems like Alphonso is dubbed through the entire film… was that his own voice?*

**AS:** That was his voice, yes.

**TH:** *Paula Sheppard?*

**AS:** My cousin was an actor and he was working for André Gregory. I don't know if you're familiar with him, he was in New York… *My Dinner with André*. Do you remember that film?

**TH:** *Yes, of course.*

**AS:** He was part of André Gregory's group. And he was studying acting. He wanted to be an actor. We're around the same age. So I asked him, how do you do it? I wanted to learn the language of actors. He told me to go to HB Studios in New York—Herbert Berghof Studios. I took acting lessons down in the Lower East Village, I think it was. So he was performing, I think in Connecticut, they had some sort of a dance program going on, and I saw her—I went up and talked to her, asked if she wanted to be in a movie. She was very interested, and I told her someday I'm going to give her a call and we're going to make this movie. When I saw her, I thought she was fabulous. She looked old, she looked young, she looked mean, she looked happy… You know what I mean? She had a *great* face. She was in this dance company and I just happened to see her.

**TH:** *Niles McMaster?*

**AS:** We put out a casting call and Niles came… So was everybody, really—Linda Miller and all the others were from a casting call.

**TH:** *Did you have difficulties with any of the actors?*

**AS:** Linda Miller was a pain in the ass. A pain in the ass. She was a good actress, but she was just a *pain*. She went out of her way to just make things difficult for me. I didn't have a good time with her. And she kind of got to the other crew and the New York actors. At the beginning she said, "Don't tell anybody that my father is Jackie Gleason. Don't you *dare*." And then she'd tell them, and they'd get mad at me because they knew that I knew. And she was having marriage problems at the time. She was married to the actor…

**TH:** *Jason Miller.*

**AS:** Jason Miller, yeah. She was a good actress. I mean, I thought she did a great job. But she had problems. She slit her wrist. She was kind of… she had a superior attitude.

**TH:** *You mentioned her slitting her wrist; didn't she do that during the actual filming?*

**AS:** Yeah, we were in the church! It was our last day filming there. She came running in and her wrist was bleeding. I thought, "Oh God, we'll never get this movie finished. It's all over. Why did she do this?!" My heart went into my throat and I thought, "This is it—it's all over." I figured she wouldn't be able to work. But she did get back to work, she finished it up… It's like anything else: there are good moments and bad moments.

**TH:** *Did she ever say why she slit her wrist? Was it just her personal problems becoming too much?*

**AS:** I think it was a combination of that… A lot of people were approaching her. She had told me not to tell anybody that she was Jackie Gleason's daughter. Then she would tell them herself, and everybody started asking all these questions about Jackie Gleason, she'd get so upset because people were bugging her. "Oh, you're Jackie Gleason's daughter!" She would get pissed off. Well, you can't have it both ways. And she wasn't a good influence on the other New York actors. It wasn't like, "OK, guys, let's go to work and make this thing happen." It was always, "I'm not happy with this, I'm not happy with that." She had just won an award, too, for the theater. But she had an attitude.

**TH:** *Did that slow down production while she recuperated—did you shut down, or were you able to film around her?*

**AS:** We had to shut down, but that wasn't uncommon. We would shoot for a few days, then we would shut down. There was always something. We ran out of money. It wasn't an easy shoot. It was hard. But that's part of the process. I could make demands only so far, but I had no money—when you don't have money, people, especially the actors out of New York, they were always worried about getting paid.

**TH:** *Lillian Roth had been a big star in the 1930s, and her story was the inspiration for the book and the film* I'll Cry Tomorrow; *how did you end up casting her in the small role of the pathologist?*

**AS:** She had a lot great stories. Somebody approached me… an agent or her manager… and asked me if I could use her. I didn't even know who she was. I knew the movie—who was it that played her?

**TH:** *Susan Hayward.*

**AS:** That's it. I saw the movie many times. Then I read the book. She told great stories. Oh *God*, the stories she told. I remember this story: she was working as a waitress. Broke. Down and out. And one of her songs was playing on the loudspeaker and there she was, working as a waitress, and nobody knew who she was. She had a lot of interesting stories.

**TH:** *Of course, it's also the debut of Brooke Shields… did you have any difficulties working with her mother?*

**AS:** We had problems with Teri [Shields], but I loved Teri. She was very helpful. Teri was a mean drunk, though. She was great until 4 or 5 in the afternoon, then she started drinking. I was amazed at how Brooke would deal with her. She was the adult in that room. But it was Teri who said she would do it. She was supportive and was so glad that Brooke was in it. She was so sweet. No, I have fond memories of Teri—except for when she got drunk. She was hard… not for me, she was just hard to be around when she was like that. She got really… you know: "fuck this, fuck that." She sounded like a truck driver.

**TH:** *Antonino Rocca?*

**AS:** I think he had the same agent that got us Lillian Roth. I think it was her agent or friend, and he knew Antonino and got him for us.

**TH:** *Did the people of Paterson support the project or did you encounter any difficulties with getting fleeced for the locations?*

**AS:** People donated things to me. People were supportive. They were happy to have a film being made. The Paterson police gave me police cars, they gave me a fire truck. Everything I needed. They helped me make *rain*. I mean, I made rain on the whole front of the building, and they were working the hoses for me. They were so, so supportive. The mayor… I was friendly with the mayor's wife. I was helping her… the Rogers locomotive building, where we filmed the father's death—I was helping her on this project of restoring all these old buildings and turning them into artists' lofts. So I was helping with that. That's how I got that building. That's where they manufactured the first locomotive engine… The Colt .45 was manufactured in that building, too.

**TH:** *The music is so chilling and effective; how did you get along with Stephen Lawrence?*

**AS:** Great. I talked to him about movies and Hitchcock. What's the name of the famous composer…?

**TH:** *Bernard Herrmann?*

**AS:** Yes! I wanted the music to be like that. We had no money to work with, but he did amazing things.

**TH:** *How deeply involved were you in the post-production?*

**AS:** Every bit of it. This was my baby. This was my *dream*. There were a lot of talented people who helped, believe me, but I was so excited. I couldn't wait to mix the soundtrack.

**TH:** *The editing is really exceptional; what are your memories of working with Edward Salier?*

**AS:** We just clicked. He was so supportive. We worked every day together. We cut it at Technicolor in New York. He and I just found a way to make things work. We would do things like blowing up close-ups, triple printing images… he also taught me a lot. He's a great editor.

**TH:** *The visual style of the film is very precise; did you storyboard the entire picture?*

**AS:** I drew little sketches. It was a kind of a storyboard. I knew, from watching too many movies… and you discover things, too. You know, the cat was eating cat food on Alphonso's belly. All these little things happen. You know that scene where you see the photograph of Brooke in the basket and it comes up?

**TH:** *Yes.*

**AS:** That was *there*. I was leaning on the counter and I said, what does this basket do? And that was just luck. I got used to that. It was all kind of a discovery process.

**TH:** *What can you tell me about Columbia's decision to not distribute the film?*

**AS:** My understanding is, Richard Rosenberg had a deal and we did a book tie-in—a paperback tie-in. They were all excited about it. I went to their office in New York and I was on cloud nine. Oh God! Then, they wanted me to cut a few things… I don't think it was anything to do with violence… but they flew me to California, where I was tightening the film up. I got a call from Rosenberg and he said, "The deal is off. They think the film is too bloody. They don't want the movie." P.S.—what I found out was, they caught Rosenberg trying to steal a lot of money from them. Somehow they were going to cover the cost of the original production. He inflated everything. They got pissed off and they dropped the picture. Then I was devastated.

**TH:** *How long of a lapse was there between that and Allied Artists picking it up?*

**AS:** You know what, I don't remember. But there was no enthusiasm from Allied Artists. When I met them at Columbia, they saw something in that movie and they really liked it. And then Allied Artists—I had one brief phone conversation with them. They weren't interested in talking to me at all. And I just felt, they saw it as a schlock movie they were putting out like so many others; they didn't see what I saw. But I was happy it got a release. It was out there. It wasn't totally dead.

**TH:** *Of course, it ended up being retitled numerous times…*

**AS:** I know! (*laughs*) This little film had some kind of a life!

**TH:** *Why were Allied Artists opposed to the* Communion *title?*

**AS:** I had no conversation with them. Richard Rosenberg called: "They don't like the title." At that time, I had no rights over the picture. I had sold everything to Richard Rosenberg. I wanted the movie to be out and I was so eager, and not being a good business person, I trusted him and thought he was doing the right things. And he did get me the money to make the movie, so I trusted him.

**TH:** *What happened with the copyright issue?*

**AS:** The copyright ran out. I found out about it, so I went and I copyrighted the movie. I have the copyright. I tell people that and nobody believes me. But I have the copyright. You know, the Blu-ray and everything, I was glad that they did that—I might do something, but I don't know. I do own the copyright. They keep on saying I don't, but they lost the copyright. And when I heard that, I went and copyright the movie.

**TH:** *When the film came out in 1976, it got some good reviews, it won some prizes, but it pretty much faded away…*

**AS:** Right. I got killed. I got killed by the Los Angeles critics. The *LA Times* just killed it.

**TH:** *At what point did you become aware that it had become a cult movie?*

**AS:** (*Struggles to remember*) Maybe something like ten years ago. I kept on hearing things that people were saying about it… It was slowly. I'm actually surprised and grateful.

**TH:** *The film was re-released at different points to cash in on the popularity of Brooke Shields…*

**AS:** Which is good. Listen, if it got people to see the movie, that's fine.

**TH:** *Did you and Brooke Shields ever talk much after the movie?*

**AS:** I got her the job on *Pretty Baby* (1978). Louis Malle was up at Technicolor while I was there editing. He was cutting some movie. We'd see each other in the hallway. "What are you doing? Blah blah blah." And I was thinking, "Oh, Louis Malle—I'm at freaking Technicolor and I'm a director." That sort of craziness. He asked me what I was doing, so I brought him in to show him Brooke Shields—how great she was, what a beautiful face she had. So I think I had some influence in her getting *Pretty Baby*.

**TH:** *I also found an article that indicated there was a lawsuit you brought against John Surgent from Horizon Films. It said you weren't paid your director's fee for* Communion *and I was wondering what his role was in the film, as neither he nor his company are credited?*

**AS:** God, I don't even remember the name. John Surgent? Who was he?

**TH:** *I was hoping you could tell me! (laughter)*

**AS:** God, my mind goes blank. I don't remember that at all. Maybe somebody got the wrong information, but I don't remember that at all.

**TH:** *You didn't get another film off the ground for several years… How did* Tanya's Island *come about?*

**AS:** I was desperate, I guess. (*laughs*) It was supposed to be… we had the idea of *Beauty and the Beast*, our own version of it, where the beast becomes a man and the man becomes the beast and the competition for the woman. We had written a script and we finally got this producer, Pierre Brousseau, to make it—and we were filming in Toronto, and then something happened because of the tax shelter… We were filming in Puerto Rico and something happened, and the Canadian tax shelter wasn't going to give us the money. We had to film a certain percentage in Canada, so we totally rewrote the whole thing to satisfy the tax shelter. So ultimately it wasn't the film I wanted to make or that Rosemary (Ritvo) wanted to make; we were just throwing shit on a wall to make this movie. I got Rick Baker, who was a great guy, to make the beast costume. We had so many production problems in Puerto Rico. Brousseau had promised us everything, but when we arrived there wasn't even a chair to sit on. The suit finally arrived and the mechanism that worked that head and face were only like two feet from the actual costume. For some reason Rick made the hair so long, so it looked more like a girl running in a monkey suit. The other problem we had was, the actor could only wear the suit for like 10 minutes; he'd pass out from the heat. So it was one mishap after another. It definitely wasn't the film I wanted to do. I was just trying to save it on a daily basis. It was very disappointing for me and Rosemary.

**TH:** *Was there anything about it that pleased you?*

**AS:** The actress [Vanity] was great. She was a waitress in Toronto when we found her. She was terrific. The people were nice, but it was tough to shoot in Puerto Rico. Then we had to shoot in Toronto and change the whole story; it became a weird, strange movie where the gorilla fucks the girl at the end. That was *not* the movie I wanted to make. It was very disappointing.

**TH:** Pandemonium *was a spoof of the horror genre; how did that project end up in your lap?*

**AS:** I wasn't meant to have a career as a director, it seems. I hadn't worked. I had no money and I was ready to pack it in. I only worked for a couple of years, really. But somebody approached me to make this movie. I had no idea about comedy. I made a bad movie. I blame myself. The one good thing was, I got all the Groundlings, I got Paul Reubens, Elvira. I was working with Phil Hartman and we were doing this thing called *The Cheeseball Special*, with our friends, and all I kept thinking was, "I'm killing Eve Arden with a fart. This gifted actress, I've seen all of her movies, she's worked with all these great actors—and I'm *killing her with a fart*." That was the final nail in my coffin, for sure.

**TH:** *You were working with some bigger name actors in* Pandemonium; *did you find it easier by that stage, having had some experiences?*

**AS:** Oh yeah. My biggest fear was, comedy was not my thing. I was experimenting. I tried to make it funny. We also didn't have money for some things, like the chase with the statue across the football field, so that came off a bit dorky. But I was happy I was directing and making a movie.

**TH:** *What was it like working for a studio as opposed to working independently?*

**AS:** Total nightmare in the sense that I had no sense of how that worked. I was an independent and I didn't know all the union stuff. I didn't know how things worked. For me it was tough. It wasn't what I was used to.

**TH:** *Was it a conscious decision on your part to stop directing, or was it more a matter of your not wanting to continue working in the studio system?*

**AS:** I couldn't get a job. I had an agent. But it was also my own arrogance and my own fault. I was with CNA when they were first starting out. Messina was my agent at the time and it was my stupidity; he would say, "I will get you work in television," and I'd say, "No, I don't want to do television." I had my own screenplay that I wanted to make, and that truly is one of the bigger regrets of my life. I was so foolish. I was young and I thought I will write and direct my own movies. No. So then I just started writing to survive, and then I got into production design.

**TH:** *What was the project you had written that you wanted to make?*

**AS:** It was a gay story, about a composer who falls in love with this violinist. The violinist works his way into the composer's life and kills him and kills his son. Ultimately the wife of the composer falls in love with this guy, not realizing that he is crazy and has killed her husband and son. We came so close so many times to getting it made. That was the movie I wanted to make. I thought it was an interesting situation for a story, so I held on to that and I got connected with various producers who said they were going to make it. Before you knew it, I was hanging out with them for a year and nothing happened. The carrot would be dangled: "Oh we're getting close." I'd hang in there, hoping, but it never happened.

**TH:** *You started working as a screenwriter after that; you even wrote a couple of episodes of one of my favorite TV shows:* Friday the 13TH: The Series... *Do you have any memories of that?*

**AS:** I kept on thinking, this has nothing to do with *Friday the 13th*! (*laughs*) You know? But the network bought the idea of the pawnshop and it got made. I switched to writing because of Elizabeth Montgomery. She actually saved me. I wasn't working. It just so happened, the producer of *Pandemonium* was the manager of Elizabeth Montgomery. We became friends. She was the Queen of Movies of the Week. I pitched her a story. She was so nice, she bought one idea and we wrote a script for her. She was a very wonderful person.

**TH:** *You've remained very active as a production designer – currently I know you've been working on the new* MacGyver *series... Do you miss directing? Do you have any projects you'd really like to direct at this point?*

**AS:** No. My cousin Dante [Tomaselli] wants to make a remake of *Communion*. I hope he gets it off the ground. I would probably enjoy production designing the remake. But no (*laughs*) my time has come and gone. I'll never direct again.

**TH:** *Were you involved in the recent Arrow Blu-ray restoration of* Communion?

**AS:** No, they stayed away from me. They didn't contact me at all. I don't know why. I spoke to the one guy at Arrow Films a few times. But no, they didn't want anything from me.

**TH:** *Were you satisfied with how it looked?*

**AS:** I haven't seen it yet!

**TH:** *Really?*

**AS:** No, I was supposed to get a copy but I haven't gotten it yet.

**TH:** *I just watched it myself, and it looks really wonderful.*

**AS:** Good. Good. I know the old edition still plays on… not Netflix… some streaming thing. I caught it and I thought it was the new version and I was disappointed, but then I realized it was the old version that's still playing.

**TH:** *It's a shame you haven't seen it, but it looks great.*

**AS:** To be honest, I'm very grateful that it is out. I'm glad they could restore it from the original negative. I'm glad it's out there and I'm happy about that.

**TH:** *Do you have any final thoughts you'd like to share about* Communion *or about your career in general?*

**AS:** I will always be a frustrated film director. (*laughs*) I managed to survive in Hollywood making somewhat of a living. And I got a lot out of that one movie, all things considered. I'm kind of proud of it. And seeing some of the reviews these days, it feels kind of good.

**TH:** *Obviously I'm a huge fan of it and of you…*

**AS:** Thank you very much; I appreciate that. Look at that. It's surviving. It's amazing. I hope Dante gets to make his own version.

**TH:** *I love his movies; I'd love to see what he could do with it.*

**AS:** He's so talented. He takes a shoestring and look what he does. He is an amazing, amazing guy.

**TH:** *I'm a great supporter of his work. I hope it happens and that you get to design it.*

**AS:** That would be great.

**TH:** *Thanks again for talking with me.*

**AS:** You're welcome. Congratulations on the book, that's a big accomplishment.

**TH:** *I hope you'll like it!*

**AS:** I'm sure I will. By the way, I just signed a deal with Netflix and a production company called Concordia—I don't know if you know of them?

**TH:** *I do.*

**AS:** They're going to do a docu-drama on the making of *Deep Sleep*.

**TH:** *Oh that's fantastic. That would make a great movie!*

**AS:** Yeah, I actually went online. You can actually watch *Deep Sleep* on there. And it was quite (*chuckles*) an amazing walk down memory lane.

Cover art for a Brazilian VHS edition of *Alice, Sweet Alice*. Artist unknown.

# Bibliography

**The following books** are a great resource for understanding the evolution of the horror genre in general. They all provide relevant contextual information, even if they don't specifically pertain to Alice, Sweet Alice. At the very least, they are highly recommended reading.

Clover, Carol J., *Men, Women, and Chain Saws: Gender in the Modern Horror Film* (Updated Edition) (Princeton: Princeton University Press, 2015)

Corman, Roger, with Jim Jerome, *How I Made a Hundred Movies in Hollywood and Never Lost a Dime* (New York, Da Capo Press, 1998)

Hardy, Phil, ed., *The Overlook Film Encyclopedia: Horror* (Woodstock: The Overlook Press, 1995)

Janisse, Kier-La, *House of Psychotic Women* (Godalming: FAB Press, 2012)

Jones, Alan, *The Rough Guide to Horror Movies* (New York: Rough Guides, 2005)

Newman, Kim, ed., *The BFI Companion to Horror* (London: British Film Institute, 1996)

Newman, Kim, *Nightmare Movies* (London: Bloomsbury, 2011)

Rigby, Jonathan, *Studies in Terror* (Cambridge: Signum Books, 2011)

Rockoff, Adam, *Going to Pieces: The Rise and Fall of the Slasher Film, 1978 to 1986* (Jefferson: McFarland & Company, 2002)

Thrower, Stephen, *Nightmare U.S.A.* (Godalming: Fab Press, 2007)

Zinoman, Jason, *Shock Value: How a Few Eccentric Outsiders Gave Us Nightmares, Conquered Hollywood, and Invented Modern Horror* (New York: Penguin Books, 2012)

# Index

**Note:** *Titles, be they films, TV shows, plays, or written works, are in italics.*

*9 ½ Weeks* 50
*Abilene Reporter News* 238
*Adventures of Ozzie and Harriet, The* 3
*Airport '79* 58
*Akron Beacon Journal* 247
*Alfred Hitchcock Presents* 41
*All My Sons* 54
Allen, Tom 17
Allen, Gary 52, 216, 217
Allen, Woody 240, 241
Altman, Robert xvi
*American Cinematographer* 17, 255
*American Soap* (lost film) 22, 24, 29, 52, 215, 233, 258-259
*Anderson Tapes, The* 55
*Andy Hardy* 3
*Animal Crackers* 57
*Anna K* 49
*Annie Hall* 52
Arden, Eve 291
Argento, Dario xvi, 10, 211, 220, 224
Arkoff, Samuel Z. 6
*Assault on Precinct 13* xvii
*Audrey Rose* 239
*Austin American-Statesman* 243

Baisley, Glen 62
Baker, Rick 38, 272
*Bamboozled* 46
*Bang the Drum Slowly* 29
*Baretta* 50
*Barnaby Jones* 47
Bava, Mario xvi, 10, 224
*Beauty and the Beast* 38, 272
*Believe in Me* 48
*Bellboy and the Playgirls, The* 17
Bergman, Ingmar xvi, 254
*Bird with the Crystal Plumage, The* 10, 211, 224
*Black Christmas* 11, 224
*Black Picture Show* 44
*Black Sabbath* 224
Blatty, William Peter 44
*Bloodsucking Freaks* 47, 52
Blowen, Michael 247
*Blue Lagoon, The* 53
*Boardwalk* 58
Bogdanovich, Peter 3
*Boston Globe* 247
Bottin, Rob 38
Brando, Marlon 4
Brousseau, Pierre 38, 272
Brownstein, Bill 235
*Buddy Buddy* 52
*Butch Cassidy and the Sundance Kid* 54

*Cactus Flower* 49
Canby, Vincent 250
*Car 54, Where Are You?* 46
Cardona, René, Jr. 36
Carpenter, John xv, xvi, 10, 11, 14, 41
*Carrie* xii, 239, 246
Cassavetes, John 10
*Castle* 41
*CBS Radio Mystery Theatre* 46
Chadwick, Bruce 25, 26, 27, 28, 30, 32, 36, 37, 47, 71
*Cheeseball Presents* 39, 273
*Chicago Sun-Times, The* 241
Christie, Julie 223
*Cincinnati Enquirer* 251
Clark, Bob 11, 224
Clark, Joe 70
Clift, Montgomery 4
Clinton, Mildred 32, 45-46, 47, 55, 63, 212, 225, 226, 229, 234, 235, 250, 264
Coen Brothers, The 53
*Communion* (novelization) 32, 34
Coppola, Francis Ford 17, 55, 216, 255
Corman, Roger 6, 7, 55
*Cosa avete fatto a Solange?*, see *What Have You Done to Solange?*
Cosford, Bill 240
*Courier-Post* 30, 38, 39
Cronenberg, David 41
*Crookylyn* 46
*Crucible, The* 49
*Cwir's Keep* 62

*Daily News* 26, 28, 30, 32, 36, 37, 47, 71
Daley, Frank 246
Dalí, Salvador 254
Dallamano, Massimo 36
Dante, Joe 10
Dassin, Jules 50
Daves, Delmer 254
*Dawn of the Dead* 15
Day, Doris 10
De Niro, Robert 19
De Palma, Brian xii, 11, 211, 239, 240

Dean, James 4
*Deathdream* 15
*Deep Red* 220, 226
*Deep Sleep* ix, 19, 20-22, 23, 24, 25, 26, 27, 30, 32, 37, 47, 63, 71, 228, 233, 255-258, 259, 260, 276
*Deep Throat* 18, 19, 20, 21
Delarose, Larry 30, 38, 39
DeMille, Cecil B. 57
DeNoble, Alphonso 14, 15, 24, 29, 37, 51-52, 66, 69, 214, 215, 219, 240, 258, 264-265
*Desecration* xii, xiv
*Devil's Disciple, The* 49
*Diabolique* 254
*Don't Answer the Phone!* 53
*Don't Look Now* ix, xvi, 11, 12, 24, 211, 223, 2462, 263-264
Donahue, Troy 254
*Dragonwyck* 4, 5
Du Maurier, Daphne 42
Dunaway, Faye 43

Ebert, Roger 241
*Edge of Night, The* 47
Edison, Thomas 30, 38, 39
*Eight is Enough* 58
Elvira 273
*Emperor Jones, The* 30
*Endless Love* 53
*Equalizer, The* 50, 55
Evans, Robert 3
*Exorcist, The* 26, 30, 44, 225, 234, 237, 246

*Fall of the House of Usher, The* 6
*Fast and the Furious, The* 6
Fellini, Federico 22, 215, 258, 259
Fleming, Victor 4
*Frankenstein* 2
*Freddy's Nightmares* 45
*Free To Be... You and Me* 29
Freeman, Morgan 70
Friburg, John 28,
*Friday the 13th* xvii, 38

*Friday the 13th: The Series* 41, 274
Friedkin, William 30, 44, 55, 225
*Fugitive, The* 55
Fulci, Lucio xvi

Gable, Clark 22
*Ganja & Hess* 62
Garland, Judy 58
*Gettysburg* 58
Gingold, Michael vii, 53, 36, 60-71
Gleason, Jackie 43, 266, 267
*Godfather, The* xii, 216
*Gods and Generals* 58
Gordon, Ruth 58
Gorman, Patrick 58-59
Gourley, D.J. 21
Greeley, Gerard 64
Greenberg, Irwin 22, 259
Gregory, André 266
Gross, Linda 244
Grunberg, Jerry 35
Gunn, Bill 44
Gunther, Marc 57

Hall, Chuck 28, 262
*Halloween* xv, xvii, 10, 11, 14, 15, 241
Hannah, Charles 28, 63
*Happy Days* 58
Hardstark, Michael 50-51, 64, 219, 227
*Hart to Hart* 53
Hartman, Phil 38, 273
*Haunted Palace, The* 6
Hayward, Susan 58, 247, 267-268
Hellman, Lillian 50
Herrmann, Bernard 29, 211, 269
*Highway to Heaven* 45
Hill, Debra 10
Hill, George Roy 54
Hitchcock, Alfred xii, 11, 14, 29, 41, 213, 222, 233, 234, 237, 240, 241, 246, 247, 254, 263, 269
Hooper, Tobe xvi, 10, 14, 41
Hopkins, Anthony 4

Horton, Louisa 72, 222, 223
*Hostel* xvii
*Hotel* 41
Hudson, Rock 10
*Hudsucker Proxy, The* 53
Huston, John 55

*I Can Get It For Your Wholesale* 58
*I Spit on Your Grave* 62
*I'll Be Your Bride* 255
*I'll Cry Tomorrow* 58, 247, 267
*In the Shadow of Kilimanjaro* 58
*Indianapolis Star* 250
*Inner Sanctum* 54
*Invasion of the Body Snatchers* 1
*Ironside* 50
Irwin, James 246
*It Came from Outer Space* 1

*Jack Benny Program, The* 46, 52
*Jaws* 36, 235
*Jeopardy!* 63

*Kentucky Fried Movie, The* 239
*Kings of the Road* 30
Kleemann, Gunter 62
Klein, Barbara 88
*Kojak* 50
Kramer, Lawrence 32, 70

Lancaster, Burt 54
*Last Horror Film, The* 29
Lauria, Frank 32, 34
*Law & Order* 55
*Law & Order: Criminal Intent* 45
Lawrence, Stephen 29, 211, 235, 244, 269
*Lean on Me* 70
*Leave it to Beaver* 52
Lee, Spike 46
Leogrande, Ernest 252
Lewton, Val 1
Leydon, Joe 248
*Lights Out* 54
*Liquid Sky* 47

*Lois & Clark: The New Adventures of Superman* 29
*Los Angeles Times* 244, 271
*Lost Boys, The* 45
*Love Parade, The* 57
Lovecraft, H.P. 6
Lovelace, Linda 19
*Lovely Sunday for Creve Coeur, A* 49
Lowry, Jane 48-49, 52, 66, 216, 217, 220
Lubitsch, Ernst 4
Lumet, Sidney 46, 55
Lustig, William xvii

*Macbeth* 3
*MacGyver* 41, 58, 257, 274
*Madam Satan* 57
Malle, Louis 26, 37, 53, 247, 248, 251, 271
*Mama's Family* 53
Mamoulian, Rouben 4
*Maniac* xvii
Mankiewicz, Joseph L. 4
Mann, Daniel 58
Mann, Michael 55
*Many Loves of Dobie Gillis, The* 50
March, Fredric 4
*Masque of the Red Death, The* 7
*Max Headroom* 29
May, Elaine 46
Mazursky, Paul 45
*McCloud* 48
McElfresh, Tom 251
McMaster, Niles 47-48, 52, 65, 217, 223, 224, 225, 226, 227, 266
Mercouri, Melina 50
*Messiah of Evil* 15
*Miami Herald, The* 240
*Miami News, The* 237
*Midsummer Night's Dream* 49
Milland, Ray 7
Miller, Jason 26, 44, 45, 266
Miller, Linda 26, 37, 43-45, 46, 47, 49, 52, 212, 220, 223, 224, 235, 244, 248, 266-267
*Minneapolis Star, The* 243

Miraglia, Emilio xv
Montgomery, Elizabeth 274
*Montreal Gazette, The* 235, 236
Morrison, Don 243
Morrow, Jennifer 63
Muskat, Andrew 63
*My Dinner with André* 266

*Nasty Habits* 239
*National Geographic* 241
*National Lampoon* 241
*NCIS* 29
*New Leaf, A* 46
*New York Daily News* 252
*New York Post* 250
*New York Times, The* 250
*Newhart* 53
*News, The* 57, 70, 234
Niccollai, John T. 21, 22, 256, 257
Nicholson, James H. 6
*Night Evelyn Came Out of the Grave, The* xv
*Night of the Juggler* 45
*Night of the Living Dead* xvi, 9, 14, 43
*Night of the Zombies* 52
*Night-Flowers* 58
*No Place to Hide* 49
*Notte che Evelyn uscì dalla tomba, La*, see *The Night Evelyn Came Out of the Grave*
*Nude Bomb, The* 58

O'Donnell, Christine 63
*Obsession* 11
Olivier, Laurence 50
*Omen, The* ix
*Omnibus* 54
*On Deadly Ground* 58
*Only Sense is Nonsense, The* 48
Oppedisano Rooney, Sandy 68
*Ottawa Journal* 246

Pacino, Al 46
Page, Geraldine 46
*Pandemonium* 38, 40, 53, 272-273, 274

Patric, Jason 45
Peckinpah, Sam 241
*People* 252
*Performance* 7
*Pittsburgh Post-Gazette* 246
Pleshette, Suzanne 254
Poe, Edgar Allan 6
Poitier, Sidney 43
Polanski, Roman 9, 14, 55, 213
*Police Story* 50
Pollock, Sydney 58
*Poor Bitos* 49
*Practice, The* 50
Price, Vincent 4, 5, 6, 9
*Prizzi's Honor* 55
*Profondo rosso*, see *Deep Red*
*Psycho* 11, 14, 213, 237
Pucillo, Jude 68

*Quantum Leap* 29

*Reazione a catena*, see *Twitch of the Death Nerve*
*Rebel Without a Cause* 4
*Rebel*, see *No Place to Hide*
Reed, Joel M. 52
*Reefer Madness* 4
*Rehearsal, The* 50
Reubens, Paul 38, 273
Rigg, Diana 38
Ritvo, Rosemary 24-25, 38, 61, 69, 71, 211, 231, 234, 235, 239, 240, 243, 244, 246, 250, 251, 258, 260, 272
Robeson, Paul 30
Robinson, Edward G. 54
Rocca, Antonino 56, 217, 268
*Rock All Night* 6
Roeg, Nicolas xvi, 7, 11, 12, 24, 211, 223, 246
*Rome Adventure* 254
Romero, George A. xvi, 9, 13, 14, 41
Rose, Joe 27, 28
Rose, Rita 250
*Rosemary's Baby* 9, 14, 55, 213

Rosenberg, Richard K. 25, 32, 33, 35, 36, 63, 233, 234, 243, 244, 247, 250, 260, 261, 270
Roth, Lillian 56, 57-58, 65, 227, 237, 247, 251, 267, 268
Rowe Kelly, Alan 62
*Run for Your Life* 55
Ruth, Daniel 239
*Ryan's Hope* 48

Sable, Dan 29
Salier, Edward 29, 212, 216, 225, 261, 269
Schell, Maximillian 50
*School That Couldn't Scream, The*, see *What Have You Done to Solange?*
Schrader, Paul 19
Scorsese, Martin xii, 19
*Secret Witness* 41
*Sentinel, The* 52
*Serpico* 46, 55, 235
*Shadow, The* 50
Sharif, Omar 38, 69
Shepherd, Cybil 19
Sheppard, Paula vii, 15, 26, 27, 46-47, 51, 63, 70, 212, 213, 219, 220, 235, 244, 250, 251, 252, 265-266
Shields, Brooke 26, 27, 38, 44, 53, 212, 218, 238, 241, 243, 244, 246, 247, 248, 249, 250, 251, 252, 261, 268, 271
Shields, Teri 26, 268
Shippy, Dick 247
*Shreveport Times* 248
Signorelli, Tom 55, 64, 219
*Silence of the Lambs, The* 4
*Silent Scream* 29
*Simon and Simon* 53
*Sisters* 11
Small, Michael 29
Smothers, Tom 38
Sole, Alfred vii, viii, ix, xii, xiv, xv, xvi, xvii, 10, 11, 12, 13, 14, 17-41, 43, 46, 51, 52, 53, 56, 57, 61, 63, 64, 66, 68, 69, 70, 71, 73, 211, 212, 213, 214, 215, 216, 217, 218, 219, 220, 221, 222,

223, 225, 226, 227, 228, 230, 231, 233, 234, 235, 236, 237, 238, 239, 240, 241, 242, 243, 244, 246, 247, 248, 250, 251, 252, 253-276
*Sorcerer* 55
Soupios, Stephanie 62
Spages, Marilyn 61
Spero, Bette 28, 30
*St. Valentine's Day Massacre, The* 55
Stallone, Sylvester 50
*Star Trek: Enterprise* 50
*Star Trek: The Next Generation* 50
*Star-Ledger* 28, 30
Stevenson, Robert Louis 4
*Sting, The* 54
*Strange Case of Dr. Jekyll and Mr. Hyde, The* 4
Strasberg, Lee 58
*Streets of San Francisco, The* 50
Streisand, Barbra 58
Sudol, Robert 62
*Summer of Sam* 46
*Summer People, The* 49
Surgent, John 30, 271-272
*Suspense* 54
*Swashbuckler* 54
*Sweet Bird of Youth, The* 46

Taggart, Patrick 243
*Tampa Tribune, The* 239
*Tanya's Island* 38, 272
*Taxi Driver* 19, 38, 87
*Terror, The* 6
*Texas Chain Saw Massacre, The* xvi, 15, 43
*Them!* 1
*Thief* 55
Thomas, Marlo 29
*Three Days of the Condor* 58
*Time of Your Life, The* 49
*Tintorera* 36
Tomaselli, Dante xii, xii, ix-xiv, 29, 60, 68, 253, 274, 275
*Tomb of Ligeia, The* 7
Tracy, Spencer 4

*Tre volti della paura, I*, see *Black Sabbath*
*Trip, The* 7, 8, 55
Truffaut, François 3
*Twitch of the Death Nerve* 10

*Uccello dalle piume di cristallo, L'*, see *Bird with the Crystal Plumage, The*
*Under Siege* 41
*Unmarried Woman, An* 45

*Vagabond King, The* 57
Vanity 272
*Variety* 24, 31, 233
*Vertigo* 11
*Vigilante* xvii
*Voice of the Turtle, The* 54
*Voices* 61
Von Mauer, Bill 237

*Wagon Train* 55
*Waltons, The* 58
Welles, Orson 3
Wenders, Wim 30
Whale, James 2
*What Have You Done to Solange?* 36
Whitaker, William 238
*Who Are We?* 49
*Wicker Man, The* 15
*Wild One, The* 4
Wilder, Billy 52
Williams, Kay 22, 24, 258, 259
Willrich, Rudolph 13, 45, 49-50, 63, 212, 235
Wilson, Chelly 19, 256
*Windy City* 47
Winner, Michael 52
Winsten, Archer 250
Wise, Robert 239
*Witchfinder General* 9

*X: The Man with the X-Ray Eyes* 7

Zarchi, Meir 62

# About the Author

Photo by Ashley Cullen-Bandzuh.

**Troy Howarth** is a Rondo Award-nominated writer who specializes in European Cult cinema. His books include *The Haunted World of Mario Bava: Revised and Expanded Edition*, *Splintered Visions: Lucio Fulci and His Films*, the three volume series *So Deadly, So Perverse*: *50 Years of Italian Giallo Films*, *Real Depravities: The Films of Klaus Kinski*, *Human Beasts: The Films of Paul Naschy*, *Assault on the System: The Nonconformist Cinema of John Carpenter*, and *Murder By Design: The Unsane Cinema of Dario Argento*. He has also contributed audio commentaries, audio essays, and liner notes to over one hundred DVD and Blu-ray releases from the U.S., the U.K., and Germany. His books *Human Beasts: The Films of Paul Naschy* and the first volume of *So Deadly, So Perverse*, as well as his commentaries on the Arrow Video edition of *Don't Torture a Duckling*, the Blue Underground edition of *Zombie*, the Synapse edition of *Suspiria*, and the Scorpion Releasing edition of *Assignment Terror* were all nominated for Rondo Awards. He resides in Pennsylvania.

www.ingramcontent.com/pod-product-compliance
Lightning Source LLC
Chambersburg PA
CBHW082110230426
43671CB00015B/2658